Human Capital Creation in an Economic Perspective

ETLA -The Research Institute of the Finnish Economy
Series B102 (ISSN 0356-7443)

The Research Institute of the Finnish Economy (ETLA) was founded in 1946 to conduct research in the fields of economics, business and social policy designed to serve financial and economic-policy decision making. At present the members of the association sponsoring ETLA are the central association of industry and employers, major banks and the central association of insurance companies. ETLA also conducts special studies financed from sources outside the association, for which a separate unit has been established. ETLA publishes monographs, reviews and forecasts in several different series.

Address: ETLA, Lönnrotinkatu 4 B, FIN-00120 Helsinki, Finland
Telephone 358-0-609900
Telefax 358-0-601753

Previous Volumes Published in Association with ETLA, Helsinki

Synnöve Vuori and Pentti Vuorinen (Eds.)
Explaining Technical Change in a Small Country

Rita Asplund (Ed.)

Human Capital Creation in an Economic Perspective

With 20 Figures

Springer-Verlag Berlin Heidelberg GmbH

Dr. Rita Asplund

ETLA
The Research Institute of the Finnish Economy
Lönnrotinkatu 4 B
FIN-00120 Helsinki
Finland

ISBN 978-3-7908-0815-5 ISBN 978-3-642-99776-1 (eBook)
DOI 10.1007/978-3-642-99776-1

Ursprünglich erschienen bei Physica-Verlag Heidelberg 1994

88/2202-5 4 3 2 1 0 – Printed on acid-free paper

FOREWORD

The past few decades have seen a revolutionary increase in interest in the economic role of education and training at the societal, business, and individual levels. This is mainly due to the strong post-war growth in industrialized economies, which has been driven by rapid technological progress and far-reaching structural change and, in the end, has resulted in increasingly skill-intensive production and growing demand for more educated labour. Today it is frequently argued that with the increasing importance of the role of know-how, the workforce has become the most important single input in the production process.

Simultaneously the dramatic increase in the availability of large micro-level databases has opened enormous possibilities to study the economic role of human capital creation also empirically.

The economic perspective of human capital accumulation is, however, of utmost importance also in times of deep economic recession. Periods of economic slowdown and rapidly increasing unemployment tend to increase the demand for advanced education and training in particular. This brings up, in turn, questions regarding overeducation and satisfying both private and social returns on investments in human capital.

The ongoing recession in combination with falling tax revenues has forced economies with large public sectors to decide on cutbacks and reallocations of educational expenses. But at the same time it may be questioned whether it is reasonable to undertake deep-going measures in order to improve the efficiency in education without having reliable information on the macro- and microeconomic effects of the vast resources annually expended on education and training. Investment in human capital at all levels of the society is a question of generations, not of business cycles.

With these points in mind a seminar on human capital creation in an economic perspective was held on May 14–15, 1992 in Helsinki. The main purpose of the seminar was to shed as much light as possible on the economic role of investment in human capital at the individual, firm and macroeconomic levels. Researchers, mainly from the Nordic countries, were invited to present theoretical and empirical results from their ongoing research projects in these particular fields.

The papers presented at the seminar spurred lively discussions and have, hopefully, also stimulated the research on the important topic of human capital not least within and across the Nordic countries. Because of the wide scope of crucial human capital-related topics covered at the seminar, it was considered worthwhile to make this information available to a broader audience by publishing up-dated versions of most of the presentations given at the seminar.

I am much indebted to several persons for help in arranging the seminar and in producing this book. Pentti Vartia was the initiator of the project. John Rogers has checked and improved the language of the chapters by non-English speaking contributers. The final layout of the book was produced by Public Design Oy.

Financial support from the Ministry of Education and the Yrjö Jahnsson Foundation is gratefully acknowledged.

Helsinki, May 1994

Rita Asplund

Contents

1 Introduction and Summary

Rita Asplund
ETLA, The Research Institute of the Finnish Economy, Helsinki, Finland

In the past few decades, there has been a revolutionary increase in interest in the role of education and training at the societal, business, and individual levels. This is mainly due to the rapid technological progress and far-reaching structural change of the industrialized world, resulting in more knowledge-intensive production and, consequently, growing demand for more educated labour.

1.1 Human Capital and Individual Earnings

For many years it has been hypothetized that, as advanced economies become more knowledge-intensive, human resources tend to become more crucial for economic progress. Today it is frequently argued that with the increasing importance of the role of know-how, the workforce has become the most important single input in the production process.

Moreover, there is empirical evidence supporting the hypothesis that the rate of technical change in an economy influences the rate of productivity growth not only directly, but also indirectly by affecting the value of education in the enhancement of productivity growth. The logic then is that when changing production processes and new technologies are introduced, general skills typically learned in school become especially valuable in fostering productivity. More educated workers are thereby seen to have a comparative advantage over less educated ones both in implementing new technologies and in adjusting themselves to the structural, institutional and organizational change process of modern industrial society.

The experiences of the past few decades clearly show that the adaptation of the labour force to new situations may be extremely painful especially in times of rapid technological change. With a broad-based educational level of relatively good quality, the possibilities of workers to respond to such structural changes are likely to increase and their (re-)employment opportunities consistently to improve. Indeed, today it is often argued that the primary role of formal schooling should be to provide adolescents with a sufficient up-to-date broad-based basic – mainly theoretical – education.

At the same time, however, quite a few societies have experienced an alarming deterioration in the educational achievement of students. This is seen to have affected the quality of the labour force and thereby contributed substantially to a slowdown in productivity growth in the past fifteen years.

Moreover, the returns measured by earnings of individuals gained from investment in education have declined considerably since the early 1960s. It has, therefore, commonly been argued that it no longer pays for the individual to invest in longer education. As shown in the OECD Employment Outlook 1993, however, a weak reversal in this trend has, in recent years, been documented in a number of industrialized economies. The trend of increasing returns on education has been especially strong in the US and the UK.

These among many other key questions concerning human capital and individual earnings are addressed in the first four articles of this book (Chapters 2–5).

1.1.1 Academic Competencies, Productivity and Earnings

In his comprehensive article, *John Bishop* highlights the complex interactions between schooling, learning and worker productivity. More precisely, he focuses on examining whether evidence from the US labour market supports recent claims that schooling and academic achievement improve worker productivity and that these impacts have strengthened during the 1980s.

Special attention is thereby paid to testing empirically the fairly common belief that in an increasingly technological society, a growing number of jobs require significant competency in mathematics and science. This is done by addressing two important questions. First, what would be the benefits of a frontline worker with a better mathematics and science education if the current job structure remained roughly unchanged? Second, is the occupational structure really changing in a way that will increase the need for higher standards and more class time devoted to math and science in secondary school?

In analyzing the first question, Bishop starts by using the standard way of inferring the impact of a worker trait on productivity, i.e. by examining its effects on earnings. His results on the impact of academic competencies on earnings in the US suggest that the effects of general academic achievement are substantial for adults and, consequently, reflect a causal relationship.

For young workers, on the other hand, the results indicate that specific academic competencies – competence in mathematical reasoning, science and language arts – have a negligible impact on earnings during the first 8 years after graduating from high school. In other words, the incentives to devote time and energy to the often difficult task of learning and developing these competencies turn out to be very weak. Bishop interprets this absence of significant labour market rewards for these competencies as an important explanation for the poor performance of US students in science and higher-level mathematics, and shows that the social costs in the US of deteriorating school quality have been and will remain substantial.

Bishop questions, however, whether the productivity effects and the earnings effects of academic competencies of students are in fact the same. When the specific competencies are not signalled to the labour market by a credential, their earnings effects are not likely to be the same as their productivity effects, he argues. Moreover, those calling for more mathematics and science education emphasize the positive effects on worker *productivity*, not on earnings.

The approach used by Bishop to analyze more directly the impact of academic competencies on worker productivity provides strong support for recommendations for major improvements in primarily mathematics education for the great mass of high school students. But in contrast to what is commonly believed, the evidence indicates that the need for higher standards in math and science education does not depend on the rate at which employers switch from traditional Tayloristic-Fordist production systems to the new high involvement work systems. On the contrary, the evidence implies that mathematical and scientific competence contributes significantly to productivity also in jobs that are structured in a traditional mass production style and that do not have college-level training in math and science as a selection requirement!

A second rationale for improving the quality of mathematics and science education is the alleged need to expand the supply of engineers, scientists, computer specialists and managers with advanced training in business and economics. The high priority given to expanding the supply of university educated workers has, in turn, been used as an argument for improving the general quality of US secondary education and, especially, secondary school preparation in mathematics and science; gaining a sound foundation in these areas in secondary school has been shown to improve chances of success in university.

In the second part of his review article, Bishop questions the justification of these arguments. In particular, he focuses on answering the following crucial questions: How rapidly has the demand for and the supply of university graduates been growing? What have been the major developments in the demand and supply of university graduates? What have been the trends in the economic payoff to university education? Which college specialties generate the largest economic payoff?

Bishop presents a multitude of evidence for the US as well as for other industrialized economies in an attempt to answer these questions. Although some trends may be distinguished, the available results, however, clearly show that much more research is needed on these subjects.

1.1.2 Educational Returns, Family Background and Earnings Differentials

The other three articles focusing on human capital and individual earnings (Chapters 3–5) all utilize a standard Mincer-type approach to analyzing a wide range of interesting aspects concerning the role and importance of human capital from the point of view of the individual.

The article by *Rita Asplund, Erling Barth, Carl le Grand, Arne Mastekaasa and Niels Westergård-Nielsen* focuses on the earnings effects of human capital in Denmark, Finland, Norway and Sweden. The strength of the study is that the results are obtained from estimating identically specified earnings equations using comparable national micro-level data sets and as comparable definitions of variables as possible.

In view of the very similar social structure of the four Nordic countries under study, it could be expected that also the earnings structure across countries is characterized rather by similarities than by dissimilarities. The analysis reveals that there are, indeed, many notable similarities but also several interesting differences between the four countries.

When limiting the analysis to employed wage earners aged 16 to 64, the overall distribution of (hourly) earnings displays a clear ordering of equality with Sweden and Norway having the most equal wage rates followed by Denmark. The most unequal distribution of earnings is obtained for Finland.

Finland also seems clearly to break the pattern of approximate similarity with respect to educational returns: the average rate of return to an additional year in postcompulsory schooling is estimated at close to 5 per cent for Denmark, Sweden and Norway and some 7 per cent for Finland. The markedly higher return on formal education estimated for Finland shows up for both genders. A common feature is, however, that the return on formal schooling turns out to be significantly lower for women than for men, except in Norway where the gender gap for returns is negligible. This finding contrasts sharply with results obtained for other industrialized economies pointing to a higher return for women than for men.

More importantly, the analysis displays areas of the educational scale where the economic incentives to continue in formal education are very small. The educational levels with the lowest incentives are vocational education in Denmark as well as BA-level and higher degrees in Norway and Finland (for men). The authors emphasize that this can be expected to affect the recruitment of educated labour in the future.

The results obtained also indicate that the earnings effects of work experience are fairly similar across countries for men but differ considerably for women. An even more mixed picture emerges when a distinction is made between private- and public-sector employment. A notable finding in this respect is that the growth in earnings with increasing work experience is higher in the public than in the private sector in Finland. The reverse seems to hold in the other three countries. A similar pattern of cross-country differences is obtained for the sectoral earnings effects of formal schooling.

These along with the multitude of other findings reported in the article raise a lot of important questions that inevitably require further research. In particular, how are the differences – and similarities – prevailing across the four Nordic countries to be explained? Which factors are most crucial in explaining the observed differences between the Nordic countries and other industrialized countries?

The article by *Anders Björklund* starts from the common observation in most societies that children of parents with high incomes, extensive schooling and high-status occupations tend to emulate the behaviour of their parents and in particular invest more in schooling than other children. A variety of educational policies have been advocated to reduce the importance of family background for schooling decisions. No country seems, however, to have succeeded in this respect.

A persistent intergenerational pattern of schooling choices is often considered a problem from both equity and efficiency points of views. Björklund emphasizes in his article that a crucial prerequisite for changing this pattern is to understand the basic mechanisms creating it. One way of obtaining useful insight into the underlying mechanisms is, he argues, to study the relationship between the length of schooling and the marginal returns to schooling.

In particular, Björklund tests two hypotheses – the financing hypothesis and the comparative advantage hypothesis – by estimating human capital earnings functions which allow the schooling coefficients to vary by family background. The financing hypothesis states that children from rich families can more easily finance their studies than children from poorer backgrounds. The comparative advantage hypothesis, in turn, states that children from rich families have more to get out of schooling in the form of a higher marginal rate of return on schooling.

Using this approach, Björklund analyzes the situation in Sweden in two years – 1968 and 1981. The results suggest that the returns on schooling are, indeed, higher for those with a strong family background. This notable impact of family background on the length of schooling indicates that there is considerable inequality of opportunity among Swedish children. Or in Björklund's own words: "those with a strong family background invest more in schooling because they get more out of it". He interprets this support of the comparative advantage hypothesis as part of an explanation for the persistent intergenerational patterns of schooling choice observed also in Sweden.

In contrast, the financing hypothesis gets no support in the estimations. When evaluated at the average length of schooling for the various social groups investigated, the marginal returns on schooling were found to be quite equal; apart from those with farmer backgrounds, there was neither a marked positive nor a negative relationship. Björklund notes that this finding is inconsistent with the notion that the existing intergenerational pattern of schooling choices represents a source of inefficiency.

The article by *Kristin Dale*, finally, focuses on regional and occupational wage differences among Norwegian manufacturing workers and, especially, on changes in these differentials over the years 1973–86. Notable changes should be expected since the structure of manufacturing industries has undergone dramatic changes in Norway during the past few decades, not least as a result of the rapidly expanding petroleum sector.

The primar hypothesis tested in the study is whether the wage agreements between the Norwegian Employers' Confederation and the Norwegian Federation of Trade Unions imply that wage differentials between branches may exist, whereas regional wage differentials among member firms within each branch are eliminated. Or is it possibly so that despite national wage agreements, regional wage differentials may persist because of the existence of local wage agreements at the firm level?

The magnitudes of existing regional wage differences are of interest in view of the overall goal for the regional policy pursued in Norway to maintain the present regional distribution of the population. In particular, the lower the wage levels in the rural districts, the smaller the needs for governmental intervention through distributional and subsidizing measures to promote the opportunities for regional firms to survive in competitive markets and thereby to keep up the regional income levels to sustain the population pattern.

The results on regional wage differentials do imply the existence of substantial regional variation in wage rates in all three years under investigation (1973, 1982, 1986). Over time there have, though, been clear shifts in the wage-level status of different regions. The results also point to marked differences in wage levels within regions and, especially, between town areas and nearby rural areas. Furthermore, the regional wage differentials are found to be much smaller among women than among men.

Not surprisingly, the results on occupational wage differentials indicate that occupational categories with higher skill levels earn higher wages also after controlling for various individual-, job- and firm-related differences across occupational groups. There are, though, substantial wage gaps between men and women in the same occupation. Moreover, the estimated wage differences among occupational categories appear to have remained relatively stable over time.

The overall conclusion drawn by the author is that time passes but relative wage differences among Norwegian workers engaged in manufacturing persist.

1.2 Competence Building in the Labour Market

With the growing importance of human skills for economic progress there is a tendency for productivity to become increasingly determined by the knowledge and skills that workers put into their tasks. Accordingly, the quality of the labour force may influence the extent to which new technology can be exploited and it may even influence the overall character of technological change.

Simultaneously it should, however, be noted that the contribution to productivity of new technology also largely depends on the way workers relate to the equipment they have to use. It has occasionally been emphasized that there are three major dimensions of human resource effectiveness – skill, motivation, and adaptability – all of which are closely interdependent. New productive investments should, therefore, always be matched by investment in training, information and workplace organization. Indeed, today the trend seems to be that the introduction of a new technology typically requires more spending on personnel retraining than on the new equipment itself. In other words, the diffusion of technology tends to take place increasingly through investment in human capital than, as was previously the case, through the acquisition of new machines.

On the whole, change is fast becoming the norm for workers throughout the industrialized world. This, in turn, creates a growing need for workers to move to other jobs in order to adjust to the consequent changes in the structure of labour demand. In the years ahead, rapidly changing production processes and new technologies can thus be expected to require a recurrent remoulding and upgrading of knowledge and skills throughout a career if the individual wants to stay abreast of current basic job requirements. A continuous updating of skills is likely to be needed even for performing the same job function. Hence, relearning is inevitably becoming a normal aspect of work life, making lifelong learning the guiding principle.

These crucial aspects of human capital accumulation in working life after completed formal education are dealt with in two articles of this book (Chapters 6 and 7).

1.2.1 Workplace Skill Accumulation, Earnings and Labour Mobility

In a most informative article, *Lisa Lynch* presents US evidence on workplace skill accumulation and its impact on earnings and labour mobility. In particular, she examines the determinants and outcomes of human capital accumulation that occurs in the workplace after formal schooling has been completed. Lynch notes that this type of human capital creation has, in recent years, received an increasing amount of attention in the US, and gives three main reasons for this: the slow growth in labour productivity in the US as compared to other countries, the dramatic changes in the skill requirements of workers and the need for massive retraining of workers due to rapid changes in technology, and the rotation of workers through a wider number of jobs as a consequence of changing work organizations.

There seems to be a growing consensus in the US that firms, on average, underinvest in training compared with their competitors mainly in Europe and Japan. The author points out, however, that such statements are at most based on very scattered evidence on post-schooling training. She, therefore, fills in the missing facts by providing a comprehensive review of training practices of US firms and individuals' post-school training experiences. In doing this, Lynch confines her investigation to the skills development of new entrants into the US labour market, i.e. to the worker category that typically experiences most of the post-school training and that also represents the workforce of the future.

A most striking finding is that by the age of 25 approximately 60 per cent of US youths have received no additional training after they have completed their formal schooling. Lynch further finds a strong positive correlation between schooling and company-provided training. In particular, most company-provided formal on-the-job training in the US turns out to be acquired by college graduates who are engaged in finance, insurance and real estate. Those who receive this type of training are also more likely to be managerial, professional or technical employees in these industry sectors and, moreover, working for larger firms.

All in all, then, the industries with the highest levels of training are definitely not the industries where most young workers are employed. In other words, the primary source of post-school skill accumulation in the US appears to be concentrated to quite a narrow worker group. Simultaneously those workers who are now expected to be most involved in more tasks and take on additional responsibilities in the workplace, i.e. those who have received the least amount of formal schooling and/or are employed in smaller firms, are the least likely to receive additional skills training in the workplace.

Lynch underscores, however, that when discussing deficiencies in the relative competitiveness and competence of the US workforce, most of the attention of policy makers is focused not on college graduates, but on the majority of workers who are not college graduates. In analyzing the impact of training and education on wages and labour mobility of young workers she, therefore, concentrates primarily on non-college graduates.

Lynch reports estimation results suggesting that all types of private-sector post-school training significantly raise the wages of the 75 per cent of young workers in the US who do not graduate from college, and that the impact of this training on wages is larger than the impact of tenure. The finding that the company-provided on-the-job training is primarily specific, in turn, induces the author to question whether US firms will be able to remain competitive in the future with this strategy of being more willing to invest in firm-specific than in general training, given the characteristics of the new entrants into the US workforce and the skill demands of new technology.

The author states that these findings have several implications for the impact of training on labour mobility. A detailed examination of the factors which influence the probability of new entrants leaving their first job points to strong links between training and the probability of young workers leaving an employer. These results also reinforce the conclusions drawn from the results on training and wages suggesting that most company-provided training is firm specific, whereas off-the-job training is more general.

1.2.2 Lifelong Learning

The competitiveness of European industry is the key factor to Europe's future wealth. This is the point of departure for the extensive review article by *Leenamaija Otala* in which she analyzes in detail the strong link between education and training systems and a country's level of industrial productivity and competitiveness.

The competitiveness of Europe is at stake, and industry is slipping behind. Moreover, companies have realized that the educational level of their workforce in combination with their current training focusing on operational capabilities is not sufficient to maintain their core competence and increase competitiveness. The most serious educational problem facing Europe is how to update and upgrade the skills and competence of its "greying" working-age population in the rapidly advancing techno-economic environment. This, in turn, has put more pressure on public education and on educational institutions.

Otala emphasizes that there are many simultaneous changes in working life and the business environment that force us to re-think the demands and ways of developing the competence of the workforce and, in particular, to notify the new requirements vis-à-vis lifelong learning. Success in the continuously changing economic environment depends on the ability of businesses to meet the new competitive standards, i.e. to run faster in the productivity race while simultaneously delivering to consumers quality, variety, customisation, convenience, and timeliness. Each of these new success factors depends on the competence of the workforce.

The author illustrates the need for continuous competence development caused by rapidly developing technology, the new demands on human resource development policies and practices arising from the internationalization of businesses, and the rapidly growing need for training programmes for all ages due to an ageing population. Simultaneously she stresses the negative consequences that may result from human resource development being downsized and the responsibility of personnel training being decentralized to operational units.

In addition, demands for cost-awareness and cost-effectiveness in training and education have resulted in company training being strongly focused on short-term needs. An implication of this short-term focus is that a career in a single company is becoming more rare. The increasing mobility of employees, in turn, makes degrees, especially higher degrees, more and more important. This development also implies that the responsibility for competence development is shifted from the company towards the employee.

Otala also points to the crucial role played by small and medium sized enterprises (SMEs) in all European economies. Much of the industrial competitiveness depends, in effect, on the competence of SMEs. Nevertheless the development of competence and, especially, of lifelong learning in these companies is still a more or less unsolved problem.

1.3 Human Capital and Economic Performance

The importance of the human capital component for the operation of the economy has been widely recognized in recent decades. Specifically, human investment is seen to contribute to economic growth not least through its effects on productivity, earnings, job mobility, entrepreneurial skills, and technological innovation.

Until recently, human capital accumulation has, however, been studied in an essentially static theoretical framework. These models can be argued to have the scope but also the shortcomings of aggregate models. Most important, they overlook the need for careful analyses of key accumulation processes at the microeconomic level of the individual as well as the firm. These limitations of traditional neoclassical growth models have, in recent years, resulted in the development of a multitude of endogenous growth models. A common feature of these "new" growth models is that long-run growth is explained by endogenously driven technical change which, depending on the model in question, is seen to be brought about mainly by some specific microeconomic phenomenon, such as human capital accumulation.

The third part of this book, which focuses on human capital and economic performance, includes three articles which provide primarily theoretical foundations for a micro-macro analysis of the effects of education on economic growth (Chapters 8–10).

The article by *Gérard Ballot* analyzes the role of continuing education in an economy characterized by Schumpeterian competition, i.e. in an economy driven by a process of creative destruction. Since the competition between firms and countries depends largely on innovation in goods and processes as well as on competition via prices, Ballot argues, also education processes and normative decisions on continuing education should be examined within that framework. He finds the normative question of who should pay for the accumulation of general human capital to be of highest social and economic importance, mainly because lack of competitiveness and unemployment seem to be largely attributable to underprovision of training.

It is, however, a formidable task to construct a model that captures the essential features of Schumpeterian competition inclusive of the impact of technical change on the demand for higher skills. Ballot, therefore, chooses first to set a general theoretical framework. In particular, he starts by summarizing the state of the debate on Becker's theorem stating that the employees alone should pay for investments in general human capital. He then continues by offering a six-step proof that Becker's theorem does not hold within a Schumpeterian framework. Instead, according to Schumpeterian competition firms should share the costs of general training.

Ballot further shows that the Schumpeterian framework is helpful not only in challenging Becker's theorem. It can also be integrated with other recent theoretical ideas in order to study carefully specific well-defined problems. Since Ballot is concerned with the demand for and financing of continuing education, both from a positive and a negative point of view, he focuses on describing some of the crucial features of human capital creation and the allocation of workers which cannot be analyzed adequately within a static framework.

Specifically, Ballot introduces in turn three distinct features into the derived paradigmatic framework: the organization of work using the tool of the hierarchical production function, general human capital as an input in the production of specific human capital in a dynamic framework and, finally, the path dependency of technology on the accumulation of competencies. All three cases point to the key role of general human capital and the importance of firms to sponsor some of the expenditures on continuing education.

Ballot concludes his article by pointing to several reasons why the rates of investment in general human capital by firms may differ across nations. In a Schumpeterian framework, the role of the government could then be to set the incentives for the firms to invest in general training.

Gunnar Eliasson focuses in his article on identifying the competence capital that drives economic growth. In providing this microeconomic explanation to macroeconomic growth, Eliasson defines knowledge capital broadly; it embraces not only the competence embodied in individuals, but also the competence embodied in teams as well as in the organization of firms, markets and the entire economic system. This definition introduces into the analysis both incentive problems and imperfections of markets for competence, micro-level factors which are shown to play a crucial role at the macro-level.

More precisely, the way individual behaviour results in macroeconomic output is argued to depend on how individuals team up in firms, how competition in markets affects firms and how rules imposed by the policy maker affect competition, i.e. on how efficiently knowledge is allocated. Therefore, to identify the knowledge factor behind microeconomic growth at the macro-level it is necessary to understand the behaviour of the micro-level agents involved – the individual, the firm, and the policy maker – and the economic environment in which they operate.

As an alternative to the classical growth model, Eliasson derives a model of dynamic markets which is characterized by an evolutionary ongoing economic process, moved by ex ante unpredictable entrepreneurial initiatives generating both success stories and a steady flow of failures. Eliasson calls his market reference model the experimentally organized economy since it involves not only the allocation of given resources but also the creation and allocation of new resources and the forcing of obsolete resources to move or exit. Education and experience accumulation of individuals is part of this selection and allocation process. Accordingly, the ability of individuals to cope with unexpected changes caused by business mistakes consitutes part of their educational experience and, consequently, of the knowledge capital of the experimentally organized economy. This ability is, in turn, largely influenced by the capacity of the economic system to provide individuals with adequate insurance in the labour market in order to make them overcome their innate risk aversion, which may otherwise impair their human capital accumulation. In contrast with firms, individuals are not expected to be able to cope with their experimentally organized market environment alone.

In order to tie the economic growth process and the incentive and educational problems together Eliasson defines what he calls "a magic variable", which can be interpreted as a rent or a profit generated from an invisible stock of competence residing in the firm. Since firms strive to keep this competence rent steadily positive through constant adaptation to their experimentally organized market environment, it acts as an important incentive variable. More importantly, he demonstrates that there is a direct relationship between the measured change in this competence rent and the rate of total factor productivity change in macroeconomic production function analysis.

The article by *Kim Huynh and Marie-Pierre Merlateau* studies the impact of investment in different kinds of human capital within an endogenous growth model. In particular, the focus is on the role of the agents' specialization in one type of human capital versus the multivalence in terms of economic growth. The heterogeneity of human capital is accounted for by distinguishing between general education, which allows the agent to be efficient in many areas, and vocational training, which makes the agent specialized in one area. The main task then is to determine the agent's behaviour, i.e. his choice of investing either in general education, in vocational training, or in both.

The authors show that in contrast to the alleged advantages of specialization, it may be optimal for the agent to invest not only in vocational training but also in general education. This is done in the context of an overlapping generation model where the agent lives for two periods. During the first period, the agent can invest in heterogeneous human capital. During the second period, the agent is taken to have a full-time job whereby he earns the benefits of his investments. Each type of human capital is assumed to yield a specific return which may differ in the short and in the long run.

The returns to the different kinds of human capital are analyzed under both certainty and uncertainty with uncertainty introduced through the fluctuations of the returns to human capital. The results obtained from the two worlds of certainty and uncertainty are then compared with respect to the tendency of specialization in vocational training and the consequences in terms of economic growth.

The certainty case points to a strong tendency of the agent to specialize in old specific vocational training due to a learning effect. This specialization is shown not always to enhance economic growth. Under uncertainty, on the other hand, the agent may prefer to diversify his investment between general education and several kinds of vocational training to be able to adapt quickly to economic fluctuations that influence returns on human capital. It is further demonstrated that this choice of multivalence may also have a positive impact on economic growth.

Based on these theoretical outcomes, the authors conclude that since the agents' behaviour when investing in human capital seems to affect economic growth, government policies should aim at inducing agents to choose the investment structure which enhances growth.

2 Schooling, Learning and Worker Productivity

John Bishop
Cornell University, New York, United States[1]

2.1 Introduction

"Knowledge and Human Power are Synonymous"
Francis Bacon

Concern about slackening productivity growth and deteriorating competitiveness has in many countries resulted in a new focus on the skills and education of frontline workers. The introduction of Lean Production and Total-Quality-Management is apparently raising the cognitive demands placed on blue collar workers (Womack, Jones and Roos 1991). Increasingly they are working in production cells in which every member of the team is expected to learn every job and to take on responsibilities formerly the sole province of supervisors, specialized technicians and industrial engineers. Higher order thinking and problem solving skills are believed to be in particularly short supply so much attention has been given to mathematics and science education because it is thought that these subjects are particularly relevant to their development (Secretary's Commission on Achieving Necessary Skills 1991).

[1] The work reported herein was supported in part under the Educational Research and Development Center program, agreement number R117Q00011-91, as administered by the Office of Educational Research and Improvement, US Department of Education and a grant to Cornell from the Pew Charitable Trust. I would like to thank John Gary and George Jakubson for their assistance in creating the extract of the NLS Youth analyzed in Section 2.2. I would also like to express my appreciation to Lauress Wise, Jeffrey McHenry, Milton Maier, Jim Harris, Jack Hunter and Frank Schmidt for their assistance in locating and interpreting the various studies of job performance in the military and Peter Mueser, Marc Bendick, David Levine, Paul Ong, Andrew Weiss, Sheldon Zedeck and Nambury Raju for helpful comments on an earlier version of this paper. The findings and opinions expressed in this report do not reflect the position or policies of the Office of Educational Research and Improvement or the US Department of Education.

The debate has been enlivened by the availability of comparative data on mathematics and science achievement of representative samples of secondary school students from many industrialized nations. At age 13 the mathematical achievement of Finnish students (48.4 percent correct on the SIMS test) is roughly equal to England and Scotland, slightly ahead of the New Zealand and the United States (46.2 percent) and substantially below France (53.6 percent), Belgium (52.8 percent), the Netherlands (58 percent), and Japan (63.6 percent). Swedish students got only 43.4 percent of the questions correct and rank below all of the industrialized nations with the exception of Luxembourg.

By the end of secondary school, however, the Finnish and Swedish students who are taking advanced mathematics courses intended to prepare for university education were substantially ahead of university bound students in Scotland, Belgium, Canada and the United States. This group represented 13 percent of the age cohort in the US, 12 percent in Japan and Sweden, 15 percent in Finland and 50 percent in Hungary. Figure 2.1 plots the percent correct on the Algebra section of the Second International Mathematics Study against the proportion of the 18-year old population in the types of courses to which the international test was administered. Finnish students achieved the second highest mean score: 69 percent correct. Sweden's 60 percent correct was in the middle of the pack; half way between the Japanese mean of 78 percent correct and the US mean of 43 percent correct (McKnight et al. 1987).

The findings of the Second International Science Study place Finland, Norway and Sweden in the middle of the pack and the US at the bottom. For 15 year olds, the percent correct on the general science test was 72 for Hungary, 67 for Japan, 62 for Finland, 61 for Sweden, 60 for Norway and 55 for the US. Only a small share of an age cohort typically takes advanced science courses in the final year of secondary school. The IAEEA data suggests that the Finnish percentages – 14 percent in physics, 16 percent in chemistry and 42 percent in biology – are higher than in most other countries. Swedish percentages were 5 percent in biology and 13 percent in chemistry and physics. Norwegian percentages were 10 percent in physics, 6 percent in chemistry and 4 percent in biology. Clearly, large numbers of Scandinavian students take rigorous science courses in secondary school.

Normally, countries with large proportions of the age cohort in advanced courses have lower mean scores. Finnish and Swedish scores are below the grand mean primarily for this reason. The exceptions to this generalization are the standout performance of Finland in biology and of Hong Kong in chemistry and physics and the dismal performance of the very select samples (1 to 2 percent of the age cohort in chemistry and physics) in America. The 6 percent of American 17–18 year olds who were taking their second biology course knew considerably less than much less selective groups of students in Europe, Canada and Asia (Postlethwaite and Wiley 1992).

Clearly, there are large gaps between the science and math competence of young people from different nations. Do such gaps have major consequences for a nation's standard of living? In the view of many, it does:

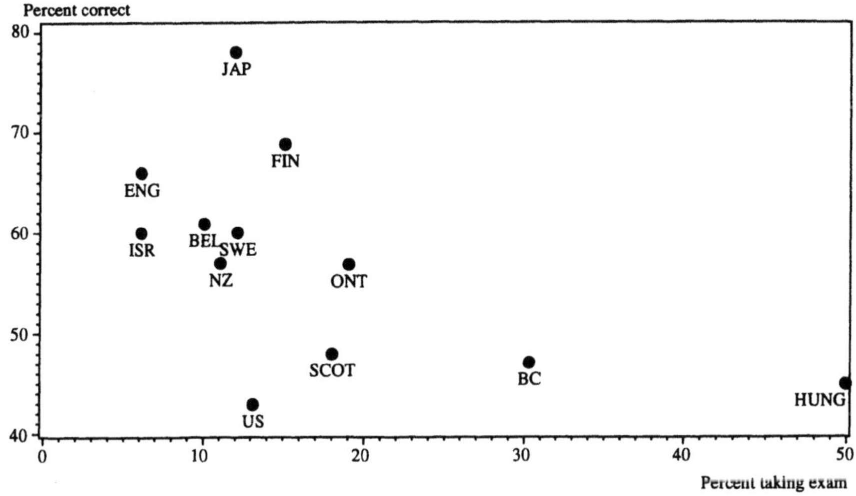

Fig. 2.1. Algebra results for 17-year-olds

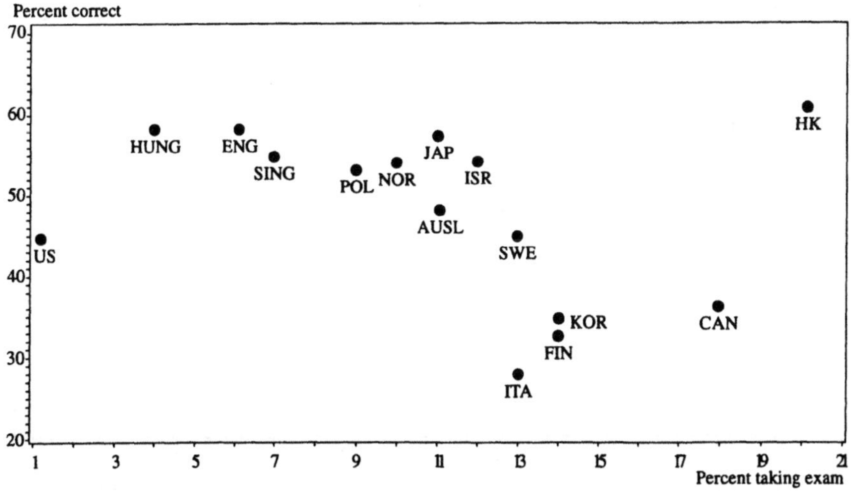

Fig. 2.2. Physics results for 18-year-olds

> Learning is the indispensable investment required for success in the "information age" we are entering (National Commission on Excellence in Education 1983, p. 7).

Behind their call for higher standards and more class time devoted to math and science is an assumption that most jobs require significant competency in these fields. There is, however, some controversy about these claims. Morris Shamos,

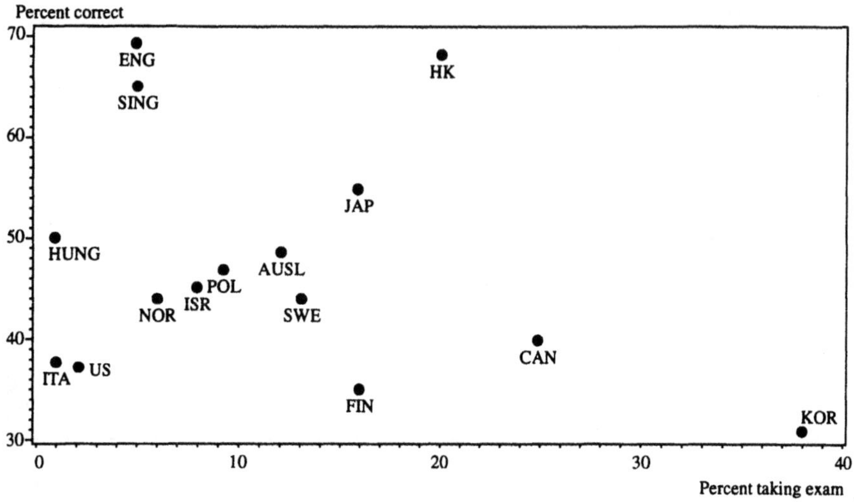

Fig. 2.3. Chemistry results for 18-year-olds

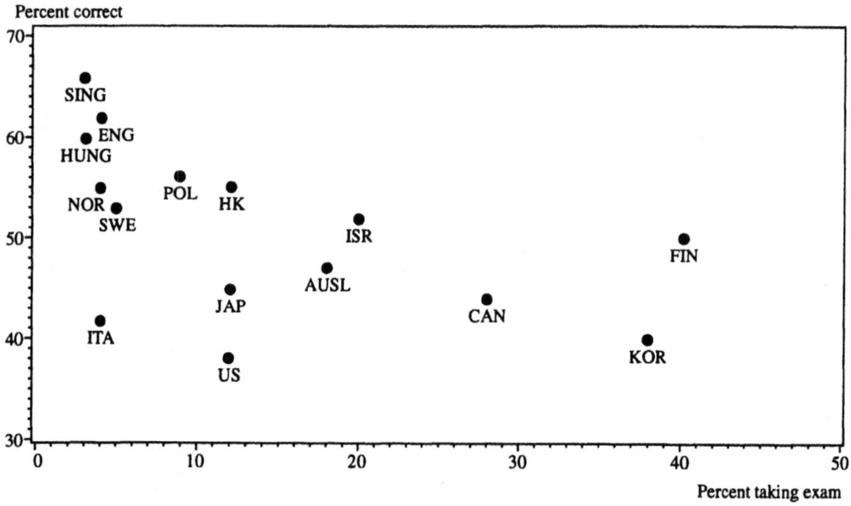

Fig. 2.4. Biology results for 18-year-olds

an emeritus professor of physics at New York University, argues, for example, that "widespread scientific literacy is *not* essential to ... prepare people for an increasingly technological society" (Education Week Nov. 23 1988, p. 28). Other commentators have questioned the relevance of algebra and geometry to the great majority of jobs that do not require technical training. It has been argued, for example, that since the great majority of employers do not currently use the new management techniques that are supposed to require a high skill work force, preparing young people for working in high performance work systems will make them unfitted for the boring and repetitive jobs that are assumed to predominate in the labor market.

This paper examines whether evidence from the labor market supports the claims that schooling and academic achievement improve worker productivity and that the impacts of schooling and achievement have increased during the 1980s. It attempts to answer two questions:

- What would be the benefits of a frontline work force that was much better prepared in mathematics and science *if current jobs remained essentially unchanged?*
- Is the occupational distribution of jobs changing in ways that increase the need for rigorous study of math and science in secondary school?

The paper has two parts. Section 2.2 examines the effects of academic competencies on productivity in traditional mass production settings. The jobs studied are not located in high involvement/lean production work systems and are occupied almost entirely by workers who have not graduated from college. Section 2.3 analyzes trends in occupational composition of employment, in supplies of highly skilled workers and in the payoff to skill.

2.2 The Impact of Academic Competencies on Worker Productivity in Current Jobs

The standard way of assessing the impact of a worker trait on productivity is to infer its effect by studying its effect on wage rates. That is what is attempted in Sections 2.2.1, 2.2.2 and 2.2.3.

Sections 2.2.1 and 2.2.2 present evidence that the effect of generalized academic competence on the wage rates of *adults* is substantial and reflects a causal relationship.

Section 2.2.3 examines the impact of the specific academic competencies on the wage rates and earnings of *young* workers in the United States. The surprising finding, here, is that competence in mathematical reasoning, science and language arts has almost no effect on wage rates during the first 8 years after graduating from high school. These results suggest an immediate explanation for the poor performance of American students in science and higher-level mathematics – the absence of significant rewards for the competencies. They appear, however, to provide only very weak support for the Excellence Commission's recommendations.

The reports recommending educational reform, however, make claims about the productivity effects not the *wage rate* effects of science, mathematics and language arts competency. Are these effects necessarily the same? This question is addressed in Section 2.2.4. It is concluded that, when the specific competencies of students are not signaled to the labor market by a credential (as is the case for math and science achievement in US high schools), there is very little reason to expect the wage rate effects of specific competencies which are highly correlated with each other to be the same as their productivity effects.

Sections 2.2.5 and 2.2.6 of the paper, therefore, tackle the productivity effects question more directly by analyzing data sets in which worker competencies have been correlated with their relative job performance in specific jobs. These analyses provide support for recommendations for better preparation in math and science, but they also reinforce the findings from the analysis of wage rates, earnings and unemployment regarding the important role of technical competence in blue collar, craft and technician jobs.

2.2.1 The Effect of General Academic Achievement on Wages of Adults

We will examine the effect of overall academic achievement on wage rates by predicting adult wage rates as a function of a *contemporaneous* measure of general academic achievement while controlling for schooling and other worker characteristics such as work experience. It is essential that the sample be representative of the nation and that academic achievement be measured long after the completion of schooling and as close as possible to the date of the wage rate observation. The difficulty, however, is that reliable academic achievement tests are time consuming and costly to administer. Consequently, data sets which measure both adult academic achievement and earnings for national probability samples are rare. There is only one American data set with these characteristics, the Panel Study of Income Dynamics. Unfortunately, the measure of academic achievement available in the survey is a short form IQ test with 13 sentence completion questions (taken from the Lorge-Thorndike intelligence test) which has a KR-20 reliability of only .652. If not corrected for, measurement error will seriously attenuate estimated relationships between wage rates and such a short form IQ test.

Consequently, the true impact of general academic achievement *(GAA)* and years of schooling on wage rates must be estimated as part of a system of equations that includes a measurement model for academic achievement, years of schooling *(SCH)* and family background.[2] When such a model is estimated, the

---

[2] The model estimated was:

$$lnWEARN = a_o + a_1 GAA + a_2 SCH + a_3 AGE + a_4 NOWHITE + \underline{a_5 TRUEBG} + u_1$$
$$TEST = GAA + u_2$$
$$YRED = SCH + u_3$$
$$\underline{MEASBG} = \underline{c} \cdot \underline{TRUEBG} + \underline{u_4}$$

true effect of general academic achievement is calculated to be a 20.9 percent increase in earnings per population standard deviation change/difference in achievement. These results suggest that if the *GAA* of people with given levels of schooling either changes over historical time or differs across societies, these differences need to be explicitly included in any accounting of differences in labor quality across space or time.

2.2.2 Are Regression Estimates of the Economic Payoff to Knowledge and Skill Biased?

Will, however, improvements in performance on such tests resulting from a more rigorous, higher quality education have a similar effect on productivity? The absence of controls for the individual's genetic endowment in the above analysis

---

MEASBG is a vector of imperfectly measured characteristics of the individual's true family background: *TRUEBG* = [father's education, father's occupation (Duncan index), number of siblings, father foreign born, born on a farm, born in the South]. *GAA*, *SCH* and the elements of *TRUEBG* are latent variables with measurement errors (u_2, u_3 and u_4) which are uncorrelated with each other and with equation error (u_1). *Var(GAA)* is normalized to 1, *Var(GAA)/Var(TEST)* = .652 and *Var(SCH)/Var (YRED)* = .915. For the three dummy variables (Father foreign born, Born on a farm, and Born in the South), reliability is assumed to be .903 and c_i is assumed to be equal to .95. For the other three background variables, c_i is assumed to be 1 and the reliabilities are assumed to be .702 for father's education, .735 for father's occupation and .927 for number of siblings (Jencks et al. 1979, Table A2.14). The results of estimating such a model predicting the log of weekly earnings in 1971 PSID data on male household heads 25 to 64 years old are:

$$\begin{aligned} lnWEARN = {} & .190GAA + .0576SCH + .004AGE - .06NOWHITE + .005FAED \\ & (6.26) \qquad (6.24) \qquad (2.92) \qquad (1.25) \qquad (.45) \\ & - .0028FAOCC - .0002SIBS + .076\,FAFOR - .152BORNFARM \\ & (1.44) \qquad (.03) \qquad (1.74) \qquad (3.58) \\ & - .009BORNSOUTH + a_o \qquad R^2 = .268 \\ & (.25) \qquad N = 1774 \end{aligned}$$

T statistics are in parenthesis below the coefficient. Except for *BORNFARM*, none of the indicators of family background have a significant direct effect on weekly earnings. The addition of these variables to the model causes a small (7 percent) reduction in the coefficient on academic achievement. If there is no correction for errors in measurement the coefficient on academic achievement (*GAA*) is .109 and the coefficient on schooling is .0596. Thus, correcting for measurement error increases the estimated effect of academic achievement by 74 percent and reduces the direct effect of years of schooling very slightly (Bishop 1989).

might mean that the 20.9 percent effect is an upward biased estimate of the true causal impact of test score gains generated by higher quality education. There are a number of reasons for believing that if such bias exists, it is small. First, while genetic endowment has probably influenced schooling and academic achievement as an adult, it appears to have no direct effect on wages in this data set, for adding the three background variables – father's education, father's occupation and number of siblings – with the highest correlation with genetic endowment did not decrease the coefficient on academic achievement. It was the addition of Born on a Farm and Father Foreign Born which lowered the coefficient on academic achievement. Secondly, controlling for family background and genetic endowment by estimating within family models comparing brothers actually increases the effect of academic ability relative to cross section regressions of earnings on education and childhood IQ in Michael Olneck's (1977) Kalamazoo data.

The test used to characterize general academic achievement in this analysis purports to be an "aptitude" test. But, verbal and mathematical aptitude tests correlate almost as highly with broad spectrum achievement tests as alternate forms of the same test correlate with each other.[3] Numerous studies have found that school attendance raises scores on these aptitude tests (Lorge 1945, Husen 1951, Department of Labor 1970), and that taking a rigorous college prep curriculum increases the gains on these tests between sophomore and senior years of high school (Bishop 1985, Hotchkiss 1984). In recognition of the fact that aptitude test scores are significantly influenced by educational background, the College Board describes the SAT as a measure of "developed verbal and mathematical reasoning abilities" (1987, p. 3).

Adult vs Childhood GAA Tests. The final piece of evidence on this issue comes from examining the results of estimations where adult GAA tests compete with childhood IQ tests in predicting adult labor market success. It is sometimes argued that aptitude tests like the Lorge-Thorndike test really measure a stable "ability to learn" which is not substantially effected by educational experiences after the age of 10, and that it is this "ability to learn" not the content of the courses taken in

[3] For example, reliabilities for the College Board's afternoon Scholastic Achievement Tests are .90 for English Literature and .87 for Math I and for the morning Scholastic Aptitude Tests are .91-.92. The correlation between Math I and the Math SAT is .83 and the correlation between English Literature and the Verbal SAT is .84 (College Board 1984, 1987). In contrast, the correlation between math and verbal SATs is .66. There are good reasons for high correlations between past achievement in a subject and scores on aptitude tests designed to predict future achievement in the subject. Past achievement aids learning because the tools (e.g. reading and mathematics) and concepts taught early in the curriculum are often essential for learning the material that comes later. Furthermore, aptitude tests are validated on later achievement levels, not on rates of change of achievement. Consequently, many of the items that are included are similar to the items that appear on achievement tests.

secondary and tertiary education which helps workers who score well on these tests to get better, higher paying jobs. If this were true, we would expect childhood IQ tests to predict adult labor market success just as well as GAA tests taken as a young adult. In fact, however, when the two tests are simultaneously entered into a model, it is the adult test not the childhood test which has by far the biggest effect on labor market success (Husen 1969). Evidence for this statement can be found in Tables 2.1 to 2.3. American data from the National Longitudinal Study of Youth (NLSY) was analyzed to determine whether 1985 wages and earnings were more influenced by a test taken in 1980 (the Armed Services Vocational Aptitude Battery) or by aptitude tests taken in the early 1970s. The results reported in Table 2.1 clearly imply that the later test had by far the most significant effect, implying that the learning that occurred during the interval between test administrations had a substantial impact on subsequent labor market outcomes.

Tuijnman's (1989) analysis of occupational attainment in the Malmo Longitudinal Study is reproduced in Table 2.2. The path coefficients on the test taken at age 20 has significant positive effects on occupational status, while the childhood test often has a negative effect when the adult test is included in the model. Table 2.3 reports the results from a similar model predicting earnings rather than occupation.[4] The estimated effect of the IQ tests on earnings in the Malmo data is much smaller than the effects obtained in NLSY data. This might reflect the general compression of wage differentials in Sweden, the inclusion of technical competence and speed of numerical computation in the ASVAB test battery, or possibly a shift over time in the relative importance of the competencies assessed by these tests. But, here again, the adult test has much stronger effects on earnings than the childhood test.

These findings suggest that the associations between scores on employment aptitude and IQ tests, on the one hand, and productivity and labor market success, on the other, arise because the tests measure developed abilities that contribute to productivity. This suggests that an increase in the incidence of these developed abilities in the working population will increase national output. Left unresolved, however, is the relative importance of different types of developed abilities. It is to this issue I now turn.

---

[4] Tuijnman's (1989) estimated "true" correlations were used to estimate a model in which log earnings are a function of schooling, home background and the two tests.

Table 2.1. Effect of ASVAB and early school tests on wage rates and earnings in 1985

	ASVAB	School test	Controls for educ. & background	R^2	N	F-test of equality of coef.
Males						
Log wage rate	.119 (4.91)	-.049 (2.53)	x	.243	1244	18.7***
Log earnings	.207 (5.54)	-.067 (2.27)	x	.396	1330	21.2***
Females						
Log wage rate	.092 (3.03)	.016 (.73)	x	.274	1211	
Log earnings	.100 (1.87)	-.016 (.43)	x	.315	1199	2.0

Source: Analysis of NLS Youth Data.
Note: The ASVAB test score was an average of all 9 subtests. The school test was the Z score relative to national norms on a test taken early in the youth's school career. A full set of controls for years of schooling, school attendance, actual cumulated work experience, gender, race, Hispanic and characteristics of the local labor market was included in the models. The sample was limited to youth for whom an early test score was available.

Table 2.2. Determinants of occupation in Swedish Malmo data

	Test age 20	Test age 10	Youth educ.	Home back-ground	Adult educ.
Occ 25	.45 (3.0)	-.24 (1.8)	.39 (7.2)	.08 (1.9)	- -
Occ 30	.41 (3.0)	-.21 (1.6)	.46 (9.0)	.04 (1.1)	- -
Occ 35	.35 (2.6)	-.16 (1.3)	.45 (9.0)	.10 (2.6)	.13 (3.1)
Occ 40	.39 (2.8)	-.20 (1.6)	.38 (7.5)	.14 (3.6)	.20 (4.7)
Occ 43	.38 (2.8)	-.23 (1.9)	.34 (6.7)	.14 (3.7)	.31 (6.1)
Occ 52	.31 (2.4)	-.20 (1.7)	.33 (7.0)	.09 (2.6)	.42 (9.0)
Occ 56	.36 (2.8)	-.22 (1.9)	.31 (6.5)	.09 (2.5)	.43 (9.3)

Source: Standardized regression coefficients (with T statistics in parenthesis) for models predicting occupational attainment are from Tuijnman, 1989, Supplementary Tables A 9.2 to A 9.8.

Table 2.3. Determinants of earnings in Swedish Malmo data

	Test age 20	Test age 10	Youth educ.	Home back-ground	R^2
Earn 25	.036 (1.23)	-.002 (.09)	.056 (3.13)	.015 (1.16)	.104
Earn 30	.029 (1.05)	.008 (.36)	.129 (7.60)	.022 (1.77)	.302
Earn 35	.061 (1.89)	.018 (.66)	.161 (8.00)	.071 (4.79)	.434
Earn 40	.063 (1.69)	-.017 (.56)	.247 (10.68)	.037 (2.15)	.431
Earn 43	.066 (1.65)	-.009 (.28)	.222 (9.01)	.048 (2.64)	.385
Earn 52	.032 (.79)	.020 (.60)	.165 (6.69)	.034 (1.86)	.261
Earn 56	.059 (1.35)	.005 (.15)	.151 (5.58)	.032 (1.60)	.223

Source: For log earnings models unstandardized regression coefficients are reported so the test score coefficients provide an estimate of the percentage change in earnings that results from a one population standard deviation change in the test score. They were fitted using Tuijnman's (1989) estimated "true" correlations reported in Tables 9.2, 9.8 and Appendix C.

2.2.3 Which Competencies are Rewarded in the American Labor Market?

Which of the various subjects typically taught in secondary schools yield the largest economic return? This issue will be first addressed by estimating models predicting wage rates and earnings of young adults in the US as a function of competence in the academic fields of mathematics, science and language arts and in the trade/technical arena while controlling for years of schooling, school attendance, ethnicity, age, work experience, marital status and characteristics of the local labor market.

The Data. The Youth Cohort of National Longitudinal Survey (NLSY) is a good data base for analyzing this issue because it contains subtest scores on the Armed Services Vocational Aptitude Battery (ASVAB), a three hour battery of tests used by the armed forces for selecting recruits and assigning them to occupational specialties. The primary purpose of the ASVAB is to predict the success of new recruits in training and their subsequent performance in their occupational specialty.[5] Even though the ASVAB was developed as an "aptitude" test, the current view of testing professionals is that:

> Achievement and aptitude tests are not fundamentally different....Tests at one end of the aptitude-achievement continuum can be distinguished from tests at the other end primarily in terms of purpose. For example, a test for mechanical aptitude would be included in a battery of tests for selecting among applicants for pilot training since knowledge of mechanical principles has been found to be related to success in flying. A similar test would be given at the end of a course in mechanics as an achievement test intended to measure what was learned in the course (National Academy of Sciences Committee on Ability Testing 1982, p. 27).

The ASVAB test battery is made up of 10 subtests: Mechanical Comprehension, Auto and Shop Knowledge, Electronics Knowledge, Clerical Checking (Coding Speed), Numerical Operations (a speeded test of simple arithmetic), Arithmetic Reasoning, Mathematics Knowledge (covering the high school math curriculum), General Science, Word Knowledge and Paragraph Comprehension. (See Bishop (1990a) for sample questions.)

Two dimensions of mathematical achievement are measured: the speed of doing simple mathematical computations is measured by a three minute 50 problem arithmetic computation subtest which will be referred to as computational speed. Mathematical reasoning ability is measured by a composite of the mathematics knowledge and arithmetic reasoning subtests. Science achievement is indexed by the ASVAB's General Science subtest. This test focuses on science definitions and has minimal coverage of higher level scientific reasoning. Verbal achievement is measured by a composite made up of the word knowledge and paragraph comprehension subtests.

The universe of skills and knowledge sampled by the mechanical comprehension, auto and shop information and electronics subtests of the ASVAB roughly corresponds to the vocational fields of trades and industry and technical

---

[5] Its ability to accomplish these objectives has been thoroughly researched and the battery has been periodically modified to incorporate the findings of this research. The test is highly correlated with the cognitive subtests of the General Aptitude Test Battery, a personnel selection test battery used by the US Employment Service, the validity of which has been established by studies of over 500 occupations. A validity generalization study funded by the armed forces concluded "that ASVAB is a highly valid predictor of performance in civilian occupations" (Hunter, Crossen and Friedman 1985, p. ix). During the summer of 1980 all members of the NLS Youth sample were asked to take this test and offered a $50 honorarium as an inducement. The tests were successfully administered to 94 percent of the sample. Testing was generally conducted in groups of 5 to 10 persons. The 1980 version of the ASVAB (Form 8A) was administered by staff of the National Opinion Research Corporation according to strict guidelines conforming to standard ASVAB procedures. At the time of the testing the NLS youth were between 15 and 23 years of age.

so these subtests are aggregated into a single composite which is interpreted as an indicator of competence in the "technical" arena.[6]

Competencies that are unique to clerical and retail sales jobs do not appear to be measured by the ASVAB. The ASVAB does contain a seven minute 84 item clerical checking subtest which was intended to predict performance in clerical jobs but validity studies of clerical jobs in the military have found that it does not add to the validity of composites based on verbal, arithmetic reasoning and mathematics knowledge subtests (Wise et al. 1987). The clerical checking subtest is included in the analysis but it should not be viewed as a valid predictor of clerical competency. These seven test composites have all been normalized to have zero mean and unit variance.[7]

All of these competencies are highly correlated with years of schooling. When these composites are regressed on age, ethnicity, proportion of 1980 spent in school, region, work experience, occupation of parents and schooling, the coefficients on years of high school range between .19 for math and .28 for verbal for males and range from .12 for technical and .24 for verbal and clerical speed for females. Greater work experience significantly increased the clerical speed of women but did not have positive effects on any of the other competencies.

Results. Two measures of labor market success were studied: the log of the hourly wage rate in the current or most recent job taken from the 1983 through 1986 interviews and the log was limited to those who were not in the military in 1979. At the time of the 1986 interview the NLS Youth ranged from 21 to 28 years of age. An extensive set of controls was included in the estimating equations.[8]

---

[6] These subtests have some similarities with the occupational competency examinations developed to assess high school vocational students. However, the ASVAB technical subtests assess knowledge in a much broader domain and the individual items are, consequently, more generic and less detailed. The ASVAB technical composite is interpreted as a measure of knowledge and trainability for a large family of jobs involving the operation, maintenance and repair of complicated machinery and other technically oriented jobs.

[7] The alternate form reliabilities of these composites are approximately .92-.93 for Technical, .93 for Math, .93-.94 for Verbal, .80 for General Science, .72 for Numerical Operations and .77 for Clerical Checking (US Military Entrance Processing Command 1984, Palmer et al. 1988).

[8] Reports of weeks spent in civilian employment were available all the way back through 1975. For each individual, these weeks worked reports were aggregated across time and an estimate of cumulated civilian work experience was derived for January 1 of each year in the longitudinal file. This variable and its square was included in every model as was age, age squared and current and past military experience. School attendance was controlled by four separate variables: a dummy for respondent is in school at the time of the interview, a dummy for respondent has been in school since the last interview, a dummy for part time attendance, and the share of the calendar year that the youth reported attending school derived from the NLS's monthly time log. Years of schooling was controlled by four

The labor market consequences of the competencies that a young person develops early in life were examined by regressing log wage rates and log earnings on ASVAB subtest scores, years of schooling, and the background variables listed above. Holding academic competencies in 1980 constant, female high school dropouts with 10 years of schooling earned 10 percent less than high school graduates and college graduates earned 42 percent more. Male high school dropouts earned 21 percent less than high school graduates and college graduates earned 35 percent more. The effects of our measures of academic and technical achievement are summarized in Figures 2.5 and 2.6 (see Bishop (1988) for a more complete description of the results).

The results for young men were as follows – *high-level academic competencies do not have positive effects on wage rates and earnings.* The mathematics reasoning, verbal and science composites all had negative effects on wage rates and earnings. Speed in arithmetic computation has substantial positive effects on labor market success of young men. This competency, however, is a lower order skill that is not (and should not be) a focus of high school mathematics (National Council of Teachers of Mathematics 1980).

For young women, speed in arithmetic computation and mathematical reasoning ability both have substantial effects on wage rates and earnings. Verbal competence had somewhat more modest positive effects on wages and earnings. *Science test scores had no effect on wage rates and earnings.*

For young men, the ASVAB technical subtests measuring electronics knowledge and mechanical, auto and shop information had large and significant positive effects on wage rates and earnings. These subtests had essentially no effect on the labor market success of young women.

The clerical checking subtest had weak positive effects on wage rates of young women and large significant effects on their earnings. For young men, doing well on the clerical checking subtest appears to increase earnings very modestly but it has no effect on wage rates.

This pattern of results is not unique to this data set. Similar results were obtained in Willis and Rosen's (1979) analysis of the earnings of those who chose not to attend college in the NBER-Thorndike data, Kang and Bishop's (1986) analysis

---

variables: years of schooling, a dummy for high school graduation, years of college education completed, and years of schooling completed since the ASVAB tests were taken. The individual's family situation was controlled by dummy variables for being married and for having at least one child. Minority status was controlled by a dummy variable for Hispanic and two dummy variables for race. Characteristics of the local labor market were held constant by entering the following variables: dummy variables for the four Census regions, a dummy variable for rural residence and for residence outside an SMSA and measures of the unemployment rate in the local labor market during that year.

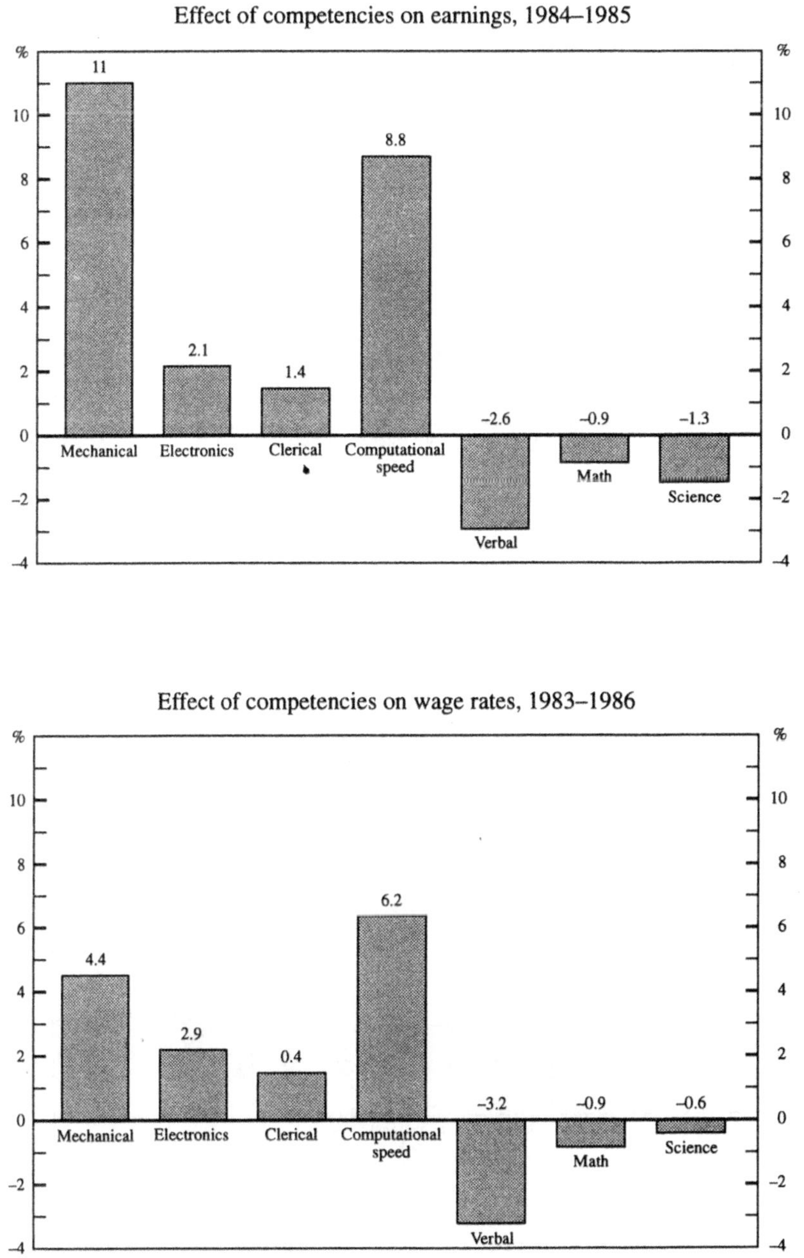

Fig. 2.5. Effect of competencies on earnings and wage rates for young men
Source: Analysis of NLS Youth data.
Note: The figure reports the effect of a one population standard deviation increase in Armed Services Vocational Aptitude Battery subtest while controlling for schooling, school attendance, age, work experience, region, SMSA residence and ethnicity.

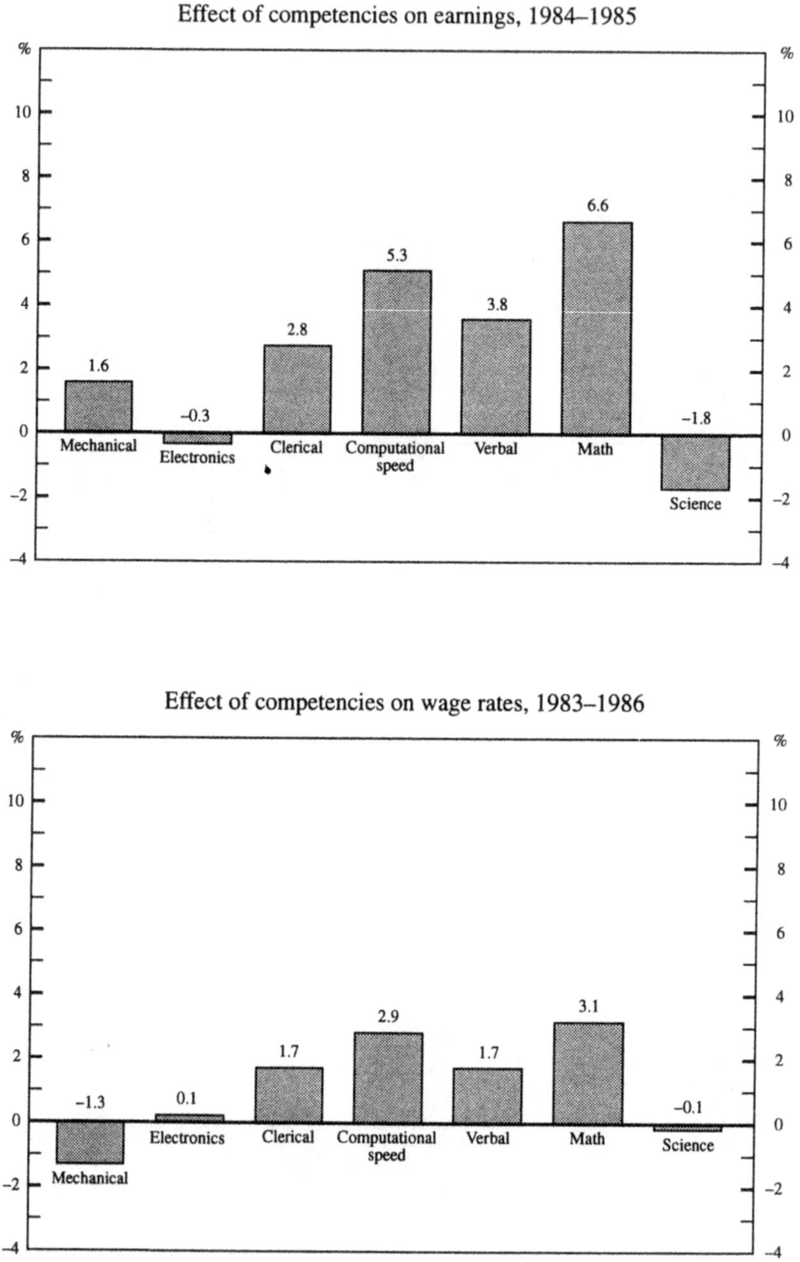

Fig. 2.6. Effect of competencies on earnings and wage rates for young women
Source: Analysis of NLS Youth data.
Note: The figure reports the effect of a one population standard deviation increase in Armed Services Vocational Aptitude Battery subtest while controlling for schooling, school attendance, age, work experience, region, SMSA residence and ethnicity.

of High School and Beyond seniors and Bishop, Blakemore and Low's (1985) analysis of both Class of 1972 and High School and Beyond data.[9]

In summary, in the United States, when years of schooling are held constant, achievement in science has no effect on wage rates, earnings or unemployment of young men and women. Achievement in mathematical reasoning has no effect on the wage rates and earnings of young men and only very modest effects on the wage rates of young women. Verbal competency has no effect on the wage rates on young men and women and no effect on the earnings of young men. These results suggest an immediate explanation for the poor performance of American students in science and higher-level mathematics. *For the 80 percent of youth who are not planning to pursue a career in medicine, science or engineering, there are no immediate labor market rewards for developing these competencies. For the great bulk of students, therefore, the incentives to devote time and energy to the often difficult task of learning these subjects are very weak.*

Do these findings also imply that if a way could be found to recruit a high quality engineering and scientific elite (possibly by recruiting scientists and engineers from abroad or early identification of mathematically and scientifically talented youth), there would be little need to worry about the poor math and science preparation of most American youth. It is to this question I now turn.

2.2.4 Is There Reason to Expect Wage Effects of Specific Competencies to be the Same as Their Productivity Effects?

Are the productivity effects of achievement in science, mathematical reasoning and English essentially zero in the types of jobs occupied by most young workers? Speed in simple arithmetic computations has large effects on the wage rates of both sexes and technical competence has large effects on wage rates of young men. Do these competencies have comparable effects on productivity?

One approach to these questions is to ask employers directly about the nature of the tasks performed by entry level workers. When the owners of small and medium sized business in the United States were asked how frequently the employee most recently hired by their firm needed to "use knowledge gained of chemistry, physics or biology" in their job, 74 percent reported that such

---

[9] Bishop, Blakemore and Low (1985) studied the effect of math, reading and vocabulary test scores on the wage rates and earnings of high school graduates for both 1972 and 1980 in a model that contained controls for grade point average and the number of credit hours of academic and vocational courses. In both these years, none of the variables representing academic performance – the three test scores, GPA and the number of academic courses – had a significant (at the ten percent level) effect on the wage rate of the first post high school job. Only one variable (the vocabulary test for female members of the class of 1972) had a significant effect on the wage 18 months after graduation.

knowledge was never required and only 12 percent reported such knowledge was used at least once a week.[10] Asked how frequently the new employee had to "use algebra, trigonometry or calculus", 68 percent reported that such skills were never required by the job and only 12 percent reported they were used at least once a week.

The skills used by entry level workers at small and medium sized firms, however, are not decisive evidence regarding employer needs for three reasons. First, the low levels of scientific and mathematical competence in the work force available to small and medium sized firms may have forced them to put off technological innovations such as statistical process control that require such skills and to simplify the functions that are performed by workers who lack technical training. If better educated workers were available, entry level workers might be given greater responsibility and become more productive. Second, the study just quoted does not tell us what is happening at large firms or in the jobs occupied by long tenure employees at small firms. The CEOs of many large technologically progressive companies such as Motorola and Xerox are insisting that their factory jobs now require workers who are much better prepared in math and science than ever before. Third, employers may not realize how the knowledge and skills developed in high school science and mathematics classes contribute to productivity in their jobs. Not knowing which employee possesses which academic skill, they would have no way of learning from experience which scientific and mathematical skills are helpful in doing a particular job. Science and mathematics are thought to teach thinking, reasoning and learning skills applicable outside the classroom and the laboratory. If these skills are indeed successfully developed by these courses, productivity might benefit even when there are no visible connections between job tasks and course content.

A second approach to estimating the effect of a trait on productivity, one favored by economists, has been to infer its effect by studying its effect on wage rates. Such an approach is not justified in this case. In the United States academic achievements in high school – particularly the fine details of achievement in a particular domain like science, mathematical reasoning or reading ability – are not well signaled to the labor market. When competencies which are highly correlated with each other are poorly signaled to the labor market, American employers have a difficult time figuring out which competencies they need and an even more difficult time finding high school graduates with the particular constellations of academic abilities they may believe they need. As a result, the relationship between their wage offers and the imperfect signals of worker competencies available to them is unlikely to reflect the true relationship between productivity and these competencies.

---

[10] The survey was of a stratified random sample of the National Federation of Independent Business membership. Larger firms had a significantly higher probability of being selected for the study. The response rate to the mail survey was 20 percent and the number of usable responses was 2014 (Bishop and Griffin, forthcoming).

The Signaling Failure in the United States. In Canada, Australia, Japan, and Europe, educational systems administer achievement exams which are closely tied to the secondary school curriculum. Students generally take between 3 and 9 different examinations. These are not pass/fail minimum competency exams. On the Baccalaureate, for example, there are four different levels of pass: *Tre's Bien, Bien, Assez Bien* and a regular pass (Noah and Eckstein 1988). In Europe, grades on these exams are requested on job applications and typically included on one's resume. Exhibit 1 in Figure 2.7 reproduces a resume used by an Irish secondary school graduate applying for a clerical job. Exhibit 2 in the figure is the first page of an application filed by a 28-year-old university graduate seeking a managerial job. While employers report they pay less attention to exam grades when hiring workers who have been out of school many years, it is nevertheless significant that the information remains on one's resume long after graduation from secondary school.

In Japan, clerical, service and blue collar jobs at the best firms are available only to those who are recommended by their high school. The most prestigious firms have long term arrangements with particular high schools to which they delegate the responsibility of selecting the new hire(s) for the firm. The criteria by which the high school is to make its selection is, by mutual agreement, grades and exam results. In addition, most employers administer their own battery of selection tests prior to hiring. The number of graduates that a high school is able to place in this way depends on its reputation and the company's past experience with graduates from the school. Schools know that they must be forthright in their recommendations because if they fail just once to make an honest recommendation, the relationship will be lost and their students will no longer be able to get jobs at that firm (Rosenbaum and Kariya 1987).

The hiring environment for clerical, service and blue collar jobs is very different in the US. American employers generally lack objective information on applicant accomplishments, skills, and productivity. Tests are available for measuring competencies, but EEOC guidelines resulted in a drastic reduction in their use after 1971. A 1987 survey of 2014 small and medium sized employers who were members of the National Federation of Independent Business found that aptitude test scores had been obtained in only 2.9 percent of the hiring decisions studied (Bishop and Griffin, forthcoming).

Other potential sources of information on effort and achievement in American high school are transcripts and referrals from teachers who know the applicant. Both are under-used. In the NFIB survey, when someone with 12 or fewer years of schooling was hired, the new hire had been referred or recommended by vocational teachers only in 5.2 percent of the cases and referred by someone else in the high school in only 2.7 percent. Transcripts had been obtained prior to the selection decision for only 14.2 percent of the hires of people with 12 or fewer years of schooling. Transcripts are not obtained because differing grading standards in different schools and courses make them difficult to interpret, because many high schools are not responding to requests for the information and because there are generally long delays before the transcripts arrive.

The only information about school experiences requested by most American employers is years of schooling, diplomas and certificates obtained, and area of

APPLICATION FOR APPOINTMENT

Appointment applied for: Distribution Projects Manager (B+Q) Ref.No. ....

PERSONAL DETAILS: (block capitals)

Surname .... Title Mr. Forenames Mervyn John

Address ....

.... Postal Code .... Tel.No.Home .... Work ....

Marital Status M Children/Dependants (with ages) 1 x 4yrs, 1 x 1yr

Age 33 Date of Birth 5-8-55 Nationality British Place of Birth ....

State of health OK Height 6' Weight 13st 12lbs

Any disabilities/recurrent medical problems? None Regd.disabled —

Driving Licenses Car Car Owner ✓ Company Car —

Endorsements, convictions, accidents, etc. None

Leisure activities and offices held in clubs and societies Cycling/Walking

EDUCATION:

Secondary Education

From	To	School	Exams Taken (inc. grades)	Other achievements
1966	1972	Barnstaple Grammar	'O' Level: Eng. Lang. (2), Maths (?), French (?), Geog. (3), Statistics (?), Chemistry (3), Add. Maths (6), Hist. (6), Physics (6); 'A' Level: Chem. (E), Physics (E), Maths (O)	Middle Sch. Games Captain

Further Education

From	To	College/Univ.	Course & results (inc.class/grades)	Other achievements
1972	1973	Univ. of Bradford	Applied Chemistry - left after 1 year - domestic reasons	

Other training and qualifications (inc. in-company and external courses, etc.)

From	To	Establishment	Training/Qualifications
1979		Farnley College, Leeds	Cert. of Prof. Competence (Transport ops)
1983	1984	Bradford College	Inst. of Industrial Management Cert.
1984	1989	In-Company	Numerous Management Classes

Membership of professional bodies

Date	Association/Institute	Grade of membership	Offices held

Application Form Completed by an Older University Dropout for a Managerial Position in the Private Sector in the United Kingdom

CURRICULUM VITAE

Name ;
Address ;
Date of Birth ;
Place of Birth ;
Nationality ;
Marital Status ;
Occupation ;
Father's name ;
Occupation ;

EDUCATION :

August 1980 – June 1985.
(All five years were spent learning through Irish.)

U.C.D.

QUALIFICATIONS :

Subject:	Intermediate Cert. (June 1983)	Leaving Cert. (June 1985)
Irish	C (H)	C (H)
English	D (H)	C (H)
Mathematics	B (H)	A (P)
French	D	C (P)
German	D	–
Science	A	–
Chemistry	–	C (H)
Physics	–	C (H)
History	B	C (H)
Geography	B	–

Reproduction of an Irish Secondary School Graduate's Resume Submitted for a Clerical Position

Fig. 2.7. Examples of resumes submitted in connection with job applications

specialization. Hiring decisions are based on easily observable characteristics which are imperfect signals of the competencies the employer cannot observe directly. As a result, hiring selections and starting wage rates are often not influenced by even very gross indicators of academic achievement such as GPA, AFQT or SAT scores (Bishop 1987b). Given the limited information available to American employers prior to hiring, it is not realistic to expect their decisions to reflect in a refined manner the specific combinations of academic competencies that students bring to the market.

But after a worker has been at a firm a while, the employer presumably learns more about the individual's capabilities and is able to observe performance on the job. Workers assigned to the same job often produce very different levels of output (Hunter, Schmidt and Judiesch 1988). Why, one might ask, are the most productive workers (those with just the right mix of specific competencies) not given large wage increases reflecting their higher productivity? The reason appears to be that workers and employers prefer employment contracts which offer only modest adjustments of relative wages in response to perceived differences in relative productivity. There are a number of good reasons for this preference: the unreliability of the feasible measures of individual productivity (Hashimoto and Yu 1980), the unwillingness of workers to risk that their wage may be reduced if their supervisor decides they are not doing a good job (Stiglitz 1974), the absence of any real danger that one's best employees will be raided because the skills of these top performers can be fully used only within the firm (Bishop 1987a), the desire to encourage cooperation among coworkers (Lazear 1986) and union preferences for pay structures which limit the power of supervisors. In addition, compensation for better than average job performance may be non-pecuniary – praise from one's supervisor, more relaxed supervision, or a high rank in the firm's social hierarchy (Frank 1984).

A study of how individual wage rates varied with initial job performance found that when people hired for the same or very similar jobs are compared, someone who is 20 percent more productive than average is typically paid only 1.6 percent more. After a year at a firm, better producers received only a 4 percent higher wage at nonunion firms with about 20 employees, and they had no wage advantage at unionized establishments with more than 100 employees or at nonunion establishments with more than 400 employees (Bishop 1987a). Over time there is some tendency for those with high test scores to be promoted more rapidly and to be employed more continuously (Wise 1975, Bishop 1991). Since, however, worker productivity cannot be measured accurately and cannot be signaled reliably to other employers, this sorting process is slow and only partially effective. Consequently, when men and women under the age of 30 are studied, the wage rate effects of specific competencies may not correspond to their true effects on productivity and, therefore, direct evidence on productivity effects of specific competencies is required before conclusions may be drawn. We turn now to an examination of direct evidence on the effects of academic and technical competencies on the job performance. Research on the determinants of job performance in the US military is examined in Section 2.2.5. Research on the determinants of job performance in the civilian sector is examined in Section 2.2.6.

2.2.5 The Impact of Academic and Generic Technical Competencies on the Job Performance in the American Military

The theoretical arguments of the previous section will now be put to an empirical test. Direct estimates of the relative importance of different competencies are obtained by estimating models in which measures of job performance in the military are regressed on all 9 subtest scores of the ASVAB battery. These direct measures of the productivity effects of the competencies measured by the ASVAB will then be compared to the wage and earnings effects of ASVAB subtests presented in Section 2.2.2. Is technical competence an important determinant of job performance as well as wages? Do verbal skills and scientific competencies which have no effects on wage rates, nevertheless, have significant positive effects on job performance? The wages and earnings of young men were influenced by computational speed not mathematical reasoning ability. Is this the case for job performance as well?

The ASVAB is one of the most thoroughly researched selection and classification batteries in existence, so there is a wealth of evidence on how its subtests effect job performance in a great variety of jobs. The test battery was developed by the US armed forces for use within the military, so military recruits have been the subject of almost all of this research. Eighty percent of the jobs held by enlisted personnel in the military have civilian counterparts (US Department of Defense 1984). The civilian occupations that are not represented in the ASVAB research are professional, manager, farmer, sales representative, and sales clerk. Since most of the soldiers studied were young and male, generalizing to other populations must be done with care. This is not a problem in this study, however, for the desired comparisons are with other young males, those in the NLS.

Studies of Training Success. Most of the validity research has involved correlating scores on ASVAB tests taken prior to induction with final grades in occupationally specific training courses (generally measured at least 4 months after induction). Since recruits are selected into the army and into the various specialties by a nonrandom process, mechanisms have been developed to correct for selection effects – what I/O psychologists call restriction of range (Thorndike 1949, Lord and Novick 1968, Dunbar and Linn 1986). These selection models assume that selection into a particular MOS is based on ASVAB subtest scores (and in some cases measures of the recruit's occupational interests). For the military environment, this appears to be a reasonable specification of the selection process for attrition is low and selection is indeed explicitly on observable test scores. This ability to model the selection process is an advantage that validity research in the military has over research in the civilian sector.

A reanalysis was conducted of data from two large scale studies of Marine recruits (Sims and Hiatt 1981 reprinted in Hunter, Crossen and Friedman 1985, Maier and Truss 1985). These studies were selected because they used versions of the ASVAB that were quite similar to the one administered to the NLS Youth Cohort. Correlation matrices which had been corrected (for restriction of range and selection effects) were obtained from the appendices of these studies and LISREL was employed to estimate models in which training grades were regressed on the full set of ASVAB subtests. The standardized regression coefficients from this analysis are reported in Table 2.4.

The results were similar to the wage and earnings regressions in only one respect: technical competency as indexed by the mechanical, auto-shop and electronics subtests had major effects on success in training for occupations involving the maintenance or use of complicated equipment. *In all other respects, however, the results contrast sharply with the wage rate regressions for young males.* The math knowledge and arithmetic reasoning subtests have much larger effects on training success than the computational speed test. Both the science and verbal subtests have strong positive impacts on success in training. It appears that the higher-level academic competencies measured by the ASVAB have much larger positive effects on success in training programs than on wage rates of young men in the civilian sector.

Reanalysis of Maier and Grafton's Data on Job Performance. In the reanalysis we reported above, training success was measured by a paper and pencil test. There is a danger that validity coefficients may be biased by common methods bias. It would be desirable to check these findings in a data set in which ASVAB subtest scores predict a hands-on measure of job performance. Maier and Grafton's (1981) study of ASVAB 6/7's ability to predict the hands-on Skill Qualification Test (SQTs) provides such a data set. Maier and Grafton described the hands-on SQTs they used in their study as follows:

> SQTs are designed to assess performance of critical job tasks. They are criterion referenced in the sense that test content is based explicitly on job requirements and the meaning of the test scores is established by expert judgement prior to administration of the test rather than on the basis of score distributions obtained from administration. The content of SQTs is a carefully selected sample from the domain of critical tasks in a specialty. Tasks are selected because they are especially critical, such as a particular weapon system, or because there is a known training deficiency. The focus on training deficiencies means that relatively few on the job can perform the tasks, and the pass rate for these tasks therefore is expected to be low. Since only critical tasks in a specialty are included in SQTs, and then only the more difficult tasks tend to be selected for testing, a reasonable inference is that performance on the SQTs should be a useful indicator of proficiency on the entire domain of critical tasks in the specialty; that is, workers who are proficient on tasks included in an SQT are also proficient on other tasks in the specialty. The list of tasks in the SQT and the measure themselves are carefully reviewed by job experts and tried out on samples of representative job incumbents prior to operational administration (pp. 4-5).

A more extensive discussion of the procedures for developing SQTs is available in a handbook (Osborn et al. 1977). A thorough discussion of their rationale is provided in Maier and Hirshfeld (1978).

Regressions were estimated using LISREL for nine major categories of Military Occupational Specialties (MOS): Skilled Technical, Skilled Electronic, General

Table 2.4. Cognitive determinants of success in Marine training programs

	Mechanicalc ompre-hension	Auto & shop knowledge	Elec-tronics	Clerical speed	Compu-tational speed	Math reasoning	Math knowledge	Verbal	Science	Spatial	R^2
Sims and Hiatt (1981): ASVAB 6/7 (23061)											
All occupations	.043*** (5.20)	.098*** (12.46)	.047*** (5.78)	.013** (2.29)	.060*** (8.96)	.116*** (14.44)	.205*** (25.26)	.086*** (11.68)	.089*** (10.68)	.037 (5.89)	.345
Maier and Truss (1985): ASVAB 8/9/10											
Electronics repair (4103)	.055*** (2.73)	.027 (1.40)	.102*** (4.81)	.009 (.69)	.062*** (3.44)	.151*** (6.41)	.256*** (11.91)	.031 (1.40)	.130*** (5.73)	–	.492
Mechanical maintenance (5841)	.058*** (3.29)	.253*** (15.02)	.094*** (5.02)	.063*** (4.44)	.014 (.87)	.086*** (4.16)	.135*** (7.14)	.120*** (6.27)	.005 (.27)	–	.444
Operators, Food (1897)	.079*** (2.72)	.063** (2.27)	.018 (.57)	.086*** (3.66)	.022 (.82)	.137*** (4.02)	.199*** (6.41)	.164*** (5.20)	.093*** (2.84)	–	.490
Clerical (5231)	.014 (.74)	-.022 (1.22)	.026 (1.33)	.136*** (9.03)	.037** (2.26)	.125*** (5.70)	.259*** (13.02)	.206*** (10.14)	-.101 (.47)	–	.443
Combat (8191)	.087*** (4.98)	.078*** (4.68)	.020 (1.09)	.027* (1.95)	.056*** (3.62)	.069** (3.40)	.143*** (7.71)	.073*** (3.88)	.061*** (3.12)	–	.251
Field artillery (1062)	.055 (1.34)	.237 (6.01)	-.009 (.21)	.178*** (5.36)	.060 (1.64)	.148*** (3.07)	.138*** (3.13)	-.011 (.24)	.065 (1.41)	–	.448

Maintenance, Mechanical Maintenance, Clerical, Missile Battery and Food Service Operators, Unskilled Electronic, Combat and Field Artillery. Except for combat and field artillery, these MOSs have close counterparts in the civilian sector. The independent variables were the 10 ASVAB 6/7 subtest scores which had counterparts in the ASVAB 8A battery used in the analysis of NLS Youth. The standardized regression coefficients from this analysis are reported in Table 2.5. These coefficients are an estimate of the effect of a one population standard deviation improvement in a test score on the hands-on job performance criterion measured in standard deviation units. Since the ASVAB subtests measure competencies with error and this error has not been corrected for, these results provide lower bound estimates of the effects of the true competencies on true job performance.

The effects of the four "technical" subtests – mechanical comprehension, auto information, shop information and electronics information – are presented in the first four columns of the table. As one might anticipate, these subtests had no effect on job performance in clerical jobs. However, they had very substantial effects on job performance in all the other occupations. The impact of a one population standard deviation increase in all four of these subtests is an increase in the SQT of .415 SD in skilled technical jobs, of .475 SD in skilled electronics jobs, of .316 SD in general maintenance jobs, of .473 SD in mechanical maintenance jobs, of .450 SD for missile battery operators and food service workers, of .170 SD in unskilled electronics jobs, of .345 SD in combat occupations and .270 SD in field artillery. The technical subtests appear to have larger effects on hands-on job performance than on training grades suggesting a common methods bias in validation studies which employ training grades as the criterion. The proportionate change in productivity that results is somewhere between 25 and 40 percent of these numbers.[11] If we assume the SD of true productivity averages 30 percent of the mean wage in these jobs, the impact of a simultaneous one SD increase in all four technical subtests is 11.5 percent of the wage (or about $2875 per year) averaging across the six non-clerical non-combat

[11] Studies that measure output for different workers in the same job at the same firm, using physical output as a criterion, can be manipulated to produce estimates of the standard deviation of non-transitory output variation across individuals. It averages about .14 in operative jobs, .28 in craft jobs, .34 in technician jobs, .164 in routine clerical jobs and .278 in clerical jobs with decision making responsibilities (Hunter, Schmidt and Judiesch 1988). Because there are fixed costs to employing an individual (facilities, equipment, light, heat and overhead functions such as hiring), the coefficient of variation of marginal products of individuals is assumed to be 1.5 times the coefficient of variation of productivity. Because about 2/3rds of clerical jobs can be classified as routine, the coefficient of variation of marginal productivity for clerical jobs is 30 percent $[1.5 \cdot (0.33 \cdot 0.278 + 0.67 \cdot 0.164)]$. Averaging operative jobs in with craft and technical jobs produces a similar 30 percent figure for blue collar jobs. The details and rationale of these calculations are explained in Bishop (1988).

Table 2.5. Effect of competencies on job performance (SQT)

	Mechanical compre-hension	Auto info.	Shop info.	Electr. info.	Attention to detail	Comp. speed	Word knowl.	Arith. reasoning	Math. knowl.	Science	R^2
Skilled technical (1324)	.092*** (3.07)	.017 (.58)	.132*** (4.28)	.174*** (5.09)	.024 (1.12)	.031 (1.17)	.215*** (6.77)	.062** (1.96)	.121*** (3.76)	.057* (1.83)	.548
Skilled electronic (349)	.086 (1.30)	.098 (1.49)	.246*** (3.64)	.045 (.60)	.084 (1.81)	-.013 (.22)	-.004 (.06)	-.021 (.30)	.26*** (3.67)	.072 (1.05)	.426
General (const.) maintenance (879)	-.004 (.11)	.082** (2.34)	.117*** (3.25)	.121*** (3.05)	.043* (1.76)	.068*** (2.19)	.066* (1.80)	-.101*** (2.73)	.441*** (11.70)	.134*** (3.67)	.592
Mechanical maintenance (131)	.042 (.38)	.314*** (2.88)	.206* (1.84)	-.089 (.71)	.055 (.72)	.235** (2.43)	-.004 (.03)	-.068 (.59)	.061 (.52)	.096 (.85)	.412
Clerical (830)	-.068 (1.59)	.087*** (2.05)	-.030 (.69)	.065 (1.33)	.015 (.50)	.085** (2.24)	.118*** (2.61)	.241*** (5.33)	.206*** (4.46)	.064 (1.44)	.425
Operators and food (814)	.109* (2.50)	.179*** (4.11)	.062 (1.39)	.100** (2.02)	.050 (1.62)	-.037 (.96)	.061 (1.33)	.114* (2.47)	.106** (2.25)	.076* (1.66)	.414
Unskilled electronic (2545)	.004 (.14)	.027 (.87)	.062* (1.93)	.077** (2.15)	.036 (1.65)	.053* (1.92)	-.010 (.31)	.058* (1.75)	.018 (.55)	-.025 (.76)	.052
Combat (5403)	.147*** (8.28)	.060*** (3.38)	.080*** (4.42)	.058*** (2.86)	.048*** (3.82)	.035** (2.23)	.069*** (3.71)	.070*** (3.74)	.139*** (7.29)	.070*** (3.82)	.358
Field artillery (534)	.059 (1.10)	.047 (.89)	.030 (.56)	.134** (2.21)	.088** (2.33)	-.009 (.19)	.000 (.01)	.186*** (3.28)	.230*** (3.99)	.061 (1.10)	.422

Source: Reanalysis of Maier and Grafton's (1981) data on the ability of ASVAB 6/7 to predict Skill Qualification Test (SQT) scores. The correlation matrix was corrected for restriction of range by Maier and Grafton.

* $p < .05$ on a one tail test. ** $p < .025$ on a one tail test. *** $p < .005$ on a one tail test. T statistics are in parenthesis under the coefficient.

occupations. The present discounted value of such a learning gain is about $50,000 (using a 5 percent real rate of discount). This is consistent with the wage rate findings presented earlier. These results imply that broad *technical literacy* is essential for workers who use and/or maintain equipment that is similar in complexity to that employed in the military.

The attention to detail subtest (which is similar to the clerical checking subtest in ASVAB 8A) has no effect on performance in clerical jobs and small effects on performance in skilled electronic, general maintenance, combat arms and field artillery.

The results for the academic subtests, however, contrast sharply with the wage rate regressions for young males. With the sole exception of the mechanical maintenance MOS cluster, the two mathematical reasoning subtests have much larger effects on SQTs than on wage rates. *The Math Knowledge subtest assessing algebra and geometry is responsible for most of this effect.* A one standard deviation increase in competence in algebra and geometry raises predicted job performance by .121 SD in skilled technical jobs, .261 SD in skilled electronic jobs, .44 SD in general maintenance jobs, .206 SD in clerical jobs, .106 SD for missile battery operators and food service jobs, .139 in combat arms and .230 in artillery. The arithmetic reasoning test was significant in 7 of the MOS clusters and had large positive effects on performance in clerical (.24 SD), missile battery and food service (.11 SD), and field artillery (.186 SD) jobs. Assuming that the standard deviation of true productivity is 30 percent of the wage, the impact of a simultaneous one SD increase in both mathematics reasoning subtests is 6.4 percent averaging across all seven non-combat occupations. The effects of the two tests of mathematical reasoning on job performance are substantial and unlike the wage rate findings much larger than the effects of computational speed. Nevertheless, they are somewhat smaller than those obtained in the models predicting training success suggesting again the possibility of methods bias.

Science knowledge which had small negative effects on wage rates, now has positive effects on hands-on measures of job performance in eight of the MOS clusters, significantly so in 4 clusters and in pooled data. A one standard deviation (SD) increase in science knowledge raises job performance by .057 SD in skilled technical jobs, .072 SD in skilled electronics jobs, .134 SD in general maintenance and construction jobs, .096 SD in mechanical maintenance jobs, .064 SD in clerical jobs, .076 SD in missile battery operator and food service jobs and .070 in combat arms. Word knowledge has significant effects on job performance in the skilled technical, general maintenance and clerical jobs and in combat arms. While statistically significant, the effects of these two competencies appear to be rather modest. Assuming that the standard deviation of true productivity is 30 percent of the wage, the effect of a one SD increase in test scores is 2 percent of the wage for science and 1.9 percent for word knowledge averaged across the seven non-combat occupations.

Differences in science or verbal competency of one population SD are quite large. In these subjects, one population SD is about the magnitude of the difference between young people with 14 years of schooling and those who left school after the 9th grade. Consequently, a productivity increase of about 2 percent per population SD on the test may appear to be only a modest return. This may be due to the inadequacies of the 11 minute long ASVAB subtests used to assess these competencies. General Science had only 24 items and Word knowledge only 35. This biases down the estimated effects of science and word knowledge on job performance. Clearly, there is a need for new research to determine whether broader and more reliable measures of verbal capacity, scientific knowledge and understanding and the ability to solve problems have more substantial effects on job performance in non-technical jobs than these ASVAB subtests.

On the other hand, however, a 2 percent increase in productivity should not be dismissed as unimportant. It is about $500 per worker per year and has a present discounted value of about $8700 (using a 5 percent real rate of interest and a 40 year working life).

Analysis of Project A Data on Core Technical Proficiency. Still more evidence on what truly determines job performance comes from Project A, a massive study (total costs of more than $100,000,000) that is developing improved methods for selecting and classifying army personnel. Wise et al. (1987) have estimated ASVAB validities for 19 very diverse jobs using Core Technical Proficiency, a MOS specific job performance measure, as the criterion. These ratings are about 50 percent based on hands-on work sample tests (the hands-on SQT) and 50 percent based on paper and pencil job knowledge exams. The ratings were obtained after the recruit had been in the army for 2 to 3 years. The study was designed to select the three or four ASVAB subtests which could be used as the aptitude composite for that MOS cluster.

Table 2.6 reports the names of the three or four subtests which in combination did the best job of predicting Core Technical Proficiency. As before, the technical subtests are important predictors of Core Technical Proficiency in all the nonclerical occupations. For the academic subtests the results are very different from the wage rate regressions but similar to the results of the reanalysis of Maier and Grafton's validity data for hands-on work samples. Computational speed is only a weak determinant of job performance. Competence in science, language arts and mathematical reasoning has very large effects on job performance.

Analysis of Project A Data on Other Performance Measures. Most of the ASVAB validity studies have studied MOS specific measures of performance which reflect the soldier's ability to do the job, not their willingness to do it on a regular basis or under adverse conditions. Do the results change when other dimensions of job performance are studied? The Project A data set again provides an opportunity to address this issue. Besides the Core Technical Proficiency construct already analyzed, Project A offers three other performance constructs which have some applicability to civilian jobs: General Soldiering Proficiency, Effort and Leadership and Maintaining Personal Discipline. General Soldiering Proficiency assesses skills that all soldiers must have (e.g. use of basic weapons, first aid, map reading, use of a gas mask) and is measured much the same way as

Table 2.6. ASVAB subtests which are the best predictors of core technical proficiency, by Military Occupational Specialty Cluster

Subtest	Technical	Speed	Quantitative	Verbal/ Science
Electronics repair (123)	Electronics	Compute-speed		Science
Skilled tech. (1329)	Mechanical comp.		Math knowledge	Science Verbal
Mechanical maintenance (716)	Auto-shop know. Mechanical comp. electronics			Science
General maintenance (272)	Auto-shop know.		Math knowledge	Science Verbal
Operators/Food (1215)	Auto-shop know.		Arith reasoning Math knowledge	Verbal
Surveillance & communication (289)	Auto-shop know.	Compute-speed	Math knowledge or Arith reason.	Verbal
Clerical (1210)			Arith reasoning Math knowledge	Verbal
Combat (1429)	Auto-shop know. Mechanical comp.		Math knowledge	Science
Field artillery (464)	Auto-shop know. Mechanical comp.	Compute-speed		Science

Source: Summarized from Table 2 of Wise, McHenry, Rossmeissl and Oppler (1987). Note: Based on an analysis of the ability of ASVAB subtests to predict Core Technical Proficiency ratings after the recruit has been in the US Army for 2 or 3 years. Core Technical Proficiency ratings are about 50 percent based on hands-on work sample tests and 50 percent based on paper and pencil job knowledge exams. The subtests listed in the table are the 3 or 4 subtests which in combination maximized the R^2 of the model predicting Core Technical Proficiency.

Core Technical Proficiency by a combination of job knowledge tests and hands-on performance tests. These two constructs are designed to measure the *can do* element of job performance.

The other two constructs attempt to measure the *will do* element of job performance. John P. Campbell (1986, p. 150) described the constructs and their measurement as follows:

> **Peer Leadership, Effort, and Self Development:** Reflects the degree to which the individual exerts effort over the full range of job tasks, perseveres under adverse or dangerous conditions, and demonstrates leadership and support of peers. That is, can the individual be counted on to carry out assigned tasks, even under adverse conditions, to exercise good judgement, and to be generally dependable and proficient? Five scales from the Army-wide Bars rating form (Technical Knowledge/Skill, Leadership, Effort, Self-development, and Maintaining Assigned Equipment), the expected combat performance rating, and the total number of commendations and awards received by the individual were summed for this factor.
>
> **Maintaining Personal Discipline:** Reflects the degree to which the individual adheres to Army regulations and traditions, exercises personal self-control, demonstrates responsibility in day-to-day behavior, and does not create disciplinary problems. Scores on this factor are composed of three Army-wide Bars scales (Following regulations, Self-control, and Integrity) and two indices from the administrative records (number of disciplinary actions and promotion rate).

It had been planned to obtain information on commendations, awards, promotions, and disciplinary actions from administrative records. However, the cost of this approach was extremely high so "everyone crossed their fingers and we collected eight archival performance indicators via a self-report questionnaire... Field tests on a sample of 500 people showed considerable agreement between self-report and archival records" (Campbell 1986, p. 144).

These two constructs are related to each other (they correlate .59) but are clearly quite distinct from the two "can do" constructs. Correlations with Core Technical Proficiency are only .28 for Effort and Leadership and .19 for Personal Discipline. The "can do" constructs are based on ratings made by the same person, so they share some common measurement error. Campbell, consequently, constructs residualized "can do" performance constructs by subtracting a ratings method factor from the raw score. With the ratings methods effect removed, Core Technical Proficiency (raw) has a correlation of .465 with Effort and Leadership (residual) and .225 with Personal Discipline (residual). In the view of the Project A team, soldiers must have both qualities – the technical competence to do their job and the willingness to do it under stressful circumstances.

Table 2.7 presents the results of using ASVAB test scores to predict General Soldiering Proficiency (raw), Effort and Leadership (both raw and residualized) and Personal Discipline (raw) (Campbell 1986, Table 10). The correlation matrices were corrected for range restriction as described by Dunbar and Linn (1986). In this analysis the 9 ASVAB subtests have been reduced to four composites: Technical, Speed (Numerical operations and Clerical checking), Quantitative (Arithmetic reasoning and Mathematics knowledge) and Verbal/Science. For General Soldiering Proficiency, the results are quite similar to the results obtained predicting hands-on SQTs and Core Technical Proficiency. The

Table 2.7. Effect of ASVAB composite on other dimensions of job performance

	Technical	Speed	Quantitative	Verbal	R^2
General soldiering proficiency (raw)	.26	.03	.20	.10	.461
Effort and leadership (residualized)	.21	.07	.08	.03	.280
Effort and leadership (raw)	.21	.09	.03	-.07	.206
Personal discipline (raw)	.06	.04	.07	-.03	.10

Source: Campbell (1986, Table 10).
Note: Standardized coefficients from an analysis of Project A Data on performance in the military.

technical and quantitative composites have the largest effects, and the verbal/science composite has a substantial effect. Speed has almost no effect. As before, the pattern of coefficients is very different from the wage regression for young men.

The pattern is different for the "will do" performance constructs. The technical composite had large positive effects on both measures of Effort and Leadership. The quantitative composite had a modest positive effect on Maintaining Personal Discipline and the residualized Effort and Leadership. Speed had a modest positive effect on Effort and Leadership. The verbal/science composite had no effect on the residualized Effort and Leadership and a small negative effect on raw score measures of both constructs. The coefficient pattern for the raw score "will do" performance constructs looks rather similar to the male wage and earnings regressions. This is an interesting result that needs to be investigated in other data sets. It should be treated with caution, however, for four reasons: the information on commendations, awards, promotions and disciplinary actions was self reported, a ratings method effect was clearly visible in the data, other researchers have expressed skepticism about the validity of military ratings (Vineberg and Joyner 1982), and there appears to be major differences between the civilian and military sectors in the effect of academic achievement tests on supervisory ratings (with the effects much larger in the civilian sector) (Hunter 1986).

In any case, even if one adopts the Project A position that ratings are a valid measure of the "will do" component of job performance, this in no way implies that the "can do" elements are subsidiary or unimportant. Consequently, the findings reviewed above that science, verbal and mathematical reasoning capability predict hands-on SQTs, Core Technical Proficiency and General Soldiering Proficiency in the military appear to provide some support to the claim that improved math, science and language arts education will add to the productivity of the work force.

Since 80 percent of the jobs held by enlisted personnel in the military have civilian counterparts, the research on the validity of the ASVAB in military settings just presented should generalize to major segments of the civilian economy (US Department of Defense 1984). Nevertheless, it would be useful to examine civilian data on the effect of technical competence on job performance. It is to the analysis of civilian data we now turn.

2.2.6 The Impact of Academic and Technical Competence on Job Performance in the Civilian Sector

Ghiselli's Review of Validation Research Prior to 1973. Over the last 50 years, industrial psychologists have conducted hundreds of studies, involving many hundreds of thousands of workers, on the relationship between supervisory assessments of job performance and various predictors of performance. In 1973 Edwin Ghiselli published a compilation of the results of this research organized by type of test and occupation. Table 2.8 presents a summary of the raw validity coefficients (correlation coefficients uncorrected for measurement error and restriction of range) for six types of tests: mechanical comprehension tests, "intelligence" tests, arithmetic tests, spatial relations tests, perceptual accuracy tests and psychomotor ability tests. As pointed out earlier, mechanical comprehension tests assess material that is covered in physics courses and applied technology courses such as auto mechanics and carpentry. The intelligence tests used in this research were paper and pencil tests assessing verbal and mathematical competency.

Intelligence tests were the best predictors of the performance of foreman. For craft occupations and semi-skilled industrial jobs, the mechanical comprehension tests are more valid predictors of job performance than any other test category. For protective occupations, mechanical comprehension tests and intelligence tests had equal validity. For clerical jobs, the best predictors of job performance were tests of intelligence, arithmetic and perceptual accuracy. These results are consistent with the analysis of job performance in the military data reported in Table 2.5.

It would appear that measures of mathematical, verbal and generic technical competence all have substantial effects on performance in technical and blue collar jobs. What about paper and pencil occupational competency tests for specific occupations? How well do they correlate with job performance?

The Relationship between Occupational Competency Tests and Job Performance. Meta-analyses of the hundreds of studies of the validity of occupational competency tests have found that content valid occupational competency tests are highly valid predictors of job performance. Dunnette's (1972) meta-

Table 2.8. Raw validity coefficients for six types of tests

	Mechanical comprehension	Intelligence	Arithmetic	Spatial relations	Perceptual accuracy	Psychomotor abilities
Foreman	23[c]	28[c]	20[d]	21[d]	27[d]	15[b]
Craftworkers	26[d]	25[f]	25[f]	23[f]	24[e]	19[f]
Industrial workers	24[d]	20[f]	21[f]	21[f]	20[f]	22[f]
Vehicle operators	22[d]	15[d]	25[c]	16[c]	17[b]	25[d]
Service occupations	–	26[d]	28[d]	13[d]	10[d]	15[d]
Protective occupations	23[b]	23[d]	18[c]	17[d]	21[c]	14[d]
Clerical	23[d]	30[f]	26[f]	16[e]	29[f]	16[f]

Source: Ghiselli's (1973) compilation of published and unpublished validity studies for job performance.

Notes: The raw validity coefficients have not been corrected for restriction of range or measurement error in the performance rating. The Perceptual Accuracy category includes number comparison, name comparison, cancellation and perceptual speed tests. They assess the ability to perceive detail quickly. Psychomotor tests measure the ability to perveive spatial patterns and to manipulate objects quickly and accurately. This category of tests includes tracing, tapping, doting, finger dexterity, hand dexterity and arm dexterity tests.

[a] Less than 100 cases. [b] 100 to 499 cases. [c] 500 to 999 cases. [d] 1,000 to 4,999 cases.
[e] 5,000 to 9,999 cases. [f] 10,000 or more cases.

analysis of 262 studies of occupational competency tests found that their average correlation with supervisory ratings was .51. This correlation was higher than the correlation of any other predictor studied including cognitive ability tests (.45), psychomotor tests (.35), interviews (.16) and biographical inventories (.34). Vineberg and Joyner's (1982) meta-analysis of military studies found that grades in training school (which were based on paper and pencil tests of occupational competency) had a higher correlation (.27) with global performance ratings by immediate supervisors than any other predictor. The correlations for the other predictors were .21 for ASVAB ability composites, .14 for years of schooling, .20 for biographical inventory and .13 for interest. Hunter's (1983a) meta-analysis found that content valid job knowledge tests had a correlation of .48 with supervisory ratings and an even higher correlation of .78 with a work sample measure of job performance, the Skill Qualification Test. Consequently, for training program graduates who are employed in the occupation for which their competency was assessed, scores on these competency exams are highly valid predictors of job performance and promotion probabilities.

Analysis of GATB Validation Studies. More recent data on what predicts job performance is available from the US Employment Service's program for revalidating the General Aptitude Test Battery (GATB). This data set contains data on job performance, the 9 GATB "aptitudes" and background data on 36,614 individuals in 159 different occupations. Professional, managerial and high-level sales occupations were not studied but the sample is quite representative of the 71,132,000 workers in the rest of the occupational distribution. It ranges from drafters and laboratory testers to hotel clerks and knitting-machine operators.

Since a major purpose of these validation studies was to examine the effects of race and ethnicity on the validity of the GATB, the firms that were selected tended to have an integrated workforce in that occupation. Firms that used aptitude tests similar to the GATB for selecting new hires for the job being studied were excluded. The employment service officials who conducted these studies report that this last requirement did not result in the exclusion of many firms. A total of 3052 employers participated.

The workers in the study were given the GATB test battery and asked to supply information on their age, education, plant experience and total experience. Plant experience was defined as years working in that occupation for the current employer. Total experience was defined as years working in the occupation for all employers. The dependent variable was an average of two ratings (generally two weeks apart) supplied by the worker's immediate supervisor. The Standard Descriptive Rating Scale obtains supervisory ratings of 5 aspects of job performance (quantity, quality, accuracy, job knowledge and job versatility) as well as an "all around" performance rating. Some studies employed rating scales specifically designed for that occupation and in one case a work sample was one of the job performance measures. None of the studies used ticket earnings from a piece rate pay system as the criterion. Studies which used course grades or tests of job knowledge as a criterion were excluded. Firms with only one employee in the job classification were excluded, as were individuals whose reported work experience was inconsistent with their age.

The mathematical achievement index (N) was an average of normalized scores on the same arithmetic reasoning test and on a numerical computations test. Verbal ability was assessed by a vocabulary test. Perceptual Speed was the sum of the P and Q aptitudes of the GATB divided by 36.72 to put it in a population SD metric. Psychomotor Ability was the sum of the K, F and M aptitudes of the GATB divided by 51.54 to put it in a population SD metric. The GATB does not contain tests assessing knowledge of electronics, mechanical comprehension, auto mechanics or shop knowledge.

Because wage rates, average productivity levels and the standards used to rate employees vary from plant to plant, mean differences in ratings across establishments have no real meaning. Therefore, normalized ratings deviations were predicted by deviations from the job/establishment's mean for gender, race,

Hispanic, age, age squared, plant experience, plant experience squared, total occupational experience, total occupational experience squared, schooling and test composites.[12]

It should be recognized that the validity literature in general and this model in particular do not yield unbiased estimates of the true structural relationships prevailing in the full population (Brown 1982, Mueser and Maloney 1987). Validity studies based on examining which job incumbents are most productive are subject to bias for three reasons: omitted variables, the selection process that determines which new hires were retained by the firm, and the selection process by which members of the population were hired for the job.

While the model used in this study is a more complete specification of the background determinants of job performance than is typically found in the validity literature, it lacks controls for important characteristics of the worker which effect worker productivity. Examples of things left out of the model are occupationally specific schooling, grades in relevant subjects in school, reputation of the school, the amount and quality of on-the-job training, performance in previous jobs, character traits like reliability and need to achieve, physical strength and a desire to work in the occupation. Exclusion of these variables from the model causes bias in the coefficients of included variables.

The second problem arises from the fact that job performance outcomes have been used to select the sample used in the analyses. Since incompetent workers were fired or induced to quit and high performing workers were probably promoted to jobs of a higher classification, the job incumbents used in this study were a restricted sample of the people originally hired for a job. The systematic

---

[12] Only deviations of rated performance ($R^m_{ij} - R^m_j$) from the mean for the establishment (R^m_j) were analyzed. The variance of the job performance distribution was also standardized across establishments by dividing ($R^m_{ij} - R^m_j$) by the standard deviation of rated performance ($SD_j\,(R^m_{ij})$) calculated for that firm (or 3 if the sample SD is less than 3). Separate models were estimated for each major occupation. They were specified as follows:

$$\frac{R^m_{ij} - R^m_j}{SD_j\,(R^m_{ij})} = \beta_0 + \beta_1\,(\underline{T}_{ij} - \underline{T}_j) + \beta_2\,(S_{ij} - S_j) + \beta_3\,(\underline{X}_{ij} - \underline{X}_j) + \beta_4\,(\underline{D}_{ij} - \underline{D}_j) + v_2$$

where

R_{ij} = ratings standardized to have a zero mean and SD of 1.

$\underline{T}_{ij}$ = a vector of the five GATB aptitude composites.

S_{ij} = the schooling of the ith individual.

$\underline{X}_{ij}$ = a vector of age and experience variables – age, age^2, total occupational experience, total occupational experience^2, plant experience and plant experience^2.

$\underline{D}_{ij}$ = a vector of dummy variables for black, Hispanic and female.

$\underline{T}_j$, S_j, $\underline{X}_j$ and $\underline{D}_j$ are the means of test composites, schooling, experience variables and race and gender dummies for the jth job/establishment combination.

nature of attrition from the job substantially reduces the variance of job performance and biases coefficients of estimated job performance models toward zero.[13]

The third source of problems is selection effects introduced by the selection that precedes the hiring decision. If hiring selections were based entirely on X variables included in the model, unstandardized coefficients such as $\hat{\beta}$ would be unbiased and correction formulas would be available for calculating standardized coefficients and validities. Unfortunately, however, incidental selection based on unobservables such as interview performance and recommendations is very probable (Thorndike 1949, Olson and Becker 1983, Mueser and Maloney 1987). In a selected sample like accepted job applicants, one cannot argue that these omitted unobservable variables are uncorrelated with the included variables that were used to make initial hiring decisions and, therefore, that coefficients on included variables are unbiased. When someone with 10 years of formal schooling is hired for a job that normally requires 12 years of schooling, there is probably a reason for that decision. The employer saw something positive in that job applicant (maybe the applicant received a particularly strong recommendation from previous employers) that led to the decision to make an exception to the rule that new hires should have 12 years of schooling. The analyst is unaware of the positive recommendations, does not include them in the job performance model and, as a result, the coefficient on schooling is biased toward zero. This phenomenon also causes the estimated effects of other worker traits used to select workers for the job such as previous relevant work experience to be biased toward zero. Consequently, the results presented below should not be viewed as estimates of the structural effect of schooling and previous work experience on worker productivity.

---

[13] When all variables are multivariate normal, the ratio of the coefficient estimated in the selected sample to the true coefficient estimated in an unselected population is equal to:

$$\tilde{\beta}/\beta = VR/(1 - R^2(1 - VR)) = VR + \tilde{R}^2(1 - VR)$$

where VR is the ratio of the variance of y in the selected sample to its variance in the full population, R^2 is the multiple coefficient of determination of y on $\underline{x}$ in the full population and $\tilde{R}^2$ is the multiple coefficient of determination of y on $\underline{x}$ in the selected population (Goldberger 1981). Estimates of VR, the ratio of incumbent job performance variance to new hire job performance variance can be derived from the NCRVE employer survey analyzed in Bishop (1987a, 1990b). Data on the reported productivity in the 3rd through 13th week after being hired of two different workers was employed to calculate a variance ratio by dividing job performance variance of incumbents (pairs of workers both of whom were still at the firm at the time of the interview a year or so after being hired) by the job performance variance of a group of very recent hires (pairs of workers both of whom stayed at least 13 weeks but who may or may not have remained at the firm through the interview). The resulting estimate of VR was .486. Assuming multivariate normality and noting that the R^2 of the models in Table 2.9 averages about .16, our estimate of $\beta/\tilde{\beta}$, the multiplier for transforming the coefficients estimated in the selected sample into estimates of population parameters, is 1.76.

The test score results are not similarly biased, however, because *very few firms use cognitive tests to select workers and those that do were not included in the sample of firms studied specifically to avoid this source of bias.*[14]

Results. The results of estimating the model are presented in Table 2.9. Mathematical achievement was clearly the most important determinant of job performance for all occupational categories except operatives. The effect of mathematical achievement on the performance of operatives was highly significant but only about one-half to two-thirds of the size of the other occupations. Verbal ability had no effect on job performance in craft and operative jobs and in clerical and service jobs its impact is roughly 40 percent of the mathematical achievement's effect.

Spatial ability had significant positive effects on performance only for craft occupations. Perceptual speed had small effects on job performance, but the coefficients are nevertheless significant in all but technical occupations (where the sample is quite small). Psychomotor skills were significantly related to performance in all occupations but in the better paid and more complex jobs the magnitude of the effect was only about one-third of that of verbal and mathematical achievement together.

The effect of psychomotor skills was larger in the two least skilled occupations – operatives and service except police and fire. For operatives the impact of psychomotor skills was roughly comparable to the impacts of mathematical and verbal achievement. These results are consistent with previous studies of these and other data sets (Hunter 1983b). Models were estimated containing squared terms for academic achievement and psychomotor skills but these additions did not produce significant reductions in the residual variance. When test scores are controlled, years of schooling had very small and sometimes negative effects on job performance.[15]

The effects of occupational experience and tenure are also quite substantial for all occupations. The negative coefficients on the square terms for occupational

---

[14] Variables which were not used to select new hires such as the GATB test scores may have a positive correlation with unobservable characteristics of the individual which are used in selection. If the unobservable has its own independent effect on job performance (i.e. it is not serving solely as a proxy for test scores), test score coefficients may be positively biased. Mueser and Maloney (1987) experimented with some plausible assumptions regarding this selection process and concluded that coefficients on education were severely biased but that coefficients on test scores were not substantially changed when these incidental selection effects were taken into account.

[15] Mueser and Maloney (1987) argue persuasively that since schooling is a very important factor in the selection process, the coefficients on schooling in estimations like these are negatively biased estimates of true population relationships. This argument probably applies as well to the coefficients on work experience in the occupation but not at the firm.

Table 2.9. Determinants of job performance

	Technician	High skill clerical	Low skill clerical	Craft workers	Operatives	Service
Mathematics	.198*** (.035)	.161*** (.033)	.207*** (.026)	.168*** (.017)	.107*** (.018)	.223*** (.039)
Verbal	.051 (.038)	.073** (.035)	.070** (.030)	-.018 (.020)	.012 (.023)	.078* (.046)
Spatial perception	.025 (.029)	-.068*** (.026)	-.002 (.021)	.075*** (.014)	.022 (.016)	.039 (.034)
Perceptual ability	.026 (.036)	.106*** (.031)	.103*** (.025)	.048*** (.018)	.082*** (.019)	.063* (.038)
Psychomotor ability	.113*** (.027)	.094*** (.026)	.091*** (.021)	.083*** (.013)	.145*** (.015)	.133*** (.030)
Years of schooling	.031* (.016)	.026 (.016)	-.014 (.013)	-.009 (.007)	-.036*** (.008)	-.020 (.017)
Relevant experience	.041*** (.014)	.019 (.015)	.042*** (.012)	.040*** (.005)	.036*** (.010)	.082*** (.016)
(Relevant experience)^2	-.00094** (.00046)	-.00012 (.00046)	-.0009** (.0004)	-.00025* (.00015)	-.0005 (.0003)	-.0021*** (.0005)
Tenure	.085*** (.015)	.113*** (.016)	-.0925*** (.014)	.0620*** (.0056)	.079*** (.011)	.054*** (.019)
Tenure^2	-.0024*** (.0006)	-.0031*** (.0006)	-.0026*** (.0006)	-.00156*** (.00018)	-.0017*** (.0004)	-.00131 (.00077)
Age-18	-.0024 (.0163)	.040*** (.015)	.037*** (.010)	.052*** (.0078)	.053*** (.007)	.044*** (.013)
(Age-18)^2	-.00012 (.00021)	-.00064*** (.00020)	-.00062*** (.00013)	-.00071*** (.00010)	-.00072*** (.00009)	-.00055* (.00017)
Female	.057 (.056)	.063 (.072)	-.024 (.063)	-.396*** (.066)	-.194*** (.043)	.166** (.073)
Black	-.138** (.060)	-.390*** (.054)	-.146*** (.042)	-.247*** (.032)	-.216*** (.029)	-.031 (.063)
Hispanic	.046 (.099)	-.286*** (.086)	.053 (.069)	-.109*** (.042)	-.053 (.049)	-.076 (.108)
R^2	.114	.167	.139	.150	.145	.153
Number of obs.	2348	2570	4123	10016	8167	1927

Source: Analysis of GATB revalidation data in the US Employment Services Individual Data File.

Note: Deviations of job performance ratings from the mean for the job/establishment are modeled as a function of deviations of worker characteristics from the mean for the job/establishment. The test scores are in a population standard deviation metric. The metric for job performance is the within job/establishment standard deviation.

experience and tenure imply they are subject to diminishing returns. For workers who have no previous experience in the field, the expected gain in job performance is about 12–13 percent of a standard deviation in the first year and about 8–9 percent of an SD in the fifth year. The effect of tenure on job performance stops rising and starts to decline somewhere between 16 and 24 years of tenure. Increases in occupational experience lose their positive effect on performance even later – at 37 years for operatives, at over 55 years for craft workers and high skill clerical workers and at 19–31 years for other occupations. Except for technicians, age has large curvilinear effects on job performance as well. Holding tenure and occupational experience constant, age had a significant positive effect on job performance in all except technical occupations. In these occupations, twenty-year-olds with no experience at all in the field were 7.2 to 10.3 percent of an SD more productive than 18-year-olds with no experience in the field. Thirty-year-olds with no occupational experience were 4.7 to 7.4 percent of an SD more productive than 28-year-olds with no experience in the field.

The substantial effects of age and previous occupational experience on job performance are consistent with current hiring practices which give great weight to these job qualifications. These results suggest that a job applicant who has age and relevant work experience in his favor but low test scores may nevertheless be preferable to a young applicant who has high test scores but no relevant work experience. This is particularly likely to be the case if turnover rates are high for the productivity benefits of age and previous relevant work experience are large initially but diminish with time on the job.

2.2.7 Policy Implications

Many believe that high involvement work systems raise the productivity payoff of the problem solving abilities taught in mathematics and science classes. This is probably the case.[16] But the need for better mathematics and science preparation does not rest on this proposition being true.

The evidence just reviewed implies that mathematical and scientific competence contributes significantly to productivity in jobs that are structured in traditional Tayloristic-Fordist style and that do not have college level training in science and mathematics as a selection requirement. The case for higher standards in education, thus, does not depend on the rate at which employers switch from traditional mass production systems to the new lean production/high performance work systems.

[16] Unfortunately, there is only limited hard scientific evidence on this issue. Projecting the future skill demands of particular occupations is a good deal more difficult than describing past changes and yet there is controversy about even such simple matters as whether word processors have raised or lowered the skills required of secretaries.

2.3 Trends in the Demand for Skill and the Payoff to Academic Competence

The second rationale for improving the quality of math and science education is the need to expand the supply of engineers, scientists, computer specialists and managers with advanced training in business and economics. Those who lack a solid background in math and science find university programs in these fields very tough going and typically drop out of college altogether or are forced to transfer out of the field. Similar arguments are made for improving the general quality of secondary education. Overall college completion rates depend on communication skills as well as competence in mathematics and science, so improvements in secondary school preparation in language arts and other fields will increase the future supply of college trained workers. Analysis of cross section and time series data on enrollment and completion of college supports the view that a strong preparation in secondary school improves chances of success in university (Bishop 1992).

This rationale for higher standards in and channeling students into secondary school programs oriented toward further education at a university assumes, however, that high priority needs to be given to expanding the supply of university educated workers. This assumption rests on two crucial judgements about the labor market for university trained workers:

1) The social payoff to university education is high.
2) The social payoff to university education is not likely to diminish in the near future as rising numbers of university graduates enter the labor market.

Are these judgements justified? A conclusion on this matter requires answers to the following questions. How rapidly have the jobs that typically recruit university graduates been growing? How rapidly has the supply of university educated workers been growing? What is the balance between demand and supply of university educated workers? What is the economic payoff to obtaining a university education? And how does that payoff vary with the field of study in college?

2.3.1 Trends in Demand for and Supply of University Graduates

Trends in Demand. The share of jobs requiring advanced education and training has been rising all over the world. Occupations at the top of the skill continuum like professionals, technicians and managers (PT&M) jobs have been growing much more rapidly than manual (service, craft, operative, laborer and farm occupations) jobs. The difference between the growth rates of these two groups of occupations is presented in columns 1 and 2 of Table 2.10. In the United States PT&M grew 2.78 percent per year more rapidly than manual jobs during the 1970s and 2.46 percent per year more rapidly in the 1980s. While the US rate of

Table 2.10. Occupational upskilling in OECD countries

	Annual rate (%) by which Prof-Tech-Managers grew more rapidly than manual workers		Prof-Tech-Managerial share (%) in 1990
	1970–1981[1]	1981–1990[2]	
Australia	2.34	2.02	24.0
Austria	–	3.67	20.8
Belgium	3.86	3.14	25.8
Canada	3.48	3.87	30.2
Denmark	6.60	2.50	28.0
Finland	6.41	5.13	28.6
Fed. Rep. of Germany	3.67	2.53	19.9
Greece	6.11	3.76	14.3
Ireland	5.97	2.10	20.3
Japan	4.27	3.26	14.9
Korea	4.24	5.95	8.7
Malaysia	–	3.03	9.5
Netherlands	4.46	4.30	28.1
Norway	5.48	3.85	30.0
Singapore	3.77	4.79	20.3
Spain	3.34	5.88	12.8
Sweden	2.95	–	–
United Kingdom[3]	3.28	3.88	31.5
United States[4]	**2.78**	2.46	29.3

[1] Manual occupations include farming, fisheries, craft, operatives, laborers and service workers. Source: International Labour Organization, *Yearbook of Labour Statistics* for 1971, 1976, 1981 & 1991, Table 2B & Table 3C. Data availability problems resulted in somewhat different time periods being used for Belgium 1970–83, Canada 1971–81, Denmark 1965–81, Greece 1961–81, Ireland 1966–83, Japan 1970–80, Federal Republic of Germany 1970–82, Netherlands 1971–81.

[2] Source: International Labour Organization, *1991 Handbook of Labour Statistics*, Table 3. Absent data meant that shorter time periods were used for some countries: Austria 1984–89, Belgium 1983–89, Federal Republic of Germany 1982–89, Greece 1981–88, Ireland 1983–88, Malaysia 1981–87.

[3] Growth rates were calculated for 1971–1978 and 1978–1989. Source: Manpower Services Commission, *MSC Manpower Report 1980*, p. 8, and Office of Population Censuses and Surveys, *Labour Force Survey 1988 and 1989*, Table 5.11.

[4] Source: D. Klein, "Occupational Employment Statistics for 1972–82", *Employment and Earnings*, Jan. 1984, pp. 13–16; and later January issues of *Employment and Earnings*. Because of a change in occupational coding in 1972, the trend was calculated for the 1972–81 period.

occupational upskilling is impressive, most countries had even higher rates. Japan's rate was 4.27 percent per year in the 1970s and 3.26 percent per year in the 1980s. Germany's rate was 3.67 percent in the 1970s and 2.53 percent per year in the 1980s. Scandinavian rates of occupational upskilling were higher still. During the 1970s the annual rate of occupational upskilling was 2.95 percent for Sweden, 6.0 percent for Denmark, 5.48 percent for Norway and 6.4 percent for Finland. During the 1980s the upskilling proceeded at a 2.5 percent per annum rate in Denmark, a 3.85 percent per annum rate in Norway and a 5.23 percent per annum rate in Finland. As a result, the professional, technical and managerial share of employment is now 28 percent in Denmark and Finland and 30 percent in Norway. Only three other countries have as high a ratio: the Netherlands, the United Kingdom and the United States (see column 3 of Table 2.10).

Trends in Supply. The supply of college educated workers has also been increasing rapidly all over the world. During the 1970s and 80s the university graduate share of the population of working age grew at an annual rate of 3.34 percent in the United States, 3.55 percent in Japan, 5.6 percent in Sweden, 5.8 percent in Norway, 3.07 percent in Belgium and 3.97 percent in Canada. The university graduate share of the working age population grew at an annual rate of 3.32 percent from 1983 to 1988 in Australia, 12.3 percent from 1981 to 1987 in Austria and 2.75 percent from 1978 to 1987 in Germany (OECD 1989). How does this growth in the supply of college graduates compare with the growth of the jobs which college graduates typically occupy?

2.3.2 The Supply and Demand Balance

Ronald Kutscher, Associate Commissioner of the US Bureau of Labor Statistics, argues that there existed in the United States "an oversupply of college graduates during the 1980's" (Kutscher 1991). He sights as evidence for this view recent increases in the number of people with 16+ years of schooling who are coded by the Current Population Survey as having jobs which are not "traditional" for holders of a Bachelor's degree. He reports that between 1983 and 1988 workers claiming to have completed 16 years of schooling increased by 41,000 in secretarial and typist jobs, by 59,000 in factory operative jobs, and by 6,000 in bartender, waiter and waitress jobs.

But what about the opposite kind of mismatch: workers who have substantially fewer years of schooling than are "required" by the job. This kind of mismatch also increased between 1983 and 1988. The number of workers claiming to have *fewer than 16 years of schooling* increased by 23,000 among physicians, by 18,800 among lawyers and judges, by 14,500 among college teachers, by 125,000 among other teachers and by 99,000 among mathematical and computer scientists (US Bureau of Labor Statistics 1990). Don't these statistics imply a growing shortage of qualified college graduate workers?

One should not, however, give much credence to any of these estimates of mismatches between schooling and occupation. The reporting and coding of occupation is quite unreliable. Those coded as a professional, a technician or manager by a Census interviewer have a 15 to 21 percent chance of being coded in a lower level occupation by a second interviewer a few months later (US Bureau of the Census 1972). Ten percent of those who report completing 16+ years of schooling also claim not to have received a Bachelor's degree. Errors in measuring education are also quite common and the incidence of such errors appears to have risen during the 1980s (Bishop and Carter 1991). Many of the discrepancies between an individual's schooling and occupation found in CPS data are caused by reporting and coding errors. How else can one explain the 9.6 percent of college teachers and the 5.4 to 6.5 percent of lawyers, physicians and secondary school teachers who claim not to have completed 16 years of schooling (US Bureau of Labor Statistics 1990). The unreliability of individual measures of occupation and education means that counts of mismatches between schooling and occupation derived from micro data have almost no validity at all. True mismatches between education and occupation are a lot less common than these statistics suggest.

This is not to deny that mismatches occur. College graduates are incredibly diverse and seek work in very distinct labor markets. College graduates who major in subjects which have little value in the labor market, who get C's and D's in undemanding courses, who are not geographically mobile, who have a substance abuse problem or who make a poor impression in interviews, will sometimes have to accept jobs which do not appear to "require" a college degree. These graduates are included in the averages and despite the drag they represent on the mean, the average college graduate is doing very well and compared to those who did not go to college she is doing extremely well.

The fact that the BLS keeps track of only one kind of mismatch – instances where education seems to exceed job requirements – and ignores instances where individuals appear to be underqualified for their job makes matters worse. By ruling out the possibility of undereducation, the conceptual framework makes a conclusion that there are too many university graduates inevitable.

If something useful is to be said about the balance between supply and demand, one must put both price and quantity data to work and give up on the idea of measuring how many people are "underemployed".

A Framework for Interpreting Data on the Supply/Demand Balance. A much better approach to examining the supply/demand balance for highly educated workers is simply to compare percentage changes in supply of graduates and the number of people working in professional, technical and managerial occupations and interpret these changes in the light of contemporaneous shifts in the wage premium for college. Changes in the employment of college graduates can be decomposed into two components: (1) shifts that can be explained by changes in the occupational composition of employment and (2) changes in college graduate share of individual occupations. The growth of the engineering profession from 0.13 percent of the workforce in 1900 to 1.6 percent of the workforce in 1988 is an example of the first source of change. Historical rates of growth of professional, technical and managerial jobs relative to manual jobs are given in the first two columns of Table 2.10.

For the United States, the normal state of affairs has been for college graduate supply to increase more rapidly than an index driven by shifts in occupational employment shares and for the difference to be made up by increases in skill and educational requirements of specific jobs (Rumberger 1981).

Engineers work at a knowledge frontier that has been shifting out at an extraordinary pace during the twentieth century. Consequently, the skills and training required to perform satisfactorily in engineering jobs have increased. At the beginning of the century most engineers did not have a Bachelor's degree; now a Bachelor's degree is required of just about all new entrants and 20 percent of engineers have a Master's degree. This demand driven escalation of the educational requirements for being an engineer illustrates the primary reason why college graduate shares of many occupations have increased over time. More recently the advent of the personal computer has shifted out the demand for managers, technicians, sales and other workers who can keep pace with this fast changing technology (Krueger 1991).

This is not, however, the only reason why the share of college graduates in an occupation might increase. During a period when college graduates are in abundant supply, some college graduates may find themselves forced into lower paying occupations which are thought to not require the skills developed in college. The signal that this is happening is declining wage premiums for recent college graduates. If, on the other hand, wage premiums for college graduates and professional occupations are stable or growing at the same time as the share of college graduates in specific occupations is rising, it is reasonable to infer that an outward shift of demand within occupations not an increase in supply caused the increase. Shifts in unemployment rates of workers classified by occupation or education can also be used as signals of changes in the balance between supply and demand.

2.3.3 Trends in the Payoff to University Education

In free labor markets, shortages of a particular type of labor cause its relative wage to rise; surpluses cause its relative wage to decline. During the 1970s the rapid growth of professional, technical and managerial occupations was accompanied by declines in the relative wage rates of these occupations in most countries (OECD 1987) suggesting that supply was growing more rapidly than demand.

Data on the 1980s for the United States and the United Kingdom indicate, however, growing relative wages for professional, technical and managerial workers, suggesting that demand for these workers was growing more rapidly than supply.

The wage premium for attaining a Bachelor's degree in the United States fell during the 1970s – a period of surplus for college graduate labor. During the 1980s the wage premium rose again. In May/June Current Population Survey data, real hourly wage rates of workers with 16 years of schooling and 1 to 10 years of experience rose 14.7 (12.2) percent for males (females) between 1980 and 1988 while real wage rates of workers with 12 years of schooling and similar levels of experience fell 16 (5.4) percent for males (females) (Kosters 1989). Blackburn,

Bloom and Freeman (1989) report that between 1979 and 1987 the real full time earnings of 25 to 34 year old white male college graduates rose 9.2 percent while the earnings of their high school graduate counterparts fell 9.4 percent. Katz and Murphy's (1992) study of March CPS data found that between 1980 and 1987 real weekly earnings of college graduates with 1 to 5 years of work experience rose 10.6 (12.9) percent for females (males) while the real earnings of high school graduates with similar levels of experience fell 3.2 and 15 percent respectively. They conclude that "changes in education differentials ... reflect changes in 'skill prices' rather than changes in group composition. We find that rapid secular growth in the relative demand for 'more skilled' workers is a key component of any consistent explanation ... of these changes in wage structure".

Comparative data on changes in the payoff to college in other OECD countries is presented in Table 2.11. During the 1980s the relative wage of college graduates was stable in Japan, fell in the Netherlands but grew in all other countries for which the calculations could be made: Germany, Canada, Australia and the United Kingdom (Davis 1992). While the tendency of demand for university graduates in the 1980s to outstrip supply appears to be strongest in the United States, the phenomenon appears not to be limited to the US.

Unemployment Rate Differentials. An additional way of assessing the balance between supply and demand for workers categorized by education is to compare their unemployment rates. The first two columns of Table 2.11 report the ratio of unemployment rates for workers with less than 12 years of schooling to the unemployment rate of workers with a Bachelor's degree or more. These data suggest that the balance between supply and demand for university graduates varied greatly across countries. By this ratio criterion the demand/supply balance in 1988 was extremely favorable for both male and female university graduates in Finland (7.5 and 8.0) and the United States (5.9 and 4.6) and highly favorable for male graduates in Australia (3.7), Austria (6.9), Canada (3.6), Germany (4.8), Norway (5.5) and the United Kingdom (4.0). In 1988 university graduate unemployment rates were higher than the rates of less educated workers in only three OECD countries – Greece for both men and women and Spain and Switzerland for women. It appears that in most countries the demand/supply balance was more favorable for male university graduates than for female graduates. The strong relative demand for engineering, computer, scientific and business specialties in which male college graduates predominate might be able to account for the modest gender differential in the United States. Other explanations are probably necessary for countries such as Australia, Austria, Germany and Norway with very large gender differentials.

Freeman (1991) has examined trends in relative unemployment rates in the United States. He reports that unemployment rates for college graduates were unchanged at very low levels (1.5 percent for 25–64 year olds) in both 1980 and 1988, but rates rose from 4.7 to 5.4 percent for high school graduates and from 7.4 to 9.2 percent for those who had not completed high school. He concluded that

Table 2.11. The payoff to university education in OECD countries during the 1980s

Country	Ratio of unemployment rates of sec. school non-completers to college graduates[1] Men	Women	Coll/HS earnings ratio in late 80s[2]	Annual rate of change in 1980s	Initial/ second year	Education groups in the ratio
United States	5.94	4.57	1.52	.026	1979/1987	Coll.Grad/ HighSchGrad
Australia	3.65	1.42	-	.004	1982/1990	Univ/Trade
Austria	6.88	2.04	-	-	-	-
Belgium	2.81	2.91	-	-	-	-
Canada	3.59	2.42	1.43	.006	1980/1985	Univ/High School
Finland	7.50	8.00	-	-	-	-
Germany	4.80	1.87	1.42	.020	1981/1984	(14-18)/(11-13 yrs of sch)
Greece	0.93	0.49	-	-	-	-
Italy	1.87	1.66	-	-	-	-
Japan	-	-	1.26	.000	1979/1987	Coll/Upper Sec School
Netherlands	2.48	1.45	1.23	–.050	1983/1987	Univ/ Secondary
Norway	5.50	2.00	-	-	-	-
Spain	1.48	0.65	-	-	-	-
Sweden	2.63	2.75	1.19	.006	1981/1986	Univ/Post Sec
Switzerland	1.00	0.86	-	-	-	-
United Kingdom	4.00	2.40	1.65	.015	1980/1988	Univ/ No Qual.

[1] Ratio of the unemployment rate of workers who have not completed upper secondary school to the unemployment rate of workers who have one or more university degrees. Source: OECD, *Employment Outlook 1989*, p. 67.
[2] Source: Davis (1992).

"rising educational pay differentials thus understate the growing mismatch between demand and supply for labour skills in the United States" (p. 361).

Projecting the Future. The wage premium for attaining a college degree in the United States is higher now than ever before. Despite the increase in college attendance rates stimulated by the high wage premium, the supply of college graduate workers in the United States is fated to grow more slowly in the 1990s than in the 1980s. The cause of the slowdown in supply is the small size of the college age cohort during the 1990s and the growing number of retirements by workers who obtained degrees during the 1950s under the GI bill. The US Bureau of Labor Statistics predicts that the rate of growth of demand for college graduate skills will slow as well (Silvestri and Lukasiewicz 1991). If their prediction is correct, the current balance between the growth of supply and demand will be maintained.

However, the BLS projection methodology is unable to anticipate the within industry shifts in occupational employment demand that are driving the explosion of college level occupations. The BLS grossly underpredicted the growth of professional, technical and managerial occupations during the 1980s. Projected to account for 28 percent of employment growth, these occupations actually accounted for 52 percent of growth between 1978 and 1990. Their projections of growth for high level occupations during the 1990s are probably biased as well. Using an econometric methodology of projecting occupational shares, Bishop and Carter (1991) predict that the growth of professional, technical and managerial employment will not diminish during the 1990s. If their prediction is correct, the labor market for college graduates, is fated to become even tighter than it is now.

2.3.4 Which College Specialties Generate the Largest Economic Payoff?

In the United States, college graduates who have majored in physical science, engineering and business earn substantially more than graduates who have majored in education, humanities or social sciences other than economics. The first four columns of Table 2.12 present data from the College Placement Council on how field of study effected the starting salaries received by college graduates whose placement outcomes were reported to the school's placement office for 1963, for 1969–70, for 1979–80 and for 1989 (College Placement Council 1985, 1991). The differences across field are sometimes as large as the wage gains accruing to those obtaining higher-level degrees. Relative to majors in humanities and social sciences other than economics, engineers received 45–70 percent higher starting salaries in 1991, computer scientists received a 38 percent premium, physical science majors received a 24 percent premium and business majors received a 10 percent premium. Studies of the earnings of adults indicate that the salaries of business majors tend to catch up with the engineers, but education and liberal arts majors remain far behind those with engineering, physical science and business degrees (see columns 5 and 6).

Largely because of these large wage differentials, there has been a dramatic growth in the relative supply of graduates in engineering, computer science and business administration. For males degrees in engineering, computer science and business which accounted for 33.2 percent of all BA's in 1973 rose to 50.8 percent of all Bachelor's degrees in 1986. For women degrees in engineering, computer science and business grew from 3.5 percent to 26.6 percent of degrees awarded. In 1973 degrees in education, humanities and social sciences accounted for 50.5 percent of Bachelor's degrees awarded to men and 83.5 percent of the Bachelor's degrees awarded to women. By 1986 these percentages had dropped to 35.1 percent and 54.7 percent respectively. As a result, the ratio of degrees awarded in engineering and computer science to degrees awarded in humanities, social

Table 2.12. Wage premiums by college major (relative to Bachelor's degree in humanities)

	Percentage differential in starting salaries[a]				Median earnings males, age 21-70 BA's in 1966[b]	Average monthly earnings in 1984[c]
	1963	1969-70	1979-80	1991		
Bachelors in low wage major:						
Humanities	0	0	0	0	0	0
Social sciences					14	-
Economics	-	-	8	15	-	111
Other social sciences	0	0	–1	–3	-	28
Education	-	-	-	–13	–9	–6
Biological sciences	-	-	-	–1	–11	12
Agriculture	-	-	-	4	-	45
Health	-	-	-	39	-	12
Bachelors in high wage major:						
Physical science	17	17	36	24	28	93
Mathematics	18	15	36	24	-	68
Engineering					52	114
Chemical eng.	23	28	67	70	-	-
Electrical eng.	27	24	56	50	-	-
Industrial eng.	20	21	53	45	-	-
Mechanical eng.	24	23	57	54	-	-
Computer science	-	-	44	38	-	-
Business					28	103
Accounting	10	17	21	21	-	-
Other business	0	2	11	10	-	-

[a] Percentage differential between the starting salary in the designated major over that received by humanities majors. Source: The College Placement Council (1985, 1991).

[b] Percentage differential for median yearly earnings of males whose highest degree is a BA or BS in the designated major relative to median earnings of humanities majors. Source: US Bureau of the Census (1967).

[c] Percentage differential for mean monthly earnings of men and women whose highest degree is a BA or BS in the designated major relative to earnings of humanities and liberal arts majors. Source: US Bureau of the Census (1987, p. 13).

sciences or education grew 5.2 percent per year in the 1970s and 10.7 percent per year between 1980 and 1986. The ratio of business degrees to humanities, social sciences, and education degrees grew 5.8 percent per year in the 1970s and 5.1 percent in the 1980s.

The very rapid growth during the last 20 years of the relative supply of college graduates trained in business and engineering fields has surprisingly not significantly diminished the wage premiums these fields command. Trends in starting wage premiums for business and technical degrees can be followed by comparing the first four columns of Table 2.12. Relative to humanities majors, wage premiums for engineering degrees grew dramatically during the 1970s and then dropped slightly by 1991, but remained significantly above the levels that had prevailed in the 1960s. Wage premiums for chemistry and mathematics majors over humanities majors rose from 17 percent in the 1960s to 36 percent in 1979–80 and then fell to 24 percent in 1991. Starting wage premiums for business majors rose from essentially zero in the 1960s to 10–11 percent during the late 1970s and 1980s.

Trends in the effect of college major on salaries of college graduates who have been working for many years can be examined by comparing columns 5 and 6. In 1967 male college graduates 21–70 years old who had majored in business earned 28 percent more and engineers 52 percent more than those who had majored in humanities (US Bureau of the Census 1972). In 1964 college graduates who had majored in physical science earned 93 percent more, engineers earned 114 percent more and business majors 103 percent more than humanities majors (US Bureau of the Census 1987). Clearly, the economic payoff to business and technical education is considerably greater than the payoff to majors in the humanities and social sciences other than economics and the advantage of these fields of study has not diminished appreciably in the face of the massive increase in the number of students choosing these fields of study. Clearly, there has been a substantial shift in market demand in the United States favoring graduates with business and technical degrees over graduates with liberal arts and education degrees. Research is needed on how the field of study in university effects the payoff to college in Japan and Europe and how the balance between supply and demand varies with field of study.

Final Thoughts. The review in Section 2.2 of the evidence on the wage and productivity payoff to various skills generated very similar conclusions. *American studies indicate that mathematical and technical skills of average workers generate much greater wage and productivity benefits than verbal and scientific skills.* The effect of the mathematics reasoning tests is quite large (a one population SD increase appears to cause an improvement in productivity of 6.4 percent or about $1600 per year). This result suggests that the educational reformers are indeed correct in urging major improvements in mathematics education for the great mass of high school students. The policy implications of these findings, at least for the US, are that mathematics particularly algebra, geometry and statistics should receive much greater emphasis in the secondary school curriculum.

Tests assessing technical competence had very large impacts on both supervisory assessment and hands-on SQT measures of job performance in nonclerical jobs in the military and on the wages and earnings of young males. A one population SD increase in these competencies appeared to raise productivity in these jobs by 11.5 percent or about $2875 per year. These results imply that broad technical literacy is essential for workers who use and/or maintain equipment that is similar in complexity to that employed in the military. Consequently, students need to receive greater exposure to computers and other technologies.

There is no data on the productivity consequences of greater knowledge of history, geography and foreign languages. The economic case for greater emphasis on English and science in high school rests largely on the pipeline argument – these competencies are necessary for success in college. *These conclusions must for now be tentative for much more research is required on the contribution of particular skills and competencies to productivity of individuals and competitiveness of nations.*

Evidence was also presented that the effect of general academic achievement on wage rates and productivity of adults is quite large. This, in turn, implies that the 1.25 grade level equivalent decline in the test scores of American secondary school graduates between 1967 and 1980 signalled a significant deterioration in the quality of young entrants into the American work force. The decline of student test scores was unprecedented for prior to 1967, student test scores had been rising steadily for more than 50 years. Bishop (1989) has developed an index of the quality of the US work force which incorporates the effects of improvements in academic achievement at given levels of schooling as well as increases in years of schooling. Jorgenson, Gollop and Fraumeni (1987) estimate that increases in years of schooling raised labor quality in the US by .725 percent per year between 1948 and 1973. Bishop's estimates imply that improvements in academic achievement at given amounts of schooling contributed an additional .212 percent per year to the growth of the quality of labor during this period. The test score decline reduced this contribution to .16 percent per year between 1973 and 1980, and .085 percent per year in the 1980s. If the test scores of high school graduates had continued to grow at the rate that prevailed between 1942 and 1967, labor quality would now be 2.9 percent higher. The social cost in terms of foregone GNP is now 86 billion dollars annually. Even with rapid improvements in the quality of elementary and secondary education, the labor quality shortfall grows to 5.5 percent in 2000 and 6.7 percent in 2010.[17] If academic learning creates externalities, as argued above, the social costs of deteriorating school quality are even greater.

It would appear that the education enterprise has historically been an important source of economic growth. When the academic achievement of students completing their schooling declines substantially, the economic costs are large

---

[17] The only way to prevent these forecasts from being realized is to change the relationship between GIA at age 17 and GIA as an adult. This might be accomplished by attracting massive numbers of adults back into school, by expanding educational offerings on television and/or by inducing employers to provide general education to long term employees.

and last for generations. Consequently, the potential benefits of major improvements in the academic achievement of students would also appear to be substantial.

Unfortunately, less than a quarter of 10th graders in the United States believe that geometry, trigonometry, biology, chemistry and physics are needed to qualify for their first choice occupation (Longitudinal Survey of American Youth 1988). The analysis of NLS Youth data presented in Section 2.2 shows that this perception is not in error. During the first 8 years after leaving high school, young men who do not go to college receive no rewards from the labor market for developing competence in science, language arts and mathematical reasoning. It would appear that the United States needs to improve its signaling of academic competencies to employers if incentives to study mathematics and science during secondary school are ever to become as strong as they currently are in Europe and Japan.

References

Bishop, J.H. (1985), *Preparing Youth for Employment.* Columbus, Ohio: National Center for Research in Vocational Education.

Bishop, J.H. (1987a), "The Recognition and Reward of Employee Performance", *Journal of Labor Economics,* Vol. 5, pp. S36–S56.

Bishop, J.H. (1987b), *Information Externalities and the Social Payoff to Academic Achievement.* Cornell University, Center for Advanced Human Resource Research: Discussion Paper 87-06.

Bishop, J.H. (1988), *The Economics of Employment Testing.* Cornell University, Center for Advanced Human Resource Research: Discussion Paper 88-14. Forthcoming in Gifford, B. (ed.), *Testing and Public Policy.*

Bishop, J.H. (1989), "Is the Test Score Decline Responsible for the Productivity Growth Decline?", *American Economic Review,* Vol. 79, pp. 178–197.

Bishop, J.H. (1990a), "The Productivity Consequences of What is Learned in High School", *Journal of Curriculum Studies,* Vol. 22, pp. 101–126.

Bishop, J.H. (1990b), "Job Performance, Turnover and Wage Growth", *Journal of Labor Economics,* Vol. 8, pp. 363–386.

Bishop, J.H. (1991), *The Impact of Academic Competencies on Wages, Unemployment and Job Performance.* Presented at the Carnegie-Rochester Conference on Public Policy in November 1991. Cornell University, Center for Advanced Human Resource Studies: Discussion Paper 91-34.

Bishop, J.H. (1992), *The Explosion of Female College Attendance.* Cornell University, Center for Advanced Human Resource Studies: Discussion Paper 92–19.

Bishop, J.H. and S. Carter (1991), "The Worsening Shortage of College Graduate Workers", *Educational Evaluation and Policy Analysis.*

Bishop, J.H., A. Blakemore and S. Low (1985), *High School Graduates in the Labor Market: A Comparison of the Class of 1972 and 1980.* Columbus, Ohio: National Center for Research in Vocational Education.

Bishop, J.H. and K. Griffin, *Recruitment, Training and Skills of Small Business Employees.* Washington, DC: National Federation of Independent Business Foundation. (forthcoming)

Blackburn, M., D. Bloom and R. Freeman (1989), "The Declining Economic Position of Less Skilled American Men", in Burtless, G. (ed.), *A Future of Lousy Jobs?* Washington, DC: The Brookings Institution.

Brown, C. (1982), "Estimating the Determinants of Employee Performance", *Journal of Human Resources,* Vol. 62, pp. 177–194.

Bureau of Labor Statistics, *Employment and Earnings.* (various January issues)

Campbell, J.P. (1986), *Validation Analysis for New Predictors.* Paper presented at the Data Analysis Workshop of the Committee on the Performance of Military Personnel, Baltimore.

College Board (1984), *The College Board Technical Handbook for the Scholastic Aptitude and Achievement Tests.* Princeton New Jersey: College Entrance Examination Board.

College Board (1987), *ATP Guide for High Schools and Colleges.* Princeton New Jersey: College Entrance Examination Board.

College Placement Council (1985), *Inflation and the College Graduate: 1962-1985.* Bethlehem, PA.

College Placement Council (1991), *CPC Salary Survey.* Bethlehem, PA.

Davis, S. (1992), "Cross-Country Patterns of Change in Relative Wages", *NBER Macroeconomics Annual.* Cambridge, Mass: National Bureau of Economic Research.

Department of Labor (1970), *General Aptitude Test Battery Manual.* Washington, DC: US Department of Labor, Manpower Administration.

Dunbar, S.B. and R.L. Linn (1986), *Range Restriction Adjustments in the Prediction of Military Job Performance.* Committee on the Performance of Military Personnel. Commission on Behavioral and Social Sciences and Education. National Research Council/National Academy of Sciences.

Dunnette, M.D. (1972), *Validity Study Results for Jobs Relevant to the Petroleum Refining Industry.* Washington, DC: American Petroleum Institute.

Frank, R. (1984), "Are Workers Paid Their Marginal Product?", *American Economic Review,* Vol. 74, pp. 549–571.

Freeman, R. (1991), "Labour Market Tightness and the Mismatch between Demand and Supply of Less-Educated Young Men in the United States in the 1980s", in Fiorel, S. (ed.), *Mismatch and Labor Mobility.* New York, NY: Cambridge University Press.

Ghiselli, E.E. (1973), "The Validity of Aptitude Tests in Personnel Selection", *Personnel Psychology,* Vol. 26, pp. 461–477.

Goldberger, A.S. (1981), "Linear Regression after Selection", *Journal of Econometrics,* Vol. 15, pp. 357–366.

Hashimoto, M. and B. Yu (1980), "Specific Capital, Employment and Wage Rigidity", *Bell Journal of Economics,* Vol. 11, pp. 536–549.

Hotchkiss, L. (1984), *Effects of Schooling on Cognitive, Attitudinal and Behavioral Outcomes.* Columbus, Ohio: The National Center for Research in Vocational Education.

Hunter, J.E. (1983a), *Test Validation for 12,000 Jobs: An Application of Job Classification and Validity Generalization Analysis to the General Aptitude Test Battery.* Washington, DC: US Employment Service, Department of Labor.

Hunter, J.E. (1983b), "Causal Analysis, Cognitive Ability, Job Knowledge, Job Performance, and Supervisor Ratings", in Lundy, S., F. Zedeck and S. Cleveland (eds.), *Performance Measure and Theory.* Hillsdale, NJ: Lawrence Erlbaum.

Hunter, J.E. (1986), "Cognitive Ability, Cognitive Aptitudes, Job Knowledge and Job Performance", *Journal of Vocational Behavior,* Vol. 29, pp. 340–362.

Hunter, J.E., J.J. Crossen and D.H. Friedman (1985), *The Validity of the Armed Services Vocational Aptitude Battery (ASVAB) for Civilian and Military Job Performance.* Washington, DC: Department of Defense.

Hunter, J.E., F.L. Schmidt and M.K. Judiesch (1988), *Individual Differences in Output as a Function of Job Complexity.* Department of Industrial Relations and Human Resources, University of Iowa.

Husen, T. (1951), "The Influence of Schooling Upon IQ", *Theoria.*

Husen, T. (1969), *Talent Opportunity and Career.* Uppsala: Almqvist and Wiksell.

International Labour Organization (1977), *1976 Yearbook of Labour Statistics.* Geneva: ILO.

International Labour Organization (1991), *1991 Yearbook of Labour Statistics.* Geneva: ILO.

Jencks, C. et al. (1979), *Who Gets Ahead? The Determinants of Economic Success in America.* New York: Basic Books.

Jorgenson, D., F. Gollop and B. Fraumeni (1987), *Productivity and US Economic Growth.* Cambridge, Mass: Harvard University Press.

Kang, S. and J.H. Bishop (1986), "The Effect of Curriculum on Labor Market Success Immediately After High School", *Journal of Industrial Teacher Education.*

Katz, L. and K. Murphy (1992), "Changes in Relative Wages, 1963–1987: Supply and Demand Factors", *Quarterly Journal of Economics,* Vol. 107, pp. 35–78.

Klein, D. (1984), "Occupational Employment Statistics for 1972–82", *Employment and Earnings,* January 1984, pp. 13–16.

Kosters, M. (1989), *Wages and Demographics.* Paper presented at the "Wages in the 1980s" Conference, November 3 1989, American Enterprise Institute, Washington, DC.

Krueger, A.B. (1991), *How Computers Have Changed the Wage Structure: Evidence from Microdata, 1984–89.* Paper presented at the National Bureau of Economic Research Summer Labor Workshop, Cambridge, MA, July 1991.

Kutscher, R. (1991), "Reply to Bishop and Carter on the Worsening Shortage of College Graduates", *Educational Evaluation and Policy Analysis,* pp. 247–252.

Lazear, E.P. (1986), *Pay Equality and Industrial Politics.* The Hoover Institution, Stanford University.

Longitudinal Survey of American Youth (1988), *LSAY Codebook.* Edited by Linda Pifer, Dekalb, Ill: Northern Illinois University.

Lord, F. and M. Novick (1968), *Statistical Theories of Mental Test Scores.* Reading, MA: Addison-Wesley.

Lorge, I. (1945), "Schooling Makes a Difference", *Teachers College Record,* Vol. 46, pp. 483-492.

Maier, M.H. and F. Grafton (1981), *Aptitude Composites for the ASVAB 8, 9 and 10.* Alexandria, VA: US Army Research Institute for the Behavioral and Social Sciences, Research Report 1308.

Maier, M.H. and A.R. Truss (1985), *Validity of the Armed Services Vocational Aptitude Battery Forms 8, 9, and 10 with Applications to Forms 11, 12, 13, and 14.* Alexandria, VA: Center for Naval Analyses, CNR 102.

Maier, M.H. and S.F. Hirshfeld (1978), *Criterion Referenced Testing: A Large Scale Application.* Alexandria, VA: Army Research Institute, Technical Research Report 1193.

Manpower Services Commission (1985), *MSC Manpower Report 1980.* London: Her Majesty's Stationary Office.

McKnight, C.C., F.J. Crosswhite, J.A. Dossey, E. Kifer, J.O. Swafford, K.J. Travers and T.J. Cooney (1987), *The Underachieving Curriculum: Assessing US School Mathematics from an International Perspective.* A National Report on the Second International Mathematics Study. Champaign, IL: Stipes Publishing Co.

Mueser, P. and T. Maloney (1987), *Cognitive Ability, Human Capital and Employer Screening: Reconciling Labor Market Behavior with Studies of Employee Productivity.* Department of Economics, University of Missouri-Columbia.

National Academy of Sciences Committee on Ability Testing (1982), *Ability Testing: Uses, Consequences and Controversies.* Part 1: Report of the Committee. Edited by Wigdor, A.K. and W.R. Gerner. Washington, DC: National Academy Press.

National Commission on Excellence in Education (1983), *A Nation at Risk: The Imperative for Educational Reform.* A report to the nation and the Secretary of Education. Washington, DC: Government Printing Office.

National Council of Teachers of Mathematics (1980), *An Agenda for Action: Recommendations for School Mathematics of the 1980s.* Washington, DC: National Council of Teachers of Mathematics.

Noah, H.J. and M.A. Eckstein (1988), *Tradeoffs in Examination Policies: An International Perspective.* Paper presented at the Annual Meeting of the British Comparative and International Education Society, University of Bristol, September 15–17, 1988.

Office of Population Censuses and Surveys (1990), *Labour Force Survey 1988 and 1989.* London: Her Majesty's Stationary Office, Series LFS No. 8.

Olneck, M. (1977), "On the Use of Sibling Data to Estimate the Effects of Family Background, Cognitive Skills, and Schooling: Results from the Kalamazoo Brothers Study", in Taubman, P. (ed.), *Kinometrics: The Determinants of Socio-economic Success Within and Between Families.* Amsterdam: North Holland.

Olson, C.A. and B.E. Becker (1983), "A Proposed Technique for the Treatment of Restriction of Range in Selection Validation", *Psychological Bulletin,* Vol. 93, pp. 137–148.

OECD (1987), *Employment Outlook 1987.* Paris: Organization for Economic Co-operation and Development.

OECD (1989), *Employment Outlook 1989.* Paris: Organization for Economic Co-operation and Development.

Osborn, W.C., R.C. Campbell, J.P. Ford, S.F. Hirshfeld, and M.H. Maier (1977), *Handbook for the Development of Skill Qualification Tests.* Alexandria, VA: Army Research Institute, Technical Report P-77-5.

Palmer, P., D.D. Hartke, M.J. Ree, J.R. Welsh and L.D. Valentine (1988), *Armed Services Vocational Aptitude Battery (ASVAB): Alternate Forms Reliability (Forms 8, 9, 10 and 11).* Brooks Air Force Base, Texas: Air Force Systems Command, Air Force Human Resources Laboratory.

Postlethwaite, T.N. and D.E. Wiley (1992), *Science Achievement in Twenty-Three Countries.* London: Pergammon Press.

Rosenbaum, J.E. and T. Kariya (1987), "From High School to Work: Market and Institutional Mechanisms in Japan", *American Journal of Sociology,* Vol. 94, pp. 1334–1365.

Rumberger, R. (1981), "The Changing Skill Requirements of Jobs in the US Economy", *Industrial and Labor Relations Review,* Vol. 34, pp. 578–590.

Secretary's Commission on Achieving Necessary Skills (1991), *What Work Requires of Schools.* Washington, DC: Department of Labor.

Silvestri, G. and J. Lukasiewicz (1991), "Occupational Employment Projections", *Monthly Labor Review,* pp. 64–94.

Sims, W.H. and C.M. Hiatt (1981), *Validation of the Armed Services Vocational Aptitude Battery (ASVAB) Forms 6 and 7 with Applications to ASVAB Forms 8, 9, and 10.* Alexandria, VA: Marine Corps Operations Analysis Group, Center for Naval Analysis, CNS 1160.

Shamos, M. (1988), "The Flawed Rationale of Calls for 'Literacy'", *Education Week*, November 23, p. 28.

Stiglitz, J.E. (1974), "Risk Sharing and Incentives in Sharecropping", *Review of Economic Studies*, Vol. 61, pp. 219–256.

Thorndike, R.L. (1949), *Personnel Selection: Test and Measurement Techniques*. New York: Wiley.

Tuijnman, A. (1989), *Recurrent Education, Earnings and Well-being: A Fifty-Year Longitudinal Study of a Cohort of Swedish Men*. Stockholm: Almqvist & Wiksell International.

US Bureau of Labor Statistics (1990). Unpublished Table F-3, 1983–1988. Trends in the employment of persons who have 4 or more years of college education and the percent they comprise of total occupation employment, by detailed occupation, pp. 26–38.

US Bureau of the Census (1967), "Characteristics of Men with College Degrees: 1967", in *Current Population Reports, Population Characteristics*, Series P-20, No. 201, (p. 23). Washington, DC: US Government Printing Office.

US Bureau of the Census (1972), "Effects of Different Reinterview Techniques on Estimates of Simple Response Variance", in *Evaluation and Research Program of the U.S. Censuses of Population and Housing 1960*. Series ER-60, No. 11 (Tables 30 and 46).

US Bureau of the Census (1987), "What's It Worth? Educational Background and Economic Status: Spring 1984", in *Current Population Reports*, Series P-70, No. 11. Washington, DC: US Government Printing Office.

US Department of Defense (1984), *Military-civilian Occupational Crosswalk Manual*. Washington, DC: Office of the Assistant Secretary of Defense (Manpower, Installations and Logistics).

US Department of Labor (1970), *General Aptitude Test Battery Manual*. United States Department of Labor, Manpower Administration.

US Military Entrance Processing Command (1984), *Counselor's Manual for the Armed Services Vocational Aptitude Battery, Form 14*.

Vineberg, R. and J.M. Joyner (1982), *Prediction of Job Performance: Review of Military Studies*. Alexandria, AV: Human Resources Research Organization (HUMRRO).

Vineberg, R. and E.N. Taylor (1972), *Performance in Four Army Jobs by Men at Different Aptitude (AFQT) Levels*. Alexandria, VA: Human Resources Research Organization (HUMRRO).

Willis, R. and S. Rosen (1979), "Education and Self-Selection", *Journal of Political Economy*, Vol. 87, pp. S7–S36.

Wise, D.A. (1975), "Academic Achievement and Job Performance", *American Economic Review*, Vol. 65, pp. 350–366.

Wise, L., J. McHenry, P. Rossmeissl and S. Oppler (1987), *ASVAB Validities using Improved Job Performance Measures*. Washington, DC: American Institutes For Research.

Womack, J.B., D.T. Jones and D. Roos (1991), *The Machine that Changed the World*. New York: Harper Perennial.

3 Human Capital and Earnings in the Nordic Countries

Rita Asplund[1], Erling Barth[2], Carl le Grand[3], Arne Mastekaasa[2] and Niels Westergård-Nielsen[4]
[1] ETLA, The Research Institute of the Finnish Economy, Helsinki, Finland
[2] Institute for Social Research, Oslo, Norway
[3] Department of Sociology, University of Stockholm, Sweden
[4] Centre for Labour Market and Social Research, Århus, Denmark

3.1 Introduction

Earnings differentials are commonly alleged to be notably smaller in the Nordic countries than in many other industrialized countries. Substantial differences in earnings dispersion across countries may have a number of consequences for the future role of the Nordic countries in an increasingly integrated world economy. A more compressed earnings distribution in the Nordic economies may affect both the pattern of immigration and the allocation of different production processes.

More importantly, it may influence the functioning of the Nordic labour markets. In particular, it may impair the incentives for the labour force to participate in various kinds of education, training and other productivity increasing activities. As a consequence, the Nordic countries may in the future experience weaker productivity growth as compared to the countries we compete with.

Empirical evidence reported in a number of studies suggests that the rate of return to formal education is fairly low in the Nordic countries compared with the returns received in most other industrialized countries. Potential explanations for this outcome are culture and, especially, the set of policies related to education, the organization of labour markets, and tax and other policies aimed at equalizing incomes and wages that have been pursued in the Nordic countries.

As a result the Nordic countries have inevitably succeeded in creating more egalitarian societies with fewer social tensions than many other countries. This effort will, however, not necessarily be costless. On the contrary, small and diminishing earnings diffentials by education can be expected to weaken substantially the incentives to invest in one's own education and training. This, in turn, would have severe effects for the countries' future possibilities of catching up with the productivity growth of the Western World.

The above arguments are equally relevant when it comes to work experience in general and firm-specific training in particular. In some countries, the earnings effects of experience have been found to be very weak for certain employee categories. This could be interpreted as a market signal indicating that some jobs or occupations provide small, if any, opportunities for on-the-job training or other possibilities for improving the productivity of the labour force. Obviously this circumstance could be seen as offering a potential policy parameter to increase productivity and job satisfaction at the same time.

With these points in mind, the main purpose of this paper is to analyse the earnings structure in four Nordic countries – Denmark, Finland, Norway and Sweden – with respect to a few key variables. In view of the very similar social structure of these four countries, it could be expected that also the earnings structure across countries is characterized rather by similarities than by dissimilarities.

In the following this question is addressed by performing the same type of analysis on comparable national data sets. The drawback of using this approach is, of course, that it limits the use of more sophisticated databases which are available in some of the Nordic countries.

The empirical evidence presented below focuses exclusively on persons in paid employment. In other words, self-employed persons and persons not currently having earned income are excluded from the analysis. Both constraints will undoubtedly introduce an element of self-selection. This possibility of a sample selectivity problem may bias the results obtained from estimating earnings equations using ordinary least squares (OLS) techniques. Results based on the same data sets and reported in Asplund et al. (1994b) suggest, however, that the sample selectivity bias is negligible and that, as a consequence, OLS techniques will produce consistent parameter estimates.

The earnings concept used as the analytical objective is hourly earnings before tax. The samples are throughout limited to employed wage earners aged 16 to 64.

Figure 3.1 describes the overall distribution of sample hourly earnings by means of Lorenz curves. The curves in the figure display distinct differences between the four Nordic countries. In particular, there is a clear ordering of equality with Sweden and Norway having the most equal wage rates followed by Denmark. The most unequal distribution of hourly earnings is obtained for Finland. The Gini coefficients show the same picture.

Obviously many factors can be put forth as potential explanations for these differences in earnings across the four Nordic countries. This paper accounts, however, only for a limited set of measurable background factors contributing to the explanation of observed earnings differentials across individuals and countries. Specifically, the empirical analysis merely includes variables capturing the earnings effects of formal education, work experience, seniority (tenure), gender, private- and public-sector employment, and occupational social status. (For more details see Asplund et al. (1994a).)

The rest of the paper is organized as follows. The next section gives a brief presentation of the standard earnings model to be estimated and the data and variables applied. In Section 3.3 some of the main results are discussed. The stability of the estimates over time is examined briefly in Section 3.4. Concluding remarks are given in Section 3.5.

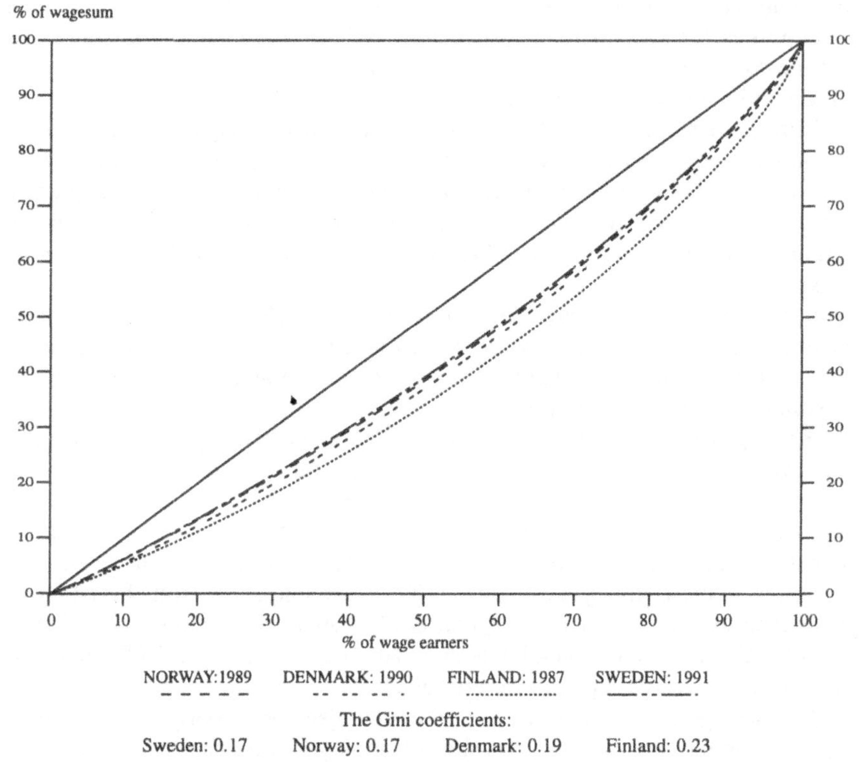

Fig. 3.1. Lorenz curves for hourly earnings in four Nordic countries

3.2 Empirical Model and Data

The theoretical background for the subsequent empirical analysis is the human capital theory. Various specifications of the standard human capital earnings function as developed by Mincer (1974) are estimated for each of the four Nordic countries under investigation. More formally, the log hourly earnings of the ith individual ($lnEARN_i$) are regressed on a vector (X_i) of human capital proxy variables, a vector (Z_i) of sector-specific characteristics, and an error term (ε_i):

$$lnEARN_i = \alpha + \Sigma \beta_j X_i + \Sigma \gamma_k Z_i + \varepsilon_i , \qquad \varepsilon_i \sim N(0, \sigma_\varepsilon^2)$$

The gender aspect is accounted for in two different ways: with gender appearing as an explanatory variable, on the one hand, and with separate estimations for each gender, on the other. This means that all model specifications are estimated both jointly and separately for male and female employees. The jointly estimated model allows for different constant terms for males and females but restricts the earnings effects of the included explanatory variables to be the same across genders. The gender-specific model allows for variation across genders in the estimates of these key variables, as well. Separate earnings equations are also estimated for the private and the public sector. As noted earlier, the earnings equations are estimated using ordinary least squares (OLS) techniques.

The data used come from national cross-section data sets found most appropriate for the purpose of the analysis. The Swedish data come from *LNU (Level of Living Survey)* for the year 1991. The Danish data come from *DLDB (Danish Longitudinal Data Base)*, which currently covers the years 1976–90. The Norwegian data were collected as part of the 1989 *Norwegian Study of Organizations and Employees*, which covers individuals employed in public- and private-sector establishments with two or more employees. The Finnish data come from the *Labour Force Survey* for 1987.

All four data sets are random draws from the whole population. The data come either entirely from surveys (Sweden), from surveys partly mixed with register data (Finland and Norway) or from drawings from various registers (Denmark). This variation clearly introduces various types of measurement errors.

Some of the data sets are longitudinal in nature. This is the case for the Danish database and partly also for the Swedish and Norwegian data sets. In Finland, on the other hand, the labour force surveys do not provide a longitudinal database because the survey sample varies from one year to another. Moreover, 1987 is the first and, until recently, only year for which the labour force surveys have been supplemented with tax-file income data. Since only a single cross-section survey is available, the stability of the Finnish estimates remains an open question.

The samples used in the subsequent empirical analysis are in all countries limited to employed persons aged 16 to 64. Despite some distinct differences between the four national data sets, there are, nevertheless, sufficient common features to make useful cross-country comparisons.

In order to further improve the comparability of results across countries, attempts have been made to use as comparable definitions of variables as possible. For variables like formal education and occupational social status, various keys made by *Nordisk statistisk sekretariat* are used fully or partly. The other variables (work experience, seniority, sector and hourly earnings) are also defined in a way that makes them comparable. The national data sets used differ, however, and this inevitably generates small differences in the definitions of some variables.

A brief summary of definitions of variables used in the subsequent empirical analysis is given in Table A3.1 of the Appendix. Sample statistics for all four countries are reported in Table A3.2 of the Appendix.

3.3 Empirical Results

This section discusses some major results concerning the estimated earnings effects of primarily human capital variables. The focus is thereby primarily on the gender-specific results. The underlying estimation results are given in Tables A3.3–A3.9 of the Appendix.

3.3.1 Returns to Years of Schooling

Formal education is measured in two different ways. In this subsection, education is defined as the number of years of formal schooling beyond the normal 9 years of compulsory basic education. In the next subsection, education is measured by means of the completed level of education.

The average rate of return to an additional year in postcompulsory schooling is estimated at about 4.5 per cent for Denmark, close to 5 per cent for Sweden and Norway and as much as some 7 per cent for Finland. Also the schooling coefficients estimated separately for Finnish males and females exceed markedly those obtained for the other three countries (Figure 3.2). Hence, Finland seems

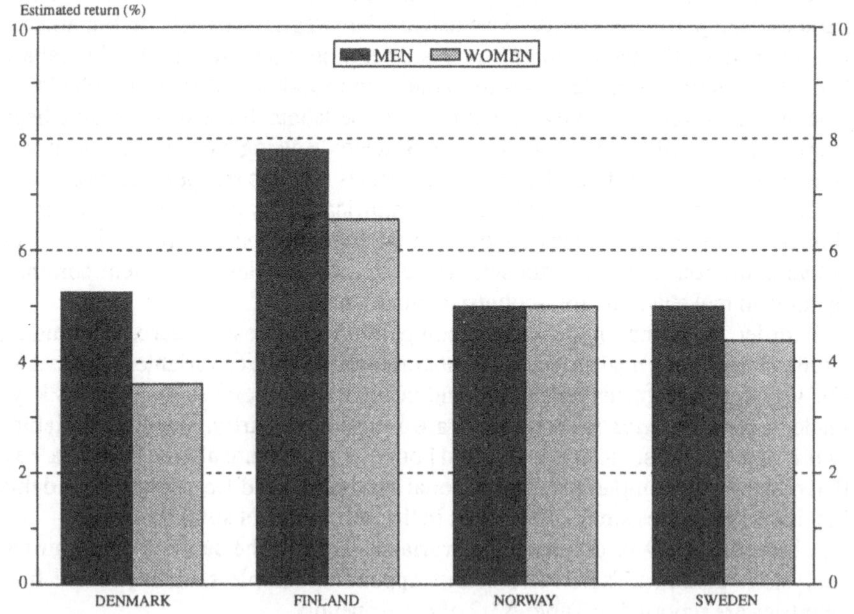

Fig. 3.2. Estimated average return to an additional year in postcompulsory schooling, by gender

clearly to break the pattern of approximate similarity with respect to educational returns across the Nordic countries.

Furthermore, the estimated return to formal education turns out to be significantly lower for women than for men. The only exception to this is Norway, where there seems to be no notable gender gap in the average rate of return to additional education. In Denmark, the difference between men and women in the rate of return to formal education amounts to about 1.3 per cent on average. This difference across genders is slightly smaller in Finland (about 1 per cent) and Sweden (some 0.8 per cent). The fairly large gap in the educational returns between Danish men and women originates in the relatively low return to education obtained for Danish women compared both to that of Danish men and to that of women in the other Nordic countries.

Allowing the estimated rates of return on formal education to vary across sectors unveils clear differences between the private and the public sector in all four countries under study. As shown in Figure 3.3, there seems to be only marginal differences in the way that the two sectors reward educational attainment in Denmark. In Norway and Sweden, the estimated return to an additional year in above-primary schooling is found to be on average higher in the private than in the public sector. In Finland, on the other hand, the public sector turns out to pay a higher return on educational attainment.

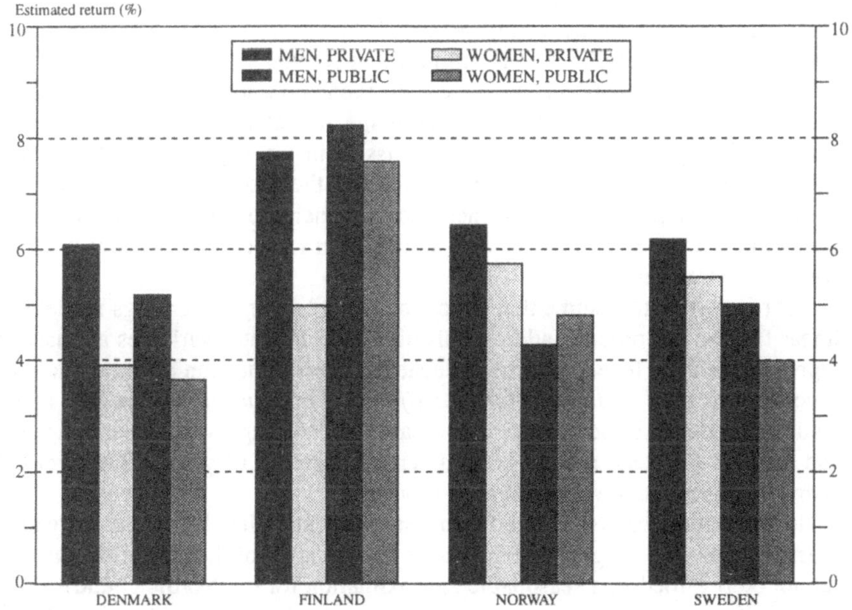

Fig. 3.3. Estimated average return to an additional year in postcompulsory schooling, by sector and gender

The figure also displays that the gender gap in the estimated returns on education is throughout fairly large in the private sector. It is notably smaller in the public sector in Denmark and Finland. In Sweden, however, the difference in the estimated return on education across genders seems to be somewhat larger in the public sector. In Norway, the return to education is found to be higher for women than for men in public-sector employment.

It would be most interesting to compare these Nordic rates of return to formal education with similar results obtained for other industrialized countries. Such a comparison could shed some light on the beliefs discussed in the outset, i.e. that the incentives to invest in further education are relatively low in the Nordic countries or in at least some of them.

Unfortunately, there are not many comparable studies, and European results are fairly rare. Estimation results for the US, in turn, are scattered and, for several reasons, not directly applicable. Compared to the present study, the data sets applied in US studies are much more exclusive, and the earnings concept used is generally not independent of the number of hours worked but covers total earnings and thus contains a supply decision together with a function describing the prevalence of unemployment.

3.3.2 Returns to Educational Degrees

The fairly low rates of return to an additional year in postcompulsory schooling estimated for the Nordic countries could, however, be due to various mis-specifications of the schooling function. One potential source of error is the way in which formal education is measured. A second non-negligible source of error originates in leaving out crucial person-specific elements, the by far most important of which is ability (see the discussion in e.g. Asplund (1993)). A third source of mis-specification is the possibility that the observed wage rate is not an equilibrium wage and that the incidence of unemployment is related to the educational level. Here only the first source of mis-specification is examined in somewhat more detail.

Is it reasonable to assume that education should enter the earnings model in a linear fashion? In order to address this question, indicator variables are used to represent the main levels of formal education. These education levels are defined according to the *Nordic Key for Classification of Education.* The five levels distinguished are: basic education (9 years of schooling), vocational education and training (12 years), short non-university degrees (14 years), BA level (16 years), and graduate level and above (18 years).

The estimation results obtained from using education level dummies instead of years of schooling suggest that the linear specification of the education variable cannot be regarded as a reasonable approximation for the Nordic countries; the pattern of educational returns turns out to be fairly segmented, especially in Denmark. The most conspicuous difference between Denmark and the other

Nordic countries is a remarkably low return to vocational education compared to the return acquired by persons with only a basic education (Figure 3.4).

Another notable difference across the four Nordic countries under study is that all educational groups investigated tend to receive a lower return in Denmark. But as can be seen from Figure 3.4, this differential is by no means equal across educational levels. The absolutely largest difference occurs in short non-university education; the estimated return to graduation at this level is remarkably high for men in Norway and Finland. This points to little, if any, incentives to continue for a degree at the BA or higher levels.

In sum, the overall structure of estimated returns on formal education is found to be fairly similar in Norway, Sweden and Finland. Denmark is different mostly because of relatively low returns to low and medium levels of education. Indeed, there seem to be obvious problems of incentives to continue in formal education for those with only a basic education in Denmark (most severe for women) and for those with a short non-university degree in Norway and Finland (most severe for men). Since the relative number of people affected by this problem is highest in Denmark, the problem with low incentives can be expected to be most severe in the educational system in Denmark.

3.3.3 Earnings Effects of Experience

The average length of total work experience varies between 17 and 18 years in Sweden, Norway and Finland, but amounts to only 13 years in Denmark. Obviously the main reason for this difference is that the information on experience comes from register data in Denmark. In the other three countries, it is based on survey data and these self-reported years of work experience probably also include shorter periods out of the labour force or in unemployment. This difference in data sources implies that the earnings effects of experience estimated for Denmark will be downward biased compared with the experience-imputed earnings effects estimated for the other three Nordic countries.

The overall earnings effect of work experience estimated for all sample employees is found to be stronger in Sweden and Norway than in Denmark and Finland. A simple t-test indicates that the observed differences between Sweden and Norway, on the one hand, and Denmark and Finland, on the other, are significant at a 5 per cent level.

Furthermore, the estimated earnings effects turn out to be fairly similar for men in all four countries but differ significantly for women. In particular, the experience-imputed earnings effects are on average relatively strong for Norwegian women, slightly weaker for Swedish and Danish women, and very weak for Finnish women.

In view of this it is hardly surprising that the gender gap in the estimated earnings effects of work experience varies a lot across countries. It is very large in Finland, and smaller, but still large, in Denmark and Sweden. In Norway,

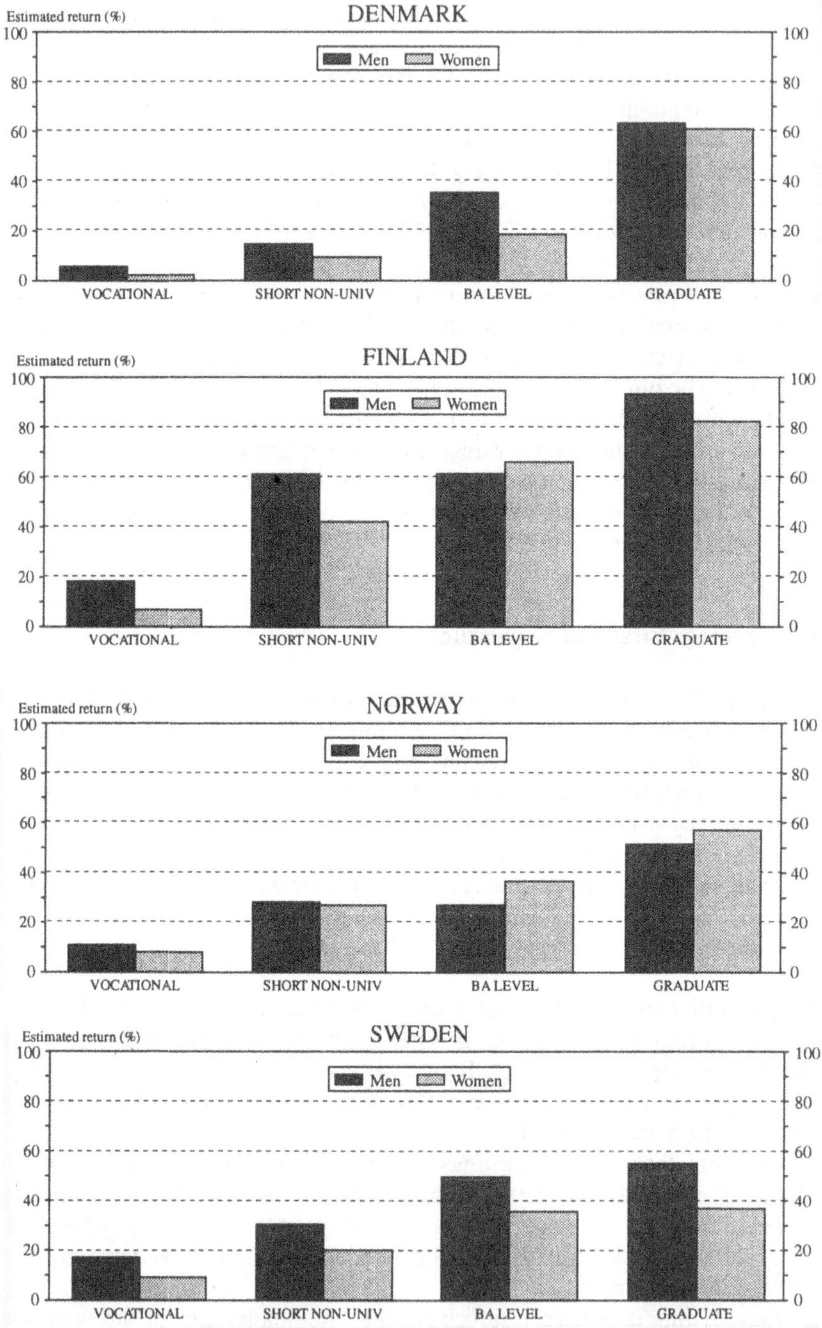

Fig. 3.4. Estimated return to levels of education compared with the return to basic education only, by gender and sector

however, there seems to be no significant gender differential in the estimated earnings effects of work experience.

The estimation results further indicate that the effects of work experience on earnings differ largely between the private and the public sector in all four countries. For convenience, these differences are highlighted by comparing the slopes of the experience-earnings profiles and the number of years it takes to reach the peak earnings level and the value of this peak level. Table 3.1 illustrates the implication of the estimated linear and quadratic experience coefficients reported in Table A3.3 of the Appendix by giving the percentage earnings growth for selected years of work experience. These calculations are based on the hypothesis that the obtained cross-sectional estimates will capture the dynamics of changes in earnings over the individuals' life cycle.

Table 3.1. Total wage growth (%) since entrance on the labour market for selected numbers of years of work experience[1]

	Experience, measured in years							
	5	10	15	20	25	30	Max of profile[2]	Obtained at
DENMARK								
Men, private	13.2	25.0	34.6	41.3	44.8	44.6	45.2	27
Women, private	11.3	20.6	26.9	30.0	29.4	25.2	30.2	22
Men, public	8.7	16.4	22.8	27.6	30.7	31.8	31.8	30
Women, public	2.5	4.7	6.7	8.5	10.1	11.4	13.2	40
FINLAND								
Men, private	12.7	24.6	35.0	43.3	49.2	52.2	52.6	32
Women, private	4.8	9.0	12.4	15.0	16.8	17.6	17.7	32
Men, public	14.0	27.3	39.2	49.2	56.6	61.1	62.4	34
Women, public	3.4	6.7	10.1	13.4	16.8	20.1	26.6	40
NORWAY								
Men, private	13.6	26.1	36.7	44.8	49.7	51.3	51.3	29
Women, private	11.9	22.3	30.6	36.6	39.1	38.7	39.3	27
Men, public	7.3	13.7	18.9	22.9	25.4	26.4	26.4	31
Women, public	10.1	19.0	26.2	31.3	34.0	34.2	34.4	28
SWEDEN								
Men, private	13.8	26.9	38.6	48.3	55.5	59.7	60.7	34
Women, private	11.3	21.4	29.8	36.1	39.8	40.8	40.8	29
Men, public	12.2	23.7	34.2	43.0	49.9	54.5	56.6	36
Women, public	7.1	13.5	19.2	23.9	27.4	29.8	31.0	37

[1] The percentage growth is calculated as the antilog of ($\beta_1 EXP + \beta_2 EXP^2$).

[2] The figures indicate the experience level where the experience-earnings profile reaches its maximum.

From Table 3.1 it can be seen that the earnings profiles with respect to work experience differ widely across genders, sectors, and countries. The highest peaks and the largest curvatures are found among Finnish and Swedish men, and this holds for both sectors. Indeed, men employed in the public sector in Finland and Sweden seem to experience approximately the same earnings growth with increasing work experience as their colleagues in the private sector. The weakest earnings growth among male employees is obtained for Danish and Norwegian men in public-sector employment.

The table also shows that in all four countries women quickly lose ground relative to their male counterparts, even though women seem to start their careers with earnings growth rates close to those of men. The experience-earnings profile estimated for Danish and Finnish women employed in the public sector is, in effect, not significantly different from zero.

To conclude, men generally tend to have steeper experience-earnings profiles than women. The exception to this conclusion is Norwegian men in public-sector employment who are found to have, on average, a surprisingly low return to work experience. Further, the growth rates in earnings with increasing experience tend to be higher in the private sector in Denmark and Norway. This holds for both genders. The same result is obtained for Swedish women, whereas the sector differentials are negligible for Swedish men. In Finland, on the other hand, the experience-imputed growth in earnings is slightly higher in the public sector.

Finally, the experience-earnings profiles in the private sector are found to have a more pronounced curvilinear character than those in the public sector. In other words, the peak earnings tend to occur at an earlier time for private-sector employees. Again the reverse situation seems to hold for Finland.

3.3.4 Earnings Effects of Experience and Seniority

The human capital literature often makes a distinction between experience acquired in the current company and/or with the present employer (i.e. seniority) and previous experience. When the earnings model is supplemented with both experience and seniority, the parameter estimate on the seniority variable may be interpreted as an upward biased estimate of the earnings effect of specific human capital, while the parameter estimate on the experience variable may be interpreted as an upward biased estimate of the earnings effect of general human capital. Accordingly, summing up the estimated coefficients on experience and seniority can be taken as partly reflecting the earnings effects of total work experience (Hashimoto and Raisan 1985).

The estimation results suggest that seniority has a much smaller impact on earnings than general experience. Moreover, the earnings effects of seniority are found to be of somewhat greater importance in Finland than in Denmark, Norway and Sweden. In particular, seniority turns out to account for up to 30 per cent of the earnings effects of total work experience estimated for Finland.

Seniority is also found to have a stronger influence on female than on male earnings. This is especially evident for Finland. At the other extreme is Norway, where seniority tends to have, on average, about the same impact on male and female earnings.

The results obtained when the earnings equation including seniority is estimated separately by country, sector and gender are summarized in Figures 3.5a–3.5d. These figures illustrate the simultaneous effects on earnings of seniority and experience. The light field (above) shows the growth in earnings determined by the length of the current employment relationship, while the dark field (below) describes the estimated growth in earnings attributable to increasing general experience. The two fields indicate, when taken together, the earnings effects of total work experience for a hypothetical individual staying with the same employer up to forty years.

Two main conclusions can be drawn from the figures. First, general experience seems to have about the same effect on the earnings of Danish, Finnish and Swedish men, irrespective of sector. The earnings effect of seniority, on the other hand, is generally larger in the public than in the private sector. This stronger effect of seniority in the public sector is most apparent for men. Accordingly, when the impact of seniority is accounted for, the estimated earnings effect of total work experience becomes larger for men in public-sector employment. The exception is, again, Norwegian men employed in the public sector, for whom the earnings effects of general experience turn out to be extremely low.

Among female employees, the earnings effect of seniority is estimated to be stronger in the public sector in Finland and Sweden. Indeed, general experience is found to have no significant effect on the earnings of Finnish public-sector women, suggesting that seniority accounts for the most part of the earnings effects of total work experience. For Danish and Norwegian women, the seniority effect is found to be of about the same magnitude in the two sectors.

Obviously the stronger seniority effects obtained for the public sector are in part attributable to the fact that public-sector wage rates are in all four countries largely regulated by relatively rigid pay schemes and seniority-based promotional patterns. Moreover, the public sector and, especially, state-owned companies are generally bigger, and also tend to act on stable, predictable product markets, often in a monopoly position. This provides state-owned companies with the prerequisites for establishing large intra-firm career labour markets which clearly increase the probability for public-sector employees to be promoted at the same employer.

A second major finding is that the earnings effects of total work experience tend to be larger for male than for female employees. This seems to be due to a much stronger impact of general experience on male earnings. In contrast, there seems to be no notable difference between men and women when it comes to the earnings effects of seniority. Possibly this finding could be interpreted as suggesting that men more often than women acquire skills which are transferable between firms and/or employers, while the skills that women acquire to a higher degree are of a firm- and/or employer-specific nature.

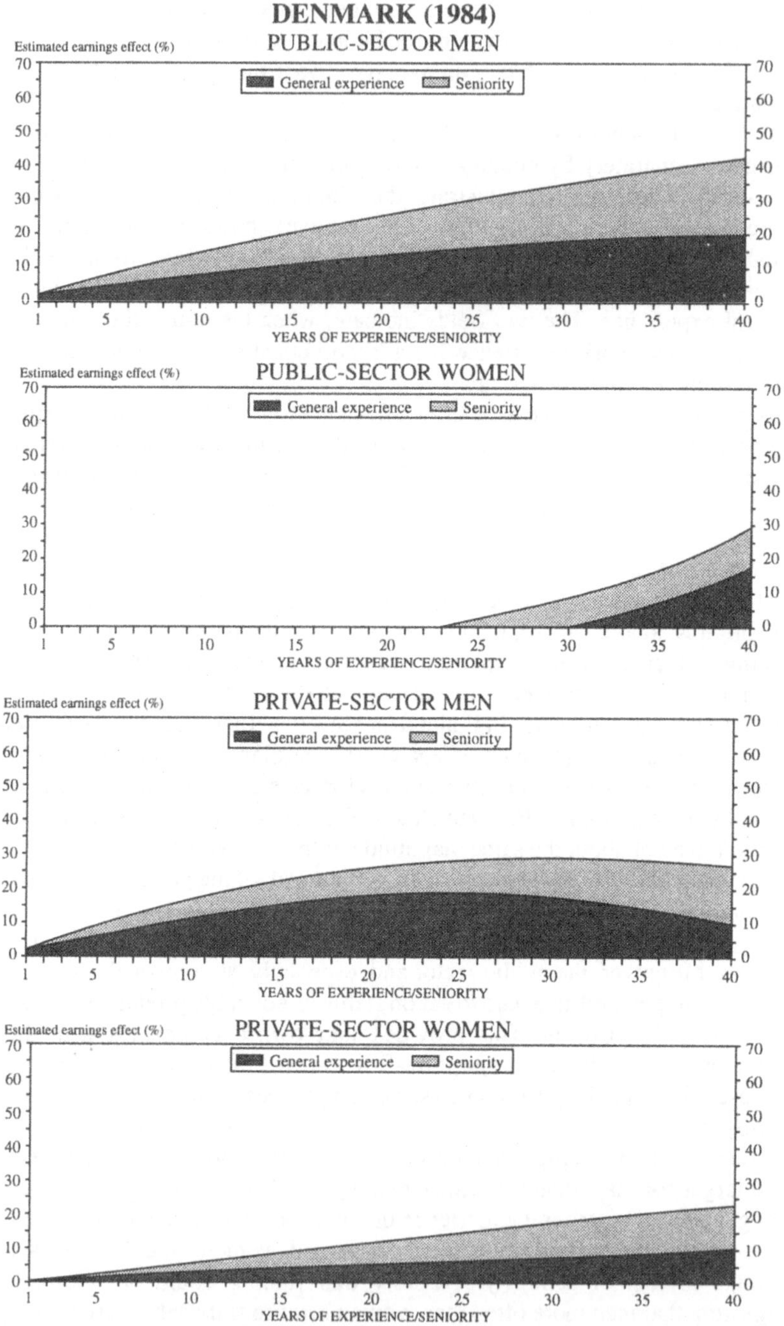

Fig. 3.5a. Simultaneous earnings effects of general experience and seniority estimated for a hypothetical individual staying with the same employer up to forty years, by gender and sector

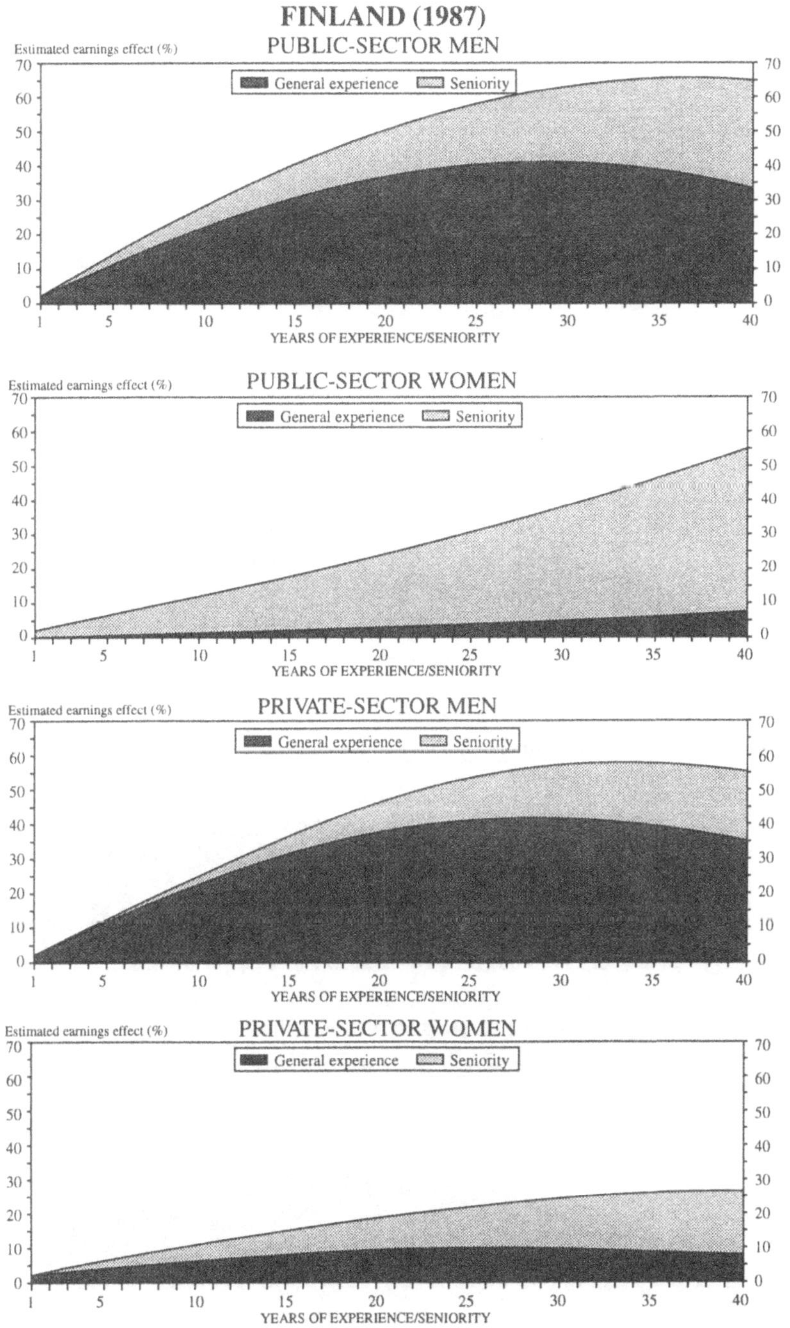

Fig. 3.5b. Simultaneous earnings effects of general experience and seniority estimated for a hypothetical individual staying with the same employer up to forty years, by gender and sector

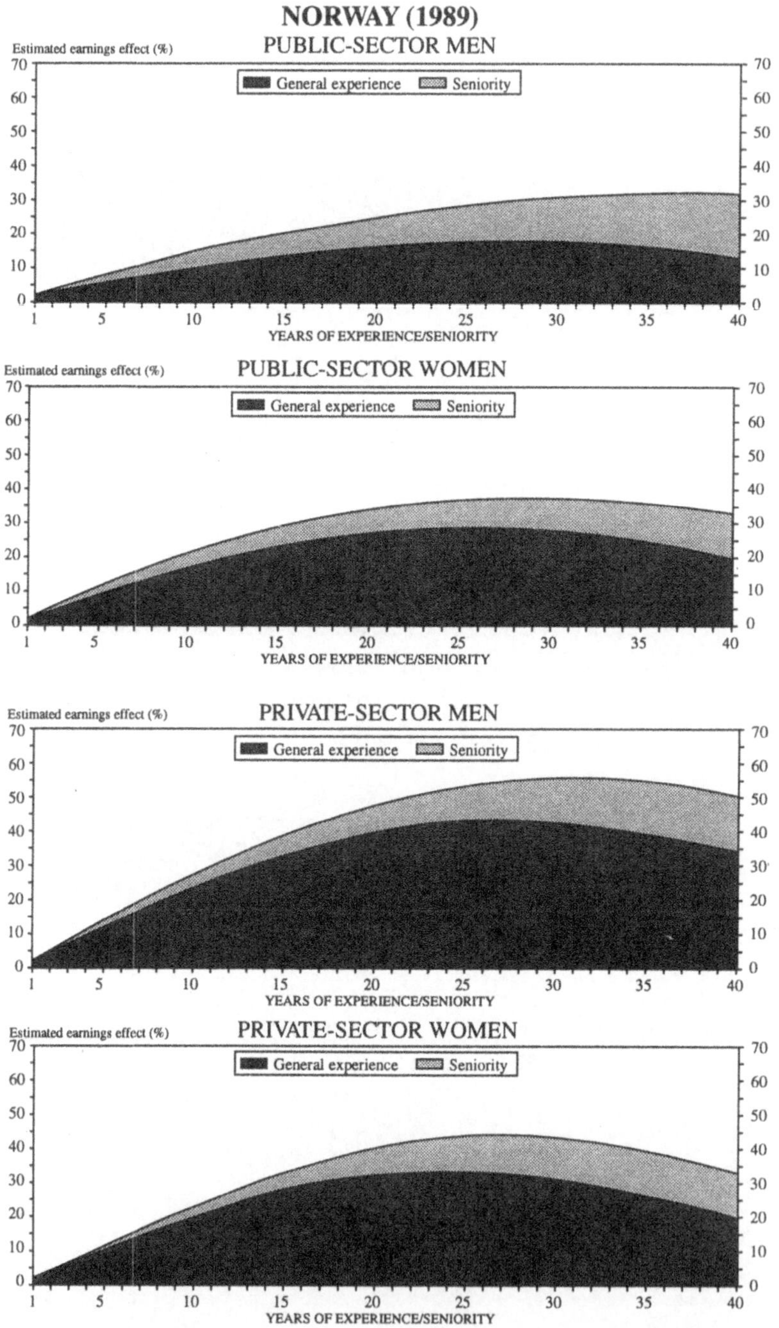

Fig. 3.5c. Simultaneous earnings effects of general experience and seniority estimated for a hypothetical individual staying with the same employer up to forty years, by gender and sector

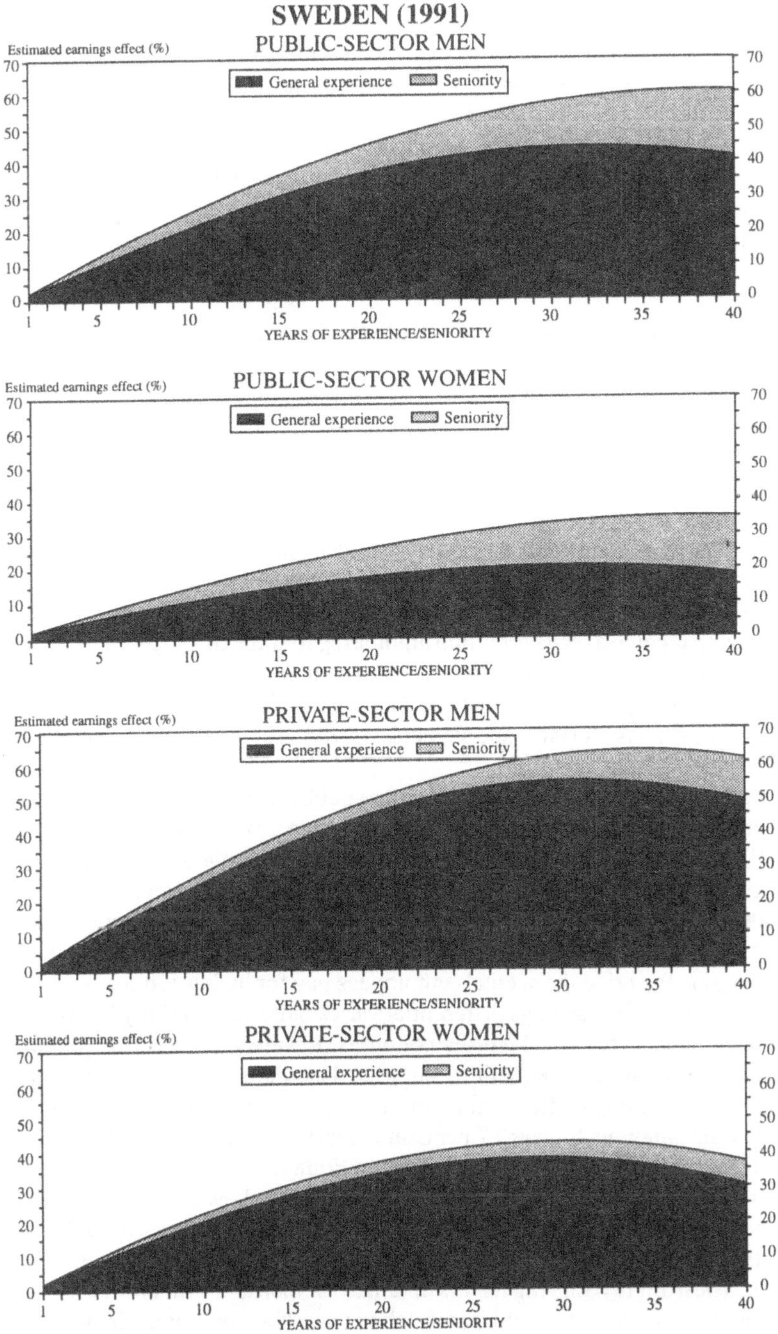

Fig. 3.5d. Simultaneous earnings effects of general experience and seniority estimated for a hypothetical individual staying with the same employer up to forty years, by gender and sector

Work experience and, especially, general experience as measured by the number of years in working life thus seems to have a substantial influence on observed earnings dispersion in all four countries under study. The estimated earnings effects of seniority and experience cannot, however, be interpreted as solely reflecting the impact on earnings of accumulated general and specific human capital, i.e. of more skills and thus higher productivity. Indeed, a number of competing theories also offer convincing alternate reasons for these positive earnings effects to occur (see the discussion in e.g. Asplund (1993)).

3.3.5 Earnings Differentials Between the Private and Public Sectors

The regression results suggest that there are notable differences between the Nordic countries when it comes to private- and public-sector earnings differentials. When estimating this sector differential by the use of a single indicator variable, it turns out that the public sectors in Denmark, Norway and Sweden have a significant and quite large negative earnings gap relative to the private sector. In contrast, no significant earnings differential shows up for Finland.

More precisely, private-sector employees in Denmark, Norway and Sweden are estimated to receive a wage premium amounting to some 6–7½ per cent, while the 1½ per cent wage premium estimated for private-sector employees in Finland is not statistically significant from zero. These gaps change only slightly when the earnings model is further supplemented with controls for the employees' occupational social status.

It may be noted that in the US, a negative public-sector earnings differential is not a general finding. Moulton (1990), for example, reviews several studies in the US, all pointing to an economic rent on the part of the public sector. An analogous interpretation of the results obtained for the Nordic countries would rather indicate an economic rent on part of private-sector employees, except in Finland. It is, however, also frequently argued that a negative public-sector earnings differential is the price the sector's employees pay for higher job security.

The private-public earnings differential varies quite substantially between male and female employees in all Nordic countries. Results obtained from estimating gender-specific earnings equations suggest that there is a significant negative public-sector earnings differential for men in all four countries. This "wage dispremium" amounts to over 12 per cent in Norway and Sweden, close to 12 per cent in Denmark and to about 5½ per cent in Finland.

For female employees, only Denmark and Sweden show a significant negative public-sector earnings differential (less than 4 per cent). For Norway and Finland, the estimation results point to no significant sector earnings differential among women. These highly varying results obtained for men and women clearly suggest that the two genders face different labour market conditions in the Nordic countries.

3.3.6 Earnings Differentials Across Occupational Social Status Categories

The addition of indicator variables capturing the earnings effects of the employees' occupational social status leads in all Nordic countries to a significant increase in the predictive power of the earnings model. The increase in R^2 from adding occupation controls vary, however, substantially among the four countries. In particular, the earnings differentials between occupational social status categories seem to be considerably larger in Finland and Sweden than in Denmark and Norway.

This difference across countries is also reflected in the estimated coefficients of the occupational social status indicator variables added to the earnings model. In Denmark and Sweden, the earnings level of upper-level salaried employees is, on average, almost 40 per cent above that of lower-level salaried employees (reference category). This difference amounts to some 27 per cent in Finland but to only about 13 per cent in Norway.

At the bottom of the traditional occupational hierarchy, the earnings level of Finnish unskilled manual workers is, on average, nearly 16 per cent below that of lower-level salaried employees. The unfavourable earnings position of unskilled workers is less pronounced in Sweden and Norway. The results obtained for Denmark point to no significant difference in the average earnings level between unskilled workers and lower-level salaried employees after controlling for differences in formal education and experience across the different occupation categories. These findings clearly strengthen the overall impression of relatively large occupational differences in earnings levels in Finland. In Norway and Denmark, on the other hand, these differences are found to be fairly small.

The addition of occupation controls to the earnings equation changes the coefficients estimated for the human capital and gender variables, given that the occupational social status of individuals is influenced by these characteristics. As far as work experience and gender are concerned, controlling for occupation leads in all four countries to minor (often negligible) declines in the coefficients estimated for these variables. Hence, the distribution of work experience seems to be fairly similar in all the occupational social status categories considered. Furthermore, differences in the distribution of men and women across occupational categories seem to explain only part of the observed male-female gap in earnings.

In contrast, the inclusion of occupation controls causes a substantial drop in the return on formal education estimated for Denmark, Finland and Sweden; the absolute size of the parameter estimate on the years of schooling variable is more than halved in Sweden and almost halved in Denmark and Finland. The reduction in the coefficient is much smaller in Norway.

Also these results point to a more important role of the individuals' occupational social status in Finland and Sweden. In particular, in these two countries a considerable part of the effects of education on earnings seems to be mediated by the employee's position in the occupational hierarchy. This seems largely to hold also for Denmark. In Norway earnings levels tend to be less strongly influenced by the employees' occupational social status. Instead the acquired formal education seems to have a more direct effect on earnings in Norway.

In assessing these results, due allowance should, however, be made for shortcomings in the occupational classification used and the assumption made that the occupational coding applied is equally valid for all four Nordic countries. Improvements in the occupational classification would possibly increase the similarity in results across countries.

3.4 Stability of Estimates over Time

In order to get comparable results for the Nordic countries, the regressions underlying the empirical evidence presented above were all done for a single year. It may, however, be questioned how stable the coefficients estimated for these selected years are over time. For example, pronounced trends will prevail if the demand for and/or the supply of educated people undergo marked changes.

The possibilities for analysing the time pattern of coefficients are, however, present only for Denmark, Norway and Sweden and, moreover, to varying degrees. For Denmark, regressions have been run for each year from 1981 to 1990. For Norway, survey data for the years 1980, 1983, 1987 and 1989 have been used. The longest time perspective is obtained for Sweden by using the LNU's from 1968, 1974, 1981 and 1991. As noted earlier, suitable historical data are not available for Finland.

In brief the analysis of the stability of estimates over time suggests the following. Results for Denmark and Norway indicate that the estimated return to an additional year in postcompulsory schooling has remained almost unchanged over the investigated time period. Results for Sweden, on the other hand, reveal a substantial fall in the estimated return to formal education from 1968 to 1974. The decline has, however, almost ceased after the mid-70s.

The regression results further indicate that the trend in the estimated earnings effects of work experience when measured at the sample mean experience level has been much the same as that in the average rate of return on formal education. This seems to hold for all three countries.

Hence, the results suggest that the earnings effects of formal education as well as work experience have been remarkably stable during the 1980s in Denmark, Norway and Sweden. The estimates for Sweden further point to sharply declining returns from the late 1960s to the early 1970s. Obviously this decline was in part caused by imbalances in the market of educated people (see OECD (1993) and the references therein). The markets in Norway and Denmark have undergone much the same changes. Accordingly there is reason to believe that a similar pattern would be found in these countries if data were available for the 1960s and 1970s.

3.5 Concluding Remarks

Estimation of identically specified human capital earnings equations for Denmark, Finland, Norway and Sweden has displayed a number of noteworthy similarities and dissimilarities in the earnings effects of key variables.

Thus the rate of return to formal education has been found to be substantially higher in Finland than in the other three Nordic countries under study. A common feature of all four countries is, however, that the returns to education tend to be significantly lower for women. Moreover, this gender gap generally seems to be larger in the private than in the public sector.

The analysis has also displayed areas of the educational scale where the economic incentives to continue in formal education are very small. This finding can be expected to affect the recruitment of educated labour in the future. The three most important education levels with low incentives are vocational education for both men and women in Denmark and BA level degrees for men and women in Norway and for men in Finland. Sweden turns out to have a fairly smooth structure of incentives.

The estimated earnings effects of work experience are fairly similar across countries for men but differ considerably for women. Consequently also the gender gap in the earnings effects of work experience varies a lot. The picture becomes even more mixed when a distinction is made between private- and public-sector employment. Two general trends emerge, though. First, irrespective of sector men have, on average, a steeper experience-earnings profile than women. Second, the growth in earnings with increasing work experience tends to be faster in the private sector in Denmark, Norway and Sweden. In Finland, on the other hand, growth rates are found to be higher in the public sector.

Seniority turns out to have a much weaker impact on earnings than general experience. Moreover, the earnings effects of seniority tend to be most pronounced in Finland, especially among women. Not surprisingly, the earnings effects of seniority are typically larger in the public sector. This is most apparent for men. The results also indicate that the stronger experience effects on male earnings originate in their much higher returns to general experience; the difference between men and women in the earnings effects of seniority is minor.

The results also point to a significant negative earnings differential on the part of public-sector employees is Denmark, Norway and Sweden. No significant differential shows up for Finland. When, however, a distinction is made between male and female employees in the two sectors, the pattern changes markedly. In all four countries, men employed in the private sector receive a substantial wage premium. In Denmark and Sweden this holds also for women. In Finland and Norway, on the other hand, this gap in sectoral earnings is non-existing.

Finally, estimation results obtained for Sweden point to a substantial drop in the returns on formal education during the end of the 1960s and the beginning of the 1970s. Since then, however, the return on education seems to have declined only slightly in the Nordic countries. A similar trend is observed in the estimated earnings effects of work experience.

References

Asplund, R. (1993), *Essays on Human Capital and Earnings in Finland.* Helsinki: ETLA, The Research Institute of the Finnish Economy, Series A18.

Asplund, R., E. Barth, C. le Grand, A. Mastekaasa and N. Westergård-Nielsen (1994a), "Wage Distribution across Individuals", in Westergård-Nielsen, N. (ed), *Wage Differentials in the Nordic Countries.* Amsterdam: North-Holland. (forthcoming)

Asplund, R., E. Barth, N. Smith and E. Wadensjö (1994b), "The Male-Female Wage Gap in the Nordic Countries", in Westergård-Nielsen, N. (ed.), *Wage Differentials in the Nordic Countries.* Amsterdam: North-Holland. (forthcoming)

Hashimoto, M. & J. Raisan (1985), "Employment, Tenure and Earnings Profiles in Japan and the United States", *American Economic Review*, Vol. 75, pp. 721–735.

Mincer, J. (1974), *Schooling, Experience, and Earnings.* New York: NBER.

Moulton, B.R. (1990), "A Reexamination of the Federal-Private Wage Differential in the United States", *Journal of Labor Economics*, Vol. 8, pp. 270–293.

OECD (1993), *Employment Outlook 1993.* Paris.

Appendix

Table A3.1. Summary of definitions of variables

Variable	Definition	Explanation
EARN	Hourly earnings including most types of compensation*	**DK:** Calculated from wage income from the tax-files using the annual ATP as amount of hours. **S & N:** Calculated from self-reported wage income. **FIN:** Calculated from annual wage income from tax-files using an estimated annual amount of working hours.
S	Schooling, years beyond the compulsory 9 years	Measured as the length of the highest postcompulsory formal education completed minus 9. **DK & N & FIN:** Data are from registers. **S:** Self-reported according to survey question.
EXP	Total work experience, number of years	**DK:** Measured as real experience according to ATP-records. **S & N & FIN:** Self-reported according to survey question.
SENIORITY	Number of years with the present employer	**DK:** Estimated from register data. **S & N & FIN:** Self-reported according to survey question.
WOMAN	Indicator variable for gender	
PUBLIC	Indicator variable for public/private sector	
OCCUP	Occupational social status	Indicator variables based on NORD-SEI**: OCCUP5: Upper-level salaried employees (NORD-SEI 005). OCCUP4: Intermediate salaried employees (NORD-SEI 004). OCCUP3: Lower-level salaried employees (NORD-SEI 003). OCCUP2: Skilled manual workers (NORD-SEI 002). OCCUP1: Unskilled manual workers (NORD-SEI 001). OCCUP0: Employees, not further specified (NORD-SEI 006). **DK:** Does roughly comply to NORD-SEI. **S & N & FIN:** Recoded, complying to NORD-SEI.

* National currency in nominal terms at the time of the investigation.

** *Nordisk Socioekonomisk Indelning*, Nordisk Statistisk Sekretariat, Tekniske Rapporter 51.

Table A3.2. Sample mean statistics by country and gender

Variables	DENMARK (1990)		FINLAND (1987)		NORWAY (1989)		SWEDEN (1991)	
	Men	Women	Men	Women	Men	Women	Men	Women
EARN	139.73	113.75	49.00	40.80	94.38	74.50	89.20	71.90
lnEARN	4.88	4.69	3.81	3.63	4.50	4.28	4.44	4.25
S	2.71	2.60	2.48	2.38	2.84	2.22	2.90	2.76
Basic education	0.35	0.40	0.35	0.36	0.20	0.24	0.27	0.24
Vocational	0.47	0.40	0.52	0.50	0.55	0.53	0.40	0.42
Short non-univ.	0.05	0.07	0.05	0.06	0.11	0.12	0.14	0.16
BA level	0.07	0.10	0.02	0.04	0.06	0.09	0.09	0.10
Graduate	0.06	0.03	0.06	0.04	0.08	0.02	0.10	0.06
EXP	15.64	11.55	17.46	16.14	19.39	14.64	20.13	16.74
EXP^2	371.83	190.60	422.19	356.83	524.34	303.74	573.48	397.12
SENIORITY	–	–	9.26	8.60	9.89	7.70	10.31	9.23
PUBLIC	0.23	0.48	0.25	0.45	0.25	0.49	0.29	0.61
OCCUP5	0.14	0.05	0.14	0.05	0.25	0.10	0.19	0.09
OCCUP4	0.12	0.07	0.18	0.18	0.35	0.24	0.18	0.20
OCCUP3	0.16	0.31	0.06	0.29	0.07	0.24	0.11	0.25
OCCUP2	0.24	0.02	0.29	0.07	0.13	0.02	0.27	0.12
OCCUP1	0.23	0.23	0.33	0.40	0.18	0.38	0.25	0.33
OCCUP0	0.12	0.32	–	–	0.03	0.02	–	–
Number of obs.	12246	11554	1908	1987	2113	1833	1658	1651

Table A3.3. Basic human capital earnings model estimated by gender

Variables	DENMARK (1990)		FINLAND (1987)		NORWAY (1989)		SWEDEN (1991)	
	Men	Women	Men	Women	Men	Women	Men	Women
Constant	4.510	4.506	3.343	3.356	4.084	3.918	3.994	3.941
	(.008)	(.008)	(.026)	(.035)	(.019)	(.017)	(.019)	(.015)
S	0.051	0.034	0.074	0.064	0.049	0.049	0.049	0.043
	(.001)	(.000)	(.003)	(.004)	(.002)	(.002)	(.002)	(.002)
EXP	0.025	0.009	0.026	0.009	0.024	0.023	0.026	0.018
	(.001)	(.001)	(.003)	(.003)	(.002)	(.002)	(.002)	(.002)
$EXP^2/100$	-0.045	-0.010	-0.039	-0.010	-0.040	-0.040	-0.038	-0.027
	(.002)	(.004)	(.006)	(.008)	(.004)	(.005)	(.004)	(.004)
R^2 adj.	0.230	0.106	0.266	0.142	0.243	0.247	0.288	0.262
Number of obs.	11330	10448	1908	1987	2019	1757	1658	1651

Table A3.4. Basic human capital earnings model estimated by gender and sector

Variables	DENMARK (1990)				FINLAND (1987)			
	PRIVATE SECTOR		PUBLIC SECTOR		PRIVATE SECTOR		PUBLIC SECTOR	
	Men	Women	Men	Women	Men	Women	Men	Women
Constant	4.484	4.459	4.521	4.542	3.359	3.387	3.257	3.335
	(.009)	(.012)	(.013)	(.011)	(.032)	(.050)	(.052)	(.051)
S	0.059	0.039	0.050	0.036	0.074	0.049	0.079	0.073
	(.002)	(.002)	(.002)	(.001)	(.005)	(.007)	(.004)	(.004)
EXP	0.028	0.017	0.013	0.0003	0.026	0.010	0.028	0.007
	(.001)	(.002)	(.001)	(.0015)	(.003)	(.004)	(.005)	(.005)
$EXP^2/100$	-0.050	-.0031	-0.018	0.014	-0.040	-0.016	-0.041	-0.000
	(.002)	(.007)	(.003)	(.005)	(.007)	(.010)	(.013)	(.011)
R^2 adj.	0.238	0.090	0.319	0.146	0.206	0.062	0.458	0.220
Number of obs.	8607	5118	2723	5330	1423	1099	485	888

Variables	NORWAY (1989)				SWEDEN (1991)			
	PRIVATE SECTOR		PUBLIC SECTOR		PRIVATE SECTOR		PUBLIC SECTOR	
	Men	Women	Men	Women	Men	Women	Men	Women
Constant	4.026	3.892	4.131	3.937	3.978	3.890	3.915	3.960
	(.022)	(.024)	(.038)	(.026)	(.023)	(.026)	(.036)	(.018)
S	0.064	0.056	0.041	0.046	0.060	0.054	0.049	0.039
	(.003)	(.004)	(.004)	(.003)	(.004)	(.004)	(.004)	(.002)
EXP	0.028	0.025	0.015	0.021	0.028	0.023	0.025	0.015
	(.002)	(.003)	(.003)	(.002)	(.002)	(.003)	(.003)	(.002)
$EXP^2/100$	-0.047	-0.046	-0.025	-0.038	-0.041	-0.040	-0.034	-0.020
	(.004)	(.008)	(.006)	(.006)	(.005)	(.007)	(.007)	(.005)
R^2 adj.	0.290	0.229	0.231	0.246	0.308	0.257	0.358	0.290
Number of obs.	1500	891	520	867	1171	651	488	1000

Table A3.5. Basic human capital earnings model including indicator variables for completed level of education, by gender (reference group is basic education)

	DENMARK (1990)		FINLAND (1987)		NORWAY (1989)		SWEDEN (1991)	
Variables	Men	Women	Men	Women	Men	Women	Men	Women
Constant	4.565 (.008)	4.567 (.008)	3.380 (.029)	3.436 (.037)	4.120 (.020)	3.972 (.018)	3.948 (.024)	3.957 (.018)
Vocational education	0.040 (.006)	0.010 (.006)	0.170 (.017)	0.075 (.018)	0.100 (.015)	0.075 (.013)	0.162 (.018)	0.074 (.013)
Short non-university	0.120 (.014)	0.086 (.011)	0.475 (.034)	0.357 (.032)	0.250 (.022)	0.247 (.019)	0.259 (.022)	0.180 (.016)
BA level	0.286 (.012)	0.170 (.010)	0.481 (.051)	0.509 (.035)	0.249 (.028)	0.307 (.021)	0.397 (.026)	0.313 (.019)
Graduate	0.483 (.013)	0.472 (.017)	0.660 (.035)	0.607 (.039)	0.414 (.024)	0.451 (.040)	0.422 (.025)	0.319 (.023)
EXP	0.027 (.001)	0.009 (.001)	0.025 (.003)	0.008 (.003)	0.025 (.002)	0.022 (.002)	0.026 (.002)	0.017 (.002)
$EXP^2/100$	-0.051 (.002)	-0.011 (.004)	-0.039 (.006)	-0.009 (.007)	-0.043 (.004)	-0.038 (.004)	-0.036 (.004)	-0.026 (.004)
R^2 adj.	0.235	0.127	0.276	0.172	0.236	0.254	0.298	0.265
Number of obs.	11330	10448	1908	1987	2019	1757	1658	1651

Table A3.6. Basic human capital earnings model including seniority, by gender

	DENMARK (1984)		FINLAND (1987)		NORWAY (1989)		SWEDEN (1991)	
Variables	Men	Women	Men	Women	Men	Women	Men	Women
Constant	4.640 (.014)	4.636 (.014)	3.350 (.027)	3.363 (.035)	4.084 (.019)	3.919 (.017)	3.990 (.019)	3.942 (.015)
S	0.047 (.001)	0.033 (.001)	0.074 (.003)	0.064 (.004)	0.049 (.002)	0.048 (.003)	0.048 (.002)	0.042 (.002)
EXP	0.013 (.001)	-0.006 (.002)	0.023 (.003)	0.005 (.003)	0.022 (.002)	0.021 (.002)	0.026 (.002)	0.016 (.002)
$EXP^2/100$	-0.026 (.003)	0.020 (.005)	-0.038 (.006)	-0.007 (.008)	-0.040 (.004)	-0.041 (.005)	-0.040 (.004)	-0.027 (.004)
SENIORITY	0.004 (.001)	0.002 (.001)	0.005 (.001)	0.007 (.001)	0.003 (.001)	0.003 (.001)	0.002 (.001)	0.003 (.001)
R^2 adj.	0.162	0.098	0.273	0.153	0.248	0.249	0.299	0.261
Number of obs.	7501	7096	1873	1974	1997	1742	1634	1619

Table A3.7. Basic human capital earnings model including seniority, by gender and sector

	DENMARK (1984)				FINLAND (1987)			
	PRIVATE SECTOR		PUBLIC SECTOR		PRIVATE SECTOR		PUBLIC SECTOR	
Variables	Men	Women	Men	Women	Men	Women	Men	Women
Constant	4.646	4.596	4.536	4.645	3.364	3.392	3.263	3.346
	(.018)	(.024)	(.022)	(.016)	(.032)	(.050)	(.054)	(.051)
S	0.055	0.038	0.050	0.035	0.074	0.049	0.078	0.074
	(.002)	(.003)	(.002)	(.001)	(.005)	(.007)	(.004)	(.004)
EXP	0.014	0.001	0.008	-0.012	0.023	0.007	0.024	0.001
	(.002)	(.003)	(.002)	(.002)	(.003)	(.005)	(.005)	(.005)
$EXP^2/100$	-0.028	0.003	-0.010	0.041	-0.038	-0.014	-0.041	-0.003
	(.003)	(.009)	(.004)	(.006)	(.007)	(.011)	(.003)	(.011)
SENIORITY	0.004	0.003	0.005	0.003	0.005	0.004	0.007	0.009
	(.001)	(.001)	(.001)	(.001)	(.001)	(.002)	(.003)	(.002)
R^2 adj.	0.159	0.067	0.319	0.157	0.212	0.066	0.466	0.241
Number of obs.	5560	3171	1941	3925	1395	1092	478	882

	NORWAY (1989)				SWEDEN (1991)			
	PRIVATE SECTOR		PUBLIC SECTOR		PRIVATE SECTOR		PUBLIC SECTOR	
Variables	Men	Women	Men	Women	Men	Women	Men	Women
Constant	4.024	3.889	4.139	3.944	3.971	3.891	3.920	3.960
	(.022)	(.024)	(.037)	(.026)	(.023)	(.027)	(.036)	(.018)
S	0.064	0.059	0.041	0.045	0.059	0.054	0.048	0.038
	(.003)	(.004)	(.004)	(.003)	(.003)	(.004)	(.004)	(.002)
EXP	0.026	0.023	0.012	0.019	0.028	0.022	0.022	0.013
	(.002)	(.003)	(.003)	(.003)	(.002)	(.003)	(.003)	(.002)
$EXP^2/100$	-0.047	-0.047	-0.021	-0.037	-0.045	-0.039	-0.034	-0.021
	(.004)	(.008)	(.006)	(.006)	(.005)	(.007)	(.007)	(.005)
SENIORITY	0.004	0.003	0.004	0.003	0.003	0.002	0.004	0.004
	(.001)	(.002)	(.001)	(.001)	(.001)	(.001)	(.001)	(.001)
R^2 adj.	0.294	0.233	0.245	0.247	0.314	0.253	0.368	0.298
Number of obs.	1481	884	515	857	1157	643	478	976

Table A3.8. Basic human capital earnings model including control for public-sector employment, by gender

Variables	DENMARK (1990)		FINLAND (1987)		NORWAY (1989)		SWEDEN (1991)	
	Men	Women	Men	Women	Men	Women	Men	Women
Constant	4.524	4.517	3.346	3.353	4.076	3.919	3.997	3.954
	(.008)	(.008)	(.026)	(.035)	(.018)	(.017)	(.019)	(.016)
S	0.055	0.036	0.076	0.063	0.056	0.050	0.055	0.044
	(.001)	(.001)	(.003)	(.044)	(.002)	(.003)	(.003)	(.002)
EXP	0.024	0.009	0.026	0.009	0.025	0.023	0.027	0.018
	(.001)	(.001)	(.003)	(.003)	(.002)	(.002)	(.002)	(.002)
$EXP^2/100$	-0.043	-0.010	-0.040	-0.010	-0.040	-0.042	-0.039	-0.028
	(.002)	(.004)	(.006)	(.008)	(.004)	(.005)	(.004)	(.004)
PUBLIC	-0.110	-0.036	-0.054	0.012	-0.120	-0.009	-0.116	-0.034
	(.007)	(.006)	(.016)	(.016)	(.036)	(.011)	(.014)	(.010)
R^2 adj.	0.248	0.109	0.270	0.142	0.270	0.246	0.314	0.267
Number of obs.	11330	10448	1908	1987	2020	1757	1658	1651

Table A3.9. Basic human capital earnings model including controls for occupational social status and public-sector employment, estimated for all employees (reference category is OCCUP3 = lower-level salaried employees)

Variables	DENMARK (1990)	FINLAND (1987)	NORWAY (1989)	SWEDEN (1991)
	All employees	All employees	All employees	All employees
Constant	4.599	3.584	4.121	4.123
	(.007)	(.024)	(.017)	(.016)
S	0.026	0.039	0.038	0.021
	(.001)	(.003)	(.002)	(.002)
EXP	0.018	0.015	0.022	0.018
	(.001)	(.002)	(.001)	(.001)
$EXP^2/100$	-0.034	-0.021	-0.037	-0.029
	(.002)	(.005)	(.003)	(.002)
WOMAN	-0.128	-0.170	-0.140	-0.119
	(.004)	(.011)	(.009)	(.008)
PUBLIC	-0.072	-0.018	-0.060	-0.068
	(.004)	(.011)	(.009)	(.008)
OCCUP5	0.320	0.243	0.125	0.306
(upper-level)	(.008)	(.024)	(.015)	(.015)
OCCUP4	0.093	0.108	0.061	0.110
(intermediate)	(.006)	(.018)	(.013)	(.013)
OCCUP2	0.008	-0.115	0.009	0.028
(skilled w.)	(.007)	(.016)	(.018)	(.013)
OCCUP1	0.010	-0.144	-0.062	-0.060
(unskilled w.)	(.005)	(.014)	(.013)	(.011)
OCCUP0	0.019	-	0.059	-
(other, unspec.)	(.009)		(.027)	
R^2 adj.	0.305	0.326	0.386	0.464
Number of obs.	21778	3895	3778	3309

4 The Impact of Family Background on the Returns on and Length of Schooling in Sweden

Anders Björklund
Swedish Institute for Social Research, Stockholm University, Sweden

4.1 Introduction

It is a common observation in most societies that children of parents with high incomes, extensive schooling and high-status occupations tend to emulate the behaviour of their parents and in particular invest more in schooling than other children. This pattern is often considered a problem from both equity and efficiency points of views. It represents inequality of opportunity and possibly also inefficiency if the intellectual capacity of all children is not fully exploited. A variety of educational policies have been advocated to reduce the importance of family background for schooling decisions. No country seems, however, to have been very successful in this respect.

In order to change the existing pattern it is crucial to understand the basic mechanisms that create this persistent intergenerational pattern of schooling choices. The idea in this paper – borrowed from Chiswick (1988) – is that useful insight into the mechanisms can be obtained from the relationship between the length of schooling and the marginal returns to schooling.

We start in Section 4.2 by describing the basic analytical idea. Then we describe the data in Section 4.3 and the empirical results in Section 4.4. The final section offers a concluding discussion of the study.

4.2 The Analytical Approach

The analytical point of departure is that the individual who is contemplating further education faces a marginal rate of return schedule for additional amounts (i.e. in practice years) of schooling. This schedule basically reflects how much the individual can raise earnings by additional schooling. The individual also faces marginal costs of financing additional schooling. These costs include first of all the interest costs to borrow the money that is necessary to finance the studies. But it also includes the disutility of postponing income to the future. It is reasonable to assume that the marginal rate of return is a decreasing function of the years of schooling and that the marginal cost of financing schooling is an increasing function of the years of schooling. By further assuming that the rational individual invests in schooling until the marginal return equals the marginal cost, the amount of schooling is determined as in part a of Figure 4.1.

Now, how can family background affect the amount of schooling in this framework? One potential explanation is that children from rich families can more easily finance their studies than children from poorer backgrounds. In this case – we call it *the financing hypothesis* – it is variation in the schedule for the marginal cost of financing education that generates the relationship between years of schooling and family background. This case is shown in part b of the figure. The interesting implication of this explanation is that there will be a negative correlation between the marginal rate of return and the length of schooling. If high financing costs represent market failures it is tempting to argue that this situation represents efficiency losses; those with a poor family background have high marginal returns on additional schooling investment but it does not take place because of high financing costs.

The other case is that those from rich families have more to get out of schooling, i.e. their marginal rate of return is higher. We call this *the comparative advantage hypothesis*. The basic explanation of such a variation in the returns to schooling could be that when rich families raise their children they emphasize skills that are useful at school more than other families do. They might also afford to invest more in activities that are useful at school.

The comparative advantage hypothesis implies the pattern shown in part c of the figure. The correlation between years of schooling and the marginal rate of return becomes positive.

A very straightforward way to implement these ideas is to estimate human-capital earnings functions which allow the schooling coefficient(s) to vary by family background. It is a well known fact that the marginal internal rate of return on schooling can be computed from regression equations with the logarithm of earnings (or wages) as a linear function of work experience and years of schooling where the latter variables might enter with quadratic or higher powered terms. It is the derivative of the logarithm of earnings with respect to years of schooling that is the marginal internal rate of return.[1]

More specifically, we propose the following equation:

$$lnW_i = \alpha_0 + \alpha_2 E_i + \alpha_2 E_i^2 + \alpha_3 S_i + \alpha_4 S_i^2 + \alpha_5 FB_i + \alpha_6 (S_i \cdot FB_i) + \alpha_7 X_i + \varepsilon_i$$

where:

lnW_i = the natural logarithm of the hourly wage for individual i

E_i = years of work experience

S_i = years of schooling

[1] The technical conditions are that there are no interactions between schooling and experience and that schooling precedes work (see Willis 1986).

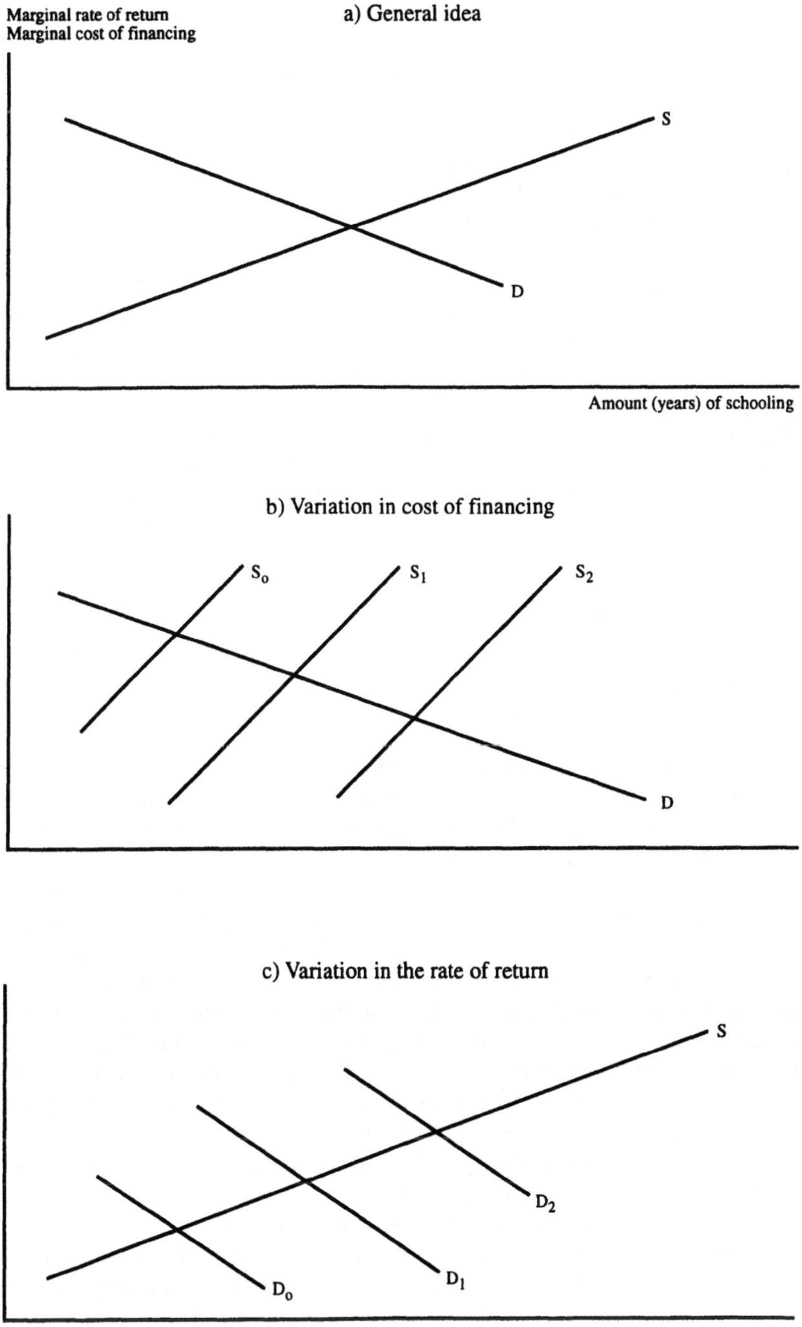

Fig. 4.1. Determination of schooling choices

FB_i = a set of family background variables
X_i = a set of control variables
ε_i = a stochastic error term.

As family background variables it is reasonable to include both such that capture the income of the parents and the educational level. Income is useful for financing studies as well as for activities that can be used to invest in skills that are useful at school. That the educational level of parents *per se* can affect the ability of children to get more out of school is rather evident.

We also suggest to use the number of siblings as a family background variable. The reason is that having many siblings can affect both the possibility of parents to help finance the studies and the time and the resources that can be spent on the "quality" of each child. The quality/quantity trade-off proposed by Gary Becker (see e.g. Becker 1991) suggests that such mechanisms can be present.

The comparative advantage hypothesis implies that α_6 is positive (negative) for those with strong (weak) family background. If there are no family background effects on the costs of financing and the cost schedule is rising, we will obtain the pattern described by Figure 4.1c. The pure version of the financing hypothesis implies that α_6 is zero and α_4 negative. We will then observe a pattern like in Figure 4.1b.

4.3 The Data

We will use the Swedish Level of Living Surveys (see Eriksson and Åberg (1987) for details) from 1968 and 1981. (In the near future we can also use the wave from 1991.) The sample is representative for the population in both 1968 and 1981. The panel property of the data is not employed in this study.

The mechanisms that we are looking for are quite general in nature, so we should be able to detect them in a homogeneous sub-sample of the population with only individuals who grew up in families with both parents present and with parents who were Swedish citizens at the birth of the individual. By restricting the sample in this way we need not control for "missing" fathers or mothers and we markedly reduce the problems of comparability between family backgrounds of immigrants and native Swedes. We also restrict the sample to those who were 26 to 65 years old in 1968 and 1981 respectively; at the age of 26 most people have completed their education and entered the labour market.

A further restriction is that only employed persons are included in the analysis. The reason is that good data on hourly wage rates are available for employed persons but not for self-employed persons and entrepreneurs.

As family background variables we use the father's social group and educational level. We use social groups 1, 2, 3 and farmers as dummy variables in our regressions with social group 3 as the base captured by the intercept. The father's educational level is divided into (i) senior high school ("gymnasium") or higher, (ii) secondary or vocational school ("real- or yrkesskola") and (iii) others. The latter group is the base.

The background of the mother is described by a dummy variable showing whether she was mainly working in the household during the childhood of the individual and another dummy variable for education above the compulsory level. We add age, age squared, marital status, living in a big city and working daytime (1981 only) as control variables. Table 4.1 contains the sample means of most of the variables used in the study.

Years of schooling vary a lot by these family background variables, which can be seen in Table 4.2. The difference between those whose father belonged to social group 1 and those with a father from social group 3 is around five years. The importance of the educational level of the father is of the same magnitude. The mother's educational level is also quite important.

In Table 4.3 we present simple regression equations which explain the years of schooling by means of these family background variables plus age and the number of siblings. The coefficients for "father social group 1" and "father high school or higher" are lower than the "raw" differences in Table 4.2, but still rather large. It is also interesting to note that the number of siblings has a strongly significant negative coefficient.

Table 4.1. Sample means

	1968		1981	
	Men	Women	Men	Women
Years of schooling	8.5	8.3	10.7	10.3
Work experience	27.2	18.4	23.8	18.0
Father, social group 1	0.04	0.04	0.05	0.06
Father, social group 2	0.20	0.26	0.29	0.30
Father, farmer[1]	0.28	0.27	0.20	0.19
Father, high school or higher	0.05	0.06	0.07	0.09
Father, secondary or vocational school	0.13	0.13	0.16	0.16
Mother, home during childhood	0.87	0.81	0.58	0.56
Mother, education above compulsory level	0.10	0.10	0.16	0.17
Number of siblings	3.3	3.4	2.4	2.5
Married	0.83	0.74	0.80	0.78
Living in big city	0.35	0.38	0.35	0.35
Working daytime	-	-	0.84	0.83
n	1303	775	1294	1161

[1] Farmers classified in social groups 2 and 3 are included as a separate category. Some very wealthy farmers who belong to social group 1 remain in this category.

Table 4.2. Years of schooling by family background

	1968		1981	
	Men	Women	Men	Women
Father, social group 1	14.2	13.2	15.8	14.2
Father, social group 2	10.0	9.4	12.1	11.4
Father, social group 3	8.1	7.8	10.0	9.4
Father, farmer	7.5	7.3	9.1	9.2
Father, high school or higher	13.6	13.2	15.2	14.4
Father, secondary or vocational school	10.1	9.6	12.7	11.6
Father, compulsory school or less	8.0	7.8	9.9	9.5
Mother, education above compulsory level	11.8	11.9	13.9	12.9
Mother, compulsory school or less	8.2	7.9	10.1	9.7
n	1303	775	1294	1161

Table 4.3. Determinants of years of schooling

	1968		1981	
	Men	Women	Men	Women
Constant	10.9	10.9	14.1	13.8
	(31.0)	(29.4)	(38.3)	(41.7)
Age	-.05	-.07	-.09	-.10
	(-7.7)	(-9.4)	(-10.6)	(-12.6)
Father, social group 1	3.51	2.12	2.56	2.02
	(6.5)	(3.4)	(5.1)	(4.9)
Father, social group 2	1.26	.94	1.02	1.09
	(6.1)	(4.5)	(4.6)	(5.8)
Father, farmer	-.43	-.42	-.59	.18
	(-2.4)	(-2.1)	(-2.5)	(0.9)
Father, high school	1.96	2.29	2.27	2.38
or higher	(4.0)	(4.0)	(5.3)	(6.8)
Father, secondary or	.98	1.09	1.58	1.11
vocational school	(4.1)	(4.4)	(6.2)	(5.1)
Mother, home	-.34	.28	-.26	-.12
during childhood	(-1.5)	(1.4)	(-1.4)	(-0.8)
Mother, education	1.25	1.81	1.43	1.19
above compulsory level	(4.3)	(5.8)	(5.2)	(5.2)
Number of	-.10	-.11	-.18	-.17
siblings	(-3.4)	(-3.6)	(-4.4)	(-4.9)
n	1303	775	1293	1161
R^2 adj.	.298	.370	.345	.388

4.4 Results

The empirical results for both sexes together and for men and women separately for 1968 and 1981 are identically organized in Tables 4.4a–4.4f. The first column in each table shows the estimates of the simple Mincer-type equation. They reveal the typical concave experience pattern and strongly significant schooling coefficients. The latter coefficients were roughly halved from 1968 to 1981, which has been noted in several previous studies. The quadratic schooling variable shown in column 2 in the tables raises the explanatory value markedly for both sexes together and for men and the precision of the two coefficients is quite good. For women, however, the precision of the two schooling coefficients becomes very low.

In column 3 we keep both the linear and the quadratic schooling variables and add separate family background variables. Even though none of these variables is strongly significantly different from zero, they raise the adjusted coefficient of determination (with the exception of women in 1981). The addition of these variables also reduces the impact of schooling on wages somewhat, but not very much.

Finally, we come to columns 4 to 6 in the six tables where the estimates central to our basic issue can be found. No coefficient of the interaction variables between the years of schooling and the family background variables is significantly different from zero for both periods and for both sexes.

Even though the level of significance is low one can, however, see two patterns in the results which at least weakly support the comparative advantage hypothesis and the quality/quantity trade off. The comparative advantage hypothesis gets some support from the predominantly positive coefficients on the interaction variable for the father's education. Actually, either "father gymnasium or higher" or "father real- or yrkesskola" has a coefficient around 0.015 for all six samples analyzed. Despite the low precision, these estimates suggest that high returns on schooling might be the reason for more years of schooling for individuals with highly educated fathers.

Even though these estimates suggest that there is some comparative advantage involved in schooling decisions, they do not necessarily rule out that differences in financing costs are important too. By using the equations in column 4 in Tables 4.4a and 4.4b and evaluating the marginal return to schooling for those with different family backgrounds, we obtain the situation depicted in Figure 4.2. We have evaluated the marginal returns for the average years of schooling for the groups. The main impression from the figure is that there is neither a marked positive nor a negative relationship. For 1968 the two groups with farmers as fathers do reveal low schooling and high marginal returns, which suggest that they had faced high financing costs. Apart from those with farmer background, however, the general impression is that the marginal returns are equal for the various groups.

Table 4.4a. Wage equations with family background variables, both sexes 1968, with t-ratios in parenthesis

	1	2	3	4	5	6
Constant	6.12 (43.0)	5.97 (36.3)	5.99 (36.2)	5.95 (34.0)	5.94 (34.0)	5.96 (34.0)
Work experience	.022 (7.4)	.022 (7.0)	.021 (6.9)	.022 (7.0)	.021 (6.9)	.022 (7.1)
Work experience squared/1000	-.38 (-6.2)	-.37 (-6.0)	-.35 (-5.8)	-.36 (-6.0)	-.36 (-5.8)	-.37 (-6.0)
Age	-.0045 (-0.6)	-.0030 (-0.4)	-.0030 (-0.4)	-.0034 (-0.5)	-.0032 (-0.4)	-.0033 (-0.4)
Age squared/1000	.051 (0.6)	.039 (0.5)	.031 (0.4)	.038 (0.4)	.034 (0.4)	.037 (0.4)
Women	-.271 (-14.8)	-.274 (-14.9)	-.272 (-14.7)	-.273 (-14.8)	-.272 (-14.7)	-.272 (-14.8)
Married	.137 (7.3)	.137 (7.4)	.136 (7.3)	.136 (7.3)	.135 (7.3)	.136 (7.3)
Living in big city	.096 (6.1)	.094 (6.0)	.094 (5.9)	.093 (5.9)	.093 (5.9)	.094 (5.9)
Years of schooling	.078 (29.4)	.102 (7.4)	.094 (6.7)	.102 (6.2)	.104 (6.4)	.099 (6.1)
Years of schooling squared	-	-.0011 (-1.8)	-.0010 (-1.6)	-.0013 (-2.0)	-.0014 (-2.1)	-.0011 (-1.7)
Father social gr. 1	-	-	.143 (2.5)	.174 (0.8)	.129 (2.2)	.050 (0.3)
Father social gr. 2	-	-	.041 (2.0)	.086 (1.3)	.042 (2.0)	.049 (0.8)
Father farmer	-	-	-.004 (-0.2)	-.109 (-1.7)	-.004 (-0.2)	-.114 (-1.8)
Father high school or higher	-	-	-.055 (-1.1)	-.252 (-1.4)	-.212 (-1.4)	-.056 (-1.1)
Father secondary or voc. school	-	-	.010 (0.4)	-.080 (-1.1)	-.055 (-0.8)	.012 (0.5)
Mother home during childhood	-	-	.040 (1.9)	.045 (0.7)	.032 (0.5)	.045 (0.7)

Table 4.4a. (cont.)

	1	2	3	4	5	6
Mother education above compulsory level	-	-	.029 (1.0)	-.008 (-0.1)	.010 (0.1)	-.037 (-0.4)
Number of siblings	-	-	-.001 (-0.3)	.012 (1.3)	.010 (1.0)	.012 (1.3)
Interactions with years of schooling:						
Father social gr. 1	-	-	-	-.004 (-0.3)	-	.007 (0.5)
Father social gr. 2	-	-	-	-.004 (-0.6)	-	-.000 (-0.0)
Father farmer	-	-	-	.014 (1.8)	-	.015 (1.9)
Father high school or higher	-	-	-	.018 (1.2)	.013 (1.1)	-
Father secondary or voc. school	-	-	-	.010 (1.4)	.007 (1.0)	-
Mother home during childhood	-	-	-	-.000 (-0.0)	.001 (0.2)	-.001 (-0.0)
Mother education above compulsory level	-	-	-	.003 (0.4)	.002 (0.2)	.006 (0.7)
Number of siblings	-	-	-	-.0016 (-1.5)	-.0013 (-1.2)	-.0016 (-1.5)
n	2078	2078	2078	2078	2078	2078
R^2 adj.	.440	.441	.443	.444	.443	.443

Table 4.4b. Wage equations with family background variables, both sexes 1981, with t-ratios in parenthesis

	1	2	3	4	5	6
Constant	7.41 (72.3)	7.10 (59.9)	7.13 (59.7)	7.13 (29.0)	7.09 (57.3)	7.14 (56.5)
Work experience	.016 (6.8)	.014 (5.9)	.015 (5.9)	.014 (5.8)	.014 (5.8)	.015 (5.9)
Work experience squared/1000	-.25 (-5.3)	-.21 (-4.6)	-.22 (-4.6)	-.21 (-4.5)	-.21 (-4.5)	-.21 (-4.6)
Age	.010 (1.9)	.015 (2.7)	.015 (2.7)	.015 (2.7)	.015 (2.7)	.015 (2.6)
Age squared/1000	-.088 (-1.4)	-.130 (-2.1)	-.129 (-2.1)	-.131 (-2.1)	-.134 (-2.2)	-.127 (-2.0)
Women	-.169 (-15.5)	-.175 (-16.0)	-.176 (-16.0)	-.177 (-16.1)	-.176 (-16.1)	-.175 (-16.0)
Married	.035 (3.0)	.035 (3.0)	.035 (2.9)	.035 (3.0)	.035 (2.9)	.035 (2.9)
Living in big city	.042 (4.1)	.040 (3.9)	.038 (3.6)	.038 (3.6)	.038 (3.6)	.038 (3.6)
Working daytime	-.041 (-3.1)	-.041 (-3.1)	-.042 (-3.2)	-.041 (-3.2)	-.041 (-3.2)	-.043 (-3.3)
Years of schooling	.041 (25.2)	.078 (10.1)	.075 (9.6)	.076 (8.0)	.080 (8.8)	.076 (8.0)
Years of schooling squared	-	-.0016 (-5.0)	-.0015 (-4.8)	-.0016 (-4.2)	-.0017 (-4.7)	-.0016 (-4.3)
Father social gr. 1	-	-	.035 (1.3)	.155 (1.3)	.029 (1.0)	.048 (0.4)
Father social gr. 2	-	-	.030 (2.4)	.008 (0.2)	.031 (2.5)	.001 (0.0)
Father farmer	-	-	.009 (0.7)	-.016 (-0.4)	.008 (0.6)	-.016 (-0.4)
Father high school or higher	-	-	.008 (0.3)	-.252 (-2.4)	-.213 (-2.2)	.004 (0.2)
Father secondary or voc. school	-	-	.000 (0.0)	.051 (1.0)	.049 (1.0)	-.002 (-0.1)

Table 4.4b. (cont.)

	1	2	3	4	5	6
Mother home during childhood	-	-	-.001 (-0.1)	-.039 (-1.2)	-.035 (1.1)	-.040 (-1.4)
Mother educ. above compulsory level	-	-	.005 (0.3)	.015 (0.3)	.025 (0.5)	-.009 (-0.2)
Number of siblings	-	-	-.0015 (-0.6)	.0080 (1.1)	.0084 (1.2)	.0069 (0.9)
Interactions with years of schooling:						
Father social gr. 1	-	-	-	-.008 (-1.0)	-	-.000 (-0.1)
Father social gr. 2	-	-	-	.002 (0.6)	-	.003 (0.8)
Father farmer	-	-	-	.003 (0.6)	-	.002 (0.6)
Father high school or higher	-	-	-	.018 (2.4)	.015 (2.3)	-
Father secondary or voc. school	-	-	-	-.004 (-1.0)	-.004 (-1.0)	-
Mother home during childhood	-	-	-	.004 (1.3)	.003 (1.2)	.004 (1.3)
Mother education above compulsory level	-	-	-	-.001 (-0.2)	-.002 (-0.4)	.001 (0.3)
Number of siblings	-	-	-	-.0010 (-1.4)	-.0011 (-1.4)	-.0009 (-1.2)
n	2455	2455	2455	2455	2455	2455
R^2 adj.	.336	.343	.343	.344	.345	.342

Table 4.4c. Wage equations with family background variables, men 1968, with t-ratios in parenthesis

	1	2	3	4	5	6
Constant	6.33 (31.7)	5.96 (26.6)	5.91 (26.3)	5.95 (25.5)	5.91 (25.4)	5.97 (25.6)
Work experience	.029 (5.0)	.027 (4.6)	.025 (4.2)	.028 (4.7)	.026 (4.4)	.028 (4.7)
Work experience squared/1000	-.53 (-5.3)	-.50 (-5.0)	-.47 (-4.7)	-.53 (-5.1)	-.49 (-4.7)	-.53 (-5.1)
Age	-.0219 (-1.9)	-.0169 (-1.4)	-.0135 (-1.1)	-.0183 (-1.5)	-.0153 (-1.3)	-.0188 (-1.6)
Age squared/1000	.267 (2.0)	.227 (1.7)	.186 (1.4)	.244 (1.8)	.204 (1.5)	.251 (1.9)
Married	.211 (8.7)	.211 (8.7)	.209 (8.6)	.207 (8.5)	.207 (8.5)	.207 (8.5)
Living in big city	.106 (5.5)	.098 (5.1)	.098 (5.1)	.096 (5.0)	.098 (5.0)	.098 (5.1)
Years of schooling	.077 (21.4)	.133 (8.4)	.127 (7.8)	.130 (6.9)	.132 (7.0)	.127 (6.8)
Years of schooling squared	-	-.0025 (-3.6)	-.0023 (-3.4)	-.0024 (-3.3)	-.0025 (-3.4)	-.0022 (-3.1)
Father social gr. 1	-	-	.117 (1.7)	.205 (0.9)	.120 (1.7)	.124 (0.6)
Father social gr. 2	-	-	.011 (0.4)	.081 (1.0)	.011 (0.4)	.025 (0.3)
Father farmer	-	-	-.037 (-1.7)	-.200 (-2.7)	-.038 (-1.7)	-.210 (-2.9)
Father high school or higher	-	-	-.103 (-1.7)	-.226 (-1.1)	-.150 (-0.9)	-.097 (-1.6)
Father secondary or voc. school	-	-	.001 (0.0)	-.135 (-1.6)	-.090 (-1.1)	-.001 (-0.0)
Mother home during childhood	-	-	.053 (1.9)	.053 (0.6)	.033 (0.4)	.056 (0.7)
Mother education above compulsory level	-	-	.044 (1.2)	.090 (0.8)	.113 (1.0)	.068 (0.6)

Table 4.4c. (cont.)

	1	2	3	4	5	6
Number of siblings	-	-	-.001 (-0.3)	.017 (1.5)	.014 (1.2)	.018 (1.6)
Interactions with years of schooling:						
Father social gr. 1	-	-	-	-.008 (-0.4)	-	.001 (0.0)
Father social gr. 2	-	-	-	-.007 (-0.8)	-	-.001 (-0.0)
Father farmer	-	-	-	.021 (2.3)	-	.023 (2.5)
Father high school or higher	-	-	-	.013 (0.8)	.005 (0.4)	-
Father secondary or voc. school	-	-	-	.014 (1.7)	.009 (1.2)	-
Mother home during childhood	-	-	-	-.000 (-0.0)	.002 (0.3)	-.000 (-0.0)
Mother education above compulsory level	-	-	-	-.004 (-0.4)	-.007 (-0.7)	-.002 (-0.2)
Number of siblings	-	-	-	-.0024 (-1.7)	-.0019 (-1.4)	-.0024 (-1.8)
n	1303	1303	1303	1303	1303	1303
R^2 adj.	.404	.410	.412	.414	.411	.414

Table 4.4d. Wage equations with family background variables, women 1968, with t-ratios in parenthesis

	1	2	3	4	5	6
Constant	5.71 (23.6)	6.16 (21.6)	6.22 (21.2)	6.09 (18.7)	6.08 (29.0)	6.10 (18.9)
Work experience	.017 (3.9)	.020 (4.5)	.020 (4.5)	.020 (4.5)	.020 (4.5)	.020 (4.5)
Work experience squared/1000	-.29 (-3.0)	-.34 (-4.2)	-.34 (-3.4)	-.34 (-3.4)	-.34 (-3.4)	-.34 (-3.4)
Age	.0094 (0.8)	.0069 (0.6)	.0045 (0.4)	.0048 (0.4)	.0046 (0.4)	.0052 (0.4)
Age squared/1000	-.115 (-0.9)	.096 (-0.7)	-.078 (-0.6)	-.079 (-0.6)	-.077 (-0.6)	-.083 (-0.6)
Married	.028 (0.9)	.022 (0.7)	.027 (0.9)	.026 (0.9)	.027 (0.9)	.027 (0.9)
Living in big city	.083 (3.1)	.089 (3.3)	.090 (3.3)	.087 (3.2)	.087 (3.2)	.088 (3.2)
Years of schooling	.077 (15.9)	-.009 (-0.3)	-.015 (-0.5)	.009 (0.2)	.013 (0.3)	.0004 (0.1)
Years of schooling squared	-	.0042 (3.0)	.0041 (2.7)	.0030 (1.5)	.0026 (1.4)	.0033 (1.8)
Father social gr. 1	-	-	.152 (1.5)	.051 (0.1)	.139 (1.4)	-.078 (-0.2)
Father social gr. 2	-	-	.071 (2.1)	.139 (1.1)	.074 (2.1)	.131 (1.1)
Father farmer	-	-	.040 (1.2)	.028 (0.2)	.040 (1.2)	.028 (0.2)
Father high school or higher	-	-	.009 (0.1)	-.181 (-0.5)	-.262 (-0.8)	.013 (0.1)
Father secondary or voc. school	-	-	.034 (0.8)	-.005 (-0.0)	.020 (0.2)	.037 (0.9)
Mother home during childhood	-	-	.032 (0.9)	.073 (0.7)	.071 (0.7)	.073 (0.7)
Mother education above compulsory level	-	-	.013 (0.2)	-.073 (-0.4)	-.067 (-0.3)	-.104 (-0.5)

Table 4.4d. (cont.)

	1	2	3	4	5	6
Number of siblings	-	-	-.003 (-0.6)	-.004 (-0.2)	-.005 (-0.3)	-.004 (-0.2)
Interactions with years of schooling:						
Father social gr. 1	-	-	-	.005 (0.1)	-	.02 (0.5)
Father social gr. 2	-	-	-	-.008 (-0.5)	-	-.007 (-0.5)
Father farmer	-	-	-	.002 (0.1)	-	.002 (0.1)
Father high school or higher	-	-	-	.017 (0.5)	.022 (0.9)	-
Father secondary or voc. school	-	-	-	.003 (0.2)	.002 (0.2)	-
Mother home during childhood	-	-	-	-.005 (-0.4)	-.005 (-0.4)	-.005 (-0.4)
Mother education above compulsory level	-	-	-	.008 (0.4)	.007 (0.4)	.011 (0.6)
Number of siblings	-	-	-	.0001 (0.0)	.0003 (0.2)	.0001 (0.1)
n	775	775	775	775	775	775
R^2 adj.	.296	.304	.306	.301	.303	.302

Table 4.4e. Wage equations with family background variables, men 1981, with t-ratios in parenthesis

	1	2	3	4	5	6
Constant	7.32 (42.4)	6.59 (32.7)	6.66 (32.8)	6.70 (32.3)	6.64 (32.3)	6.72 (32.5)
Work experience	.014 (3.0)	.005 (1.0)	.006 (1.2)	.004 (0.8)	.004 (0.8)	.005 (0.9)
Work experience squared/1000	-.285 (-3.5)	-.127 (-1.5)	-.137 (-1.6)	-.101 (-1.2)	-.104 (-1.2)	-.111 (-1.3)
Age	.013 (-1.4)	.034 (3.2)	.032 (3.0)	.035 (3.2)	.035 (3.3)	.033 (3.1)
Age squared/1000	-.068 (-0.6)	-.276 (-2.4)	-.259 (-2.2)	-.294 (-2.5)	-.294 (-2.5)	-.281 (-2.4)
Married	.091 (5.3)	.093 (5.5)	.092 (5.4)	.091 (5.4)	.091 (5.3)	.091 (5.3)
Living in big city	.072 (4.9)	.067 (4.6)	.063 (4.2)	.062 (4.2)	.063 (4.3)	.061 (4.2)
Working daytime	-.026 (-1.4)	-.029 (-1.6)	-.029 (-1.6)	-.029 (-1.5)	-.027 (-1.5)	-.031 (-1.6)
Years of schooling	.035 (12.5)	.100 (10.0)	.095 (9.3)	.087 (7.0)	.094 (7.9)	.087 (7.1)
Years of schooling squared	-	-.0026 (-6.7)	-.0025 (-6.4)	-.0024 (-5.1)	-.0026 (-5.7)	-.0025 (-5.4)
Father social gr. 1	-	-	.072 (1.8)	.230 (1.4)	.060 (1.5)	.167 (1.1)
Father social gr. 2	-	-	.035 (2.0)	-.026 (-0.5)	.036 (2.0)	-.028 (-1.1)
Father farmer	-	-	.001 (0.1)	-.067 (-1.2)	-.004 (-0.2)	-.066 (-1.1)
Father high school or higher	-	-	.011 (0.3)	-.167 (-1.2)	-.128 (-1.0)	.004 (0.1)
Father secondary or voc. school	-	-	.008 (0.4)	.058 (0.9)	.048 (0.7)	.003 (0.2)
Mother home during childhood	-	-	.015 (1.0)	-.077 (-1.7)	-.068 (-1.6)	-.077 (-1.8)

Table 4.4e. (cont.)

	1	2	3	4	5	6
Mother education above compulsory level	-	-	-.009 (-0.4)	-.030 (-0.4)	-.011 (-0.1)	-.051 (-0.7)
Number of siblings	-	-	-.005 (-1.5)	-.000 (-0.0)	-.001 (-0.1)	-.002 (-0.2)
Interactions with years of schooling:						
Father social gr. 1	-	-	-	-.010 (-0.9)	-	-.005 (-0.5)
Father social gr. 2	-	-	-	.006 (1.2)	-	.006 (1.2)
Father farmer	-	-	-	.006 (1.1)	-	.006 (1.1)
Father high school or higher	-	-	-	.011 (1.2)	.009 (1.0)	-
Father secondary or voc. school	-	-	-	-.004 (-0.8)	-.003 (-0.7)	-
Mother home during childhood	-	-	-	.008 (2.2)	.008 (2.0)	.008 (2.2)
Mother education above compulsory level	-	-	-	.002 (0.3)	.000 (0.1)	.003 (0.6)
Number of siblings	-	-	-	-.0005 (-0.5)	-.0005 (-0.5)	-.0004 (-0.4)
n	1294	1294	1294	1294	1294	1294
R^2 adj.	.256	.281	.283	.285	.284	.284

Table 4.4f. Wage equations with family background variables, women 1981, with t-ratios in parenthesis

	1	2	3	4	5	6
Constant	7.34 (55.3)	7.53 (47.1)	7.52 (46.4)	7.37 (41.3)	7.40 (42.3)	7.40 (41.7)
Work experience	.016 (5.3)	.017 (5.5)	.017 (5.5)	.017 (6.5)	.017 (5.4)	.017 (5.5)
Work experience squared/1000	-.253 (-3.9)	-.265 (-4.1)	-.265 (-4.1)	-.263 (-4.0)	-.264 (-4.1)	-.265 (-4.1)
Age	.0083 (1.2)	.0069 (1.0)	.0075 (1.1)	.0086 (1.3)	.0081 (1.2)	.0088 (1.3)
Age squared/1000	-.072 (-1.0)	-.063 (-0.8)	-.070 (-0.9)	-.081 (-1.1)	-.075 (-1.0)	.084 (-1.1)
Married	-.026 (-1.6)	-.025 (-1.5)	-.025 (-1.5)	-.025 (-1.5)	-.025 (-1.6)	-.026 (-1.6)
Living in big city	.008 (0.6)	.009 (0.6)	.008 (0.6)	.006 (0.5)	.007 (0.5)	.007 (0.5)
Working daytime	-.052 (-2.9)	-.052 (-2.9)	-.052 (-2.9)	-.052 (-2.9)	-.051 (-2.9)	-.053 (-2.9)
Years of schooling	.042 (18.4)	.012 (0.9)	.011 (0.8)	.029 (1.6)	.029 (1.7)	.022 (1.3)
Years of schooling squared	-	.0013 (2.1)	.0013 (2.1)	.0008 (1.2)	.0007 (1.0)	.0011 (1.6)
Father social gr. 1	-	-	.003 (0.1)	.122 (0.7)	.002 (0.1)	.001 (0.0)
Father social gr. 2	-	-	.028 (1.7)	.102 (1.7)	.030 (1.8)	.100 (1.7)
Father farmer	-	-	.012 (0.7)	.058 (0.9)	.013 (0.7)	.058 (0.9)
Father high school or higher	-	-	-.026 (-0.8)	-.284 (-1.8)	-.244 (-1.6)	-.024 (-0.7)
Father secondary or voc. school	-	-	-.005 (-0.3)	.043 (0.6)	.060 (0.8)	-.003 (-0.2)
Mother home during childhood	-	-	-.016 (-1.2)	.005 (0.1)	.004 (0.1)	.004 (0.1)

Table 4.4f. (cont.)

	1	2	3	4	5	6
Mother education above compulsory level	-	-	.019 (0.9)	.012 (0.1)	.017 (0.2)	-.005 (-0.1)
Number of siblings	-	-	.002 (0.7)	.014 (1.3)	.014 (1.4)	.015 (1.4)
Interactions with years of schooling:						
Father social gr. 1	-	-	-	-.010 (-0.8)	-	-.001 (-0.1)
Father social gr. 2	-	-	-	-.007 (-1.2)	-	-.007 (-1.3)
Father farmer	-	-	-	-.005 (-0.8)	-	-.005 (-0.8)
Father high school or higher	-	-	-	.019 (1.6)	.015 (1.4)	-
Father secondary or voc. school	-	-	-	-.004 (-0.6)	-.006 (-0.9)	-
Mother home during childhood	-	-	-	-.002 (-0.5)	-.002 (-0.5)	-.002 (-0.4)
Mother education above compulsory level	-	-	-	.001 (0.1)	-.000 (-0.0)	.002 (0.3)
Number of siblings	-	-	-	-.0013 (-1.2)	-.0013 (-1.2)	-.0013 (-1.2)
n	1116	1116	1116	1116	1116	1116
R^2 adj.	.240	.243	.242	.241	.242	.240

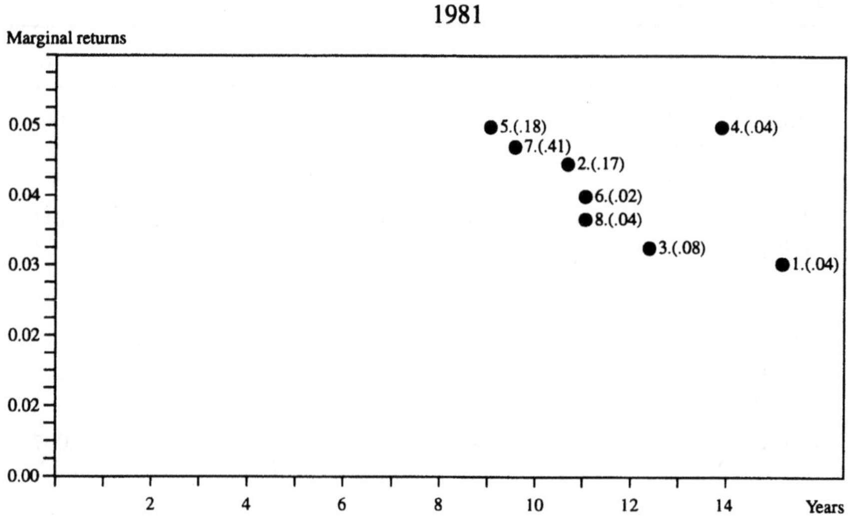

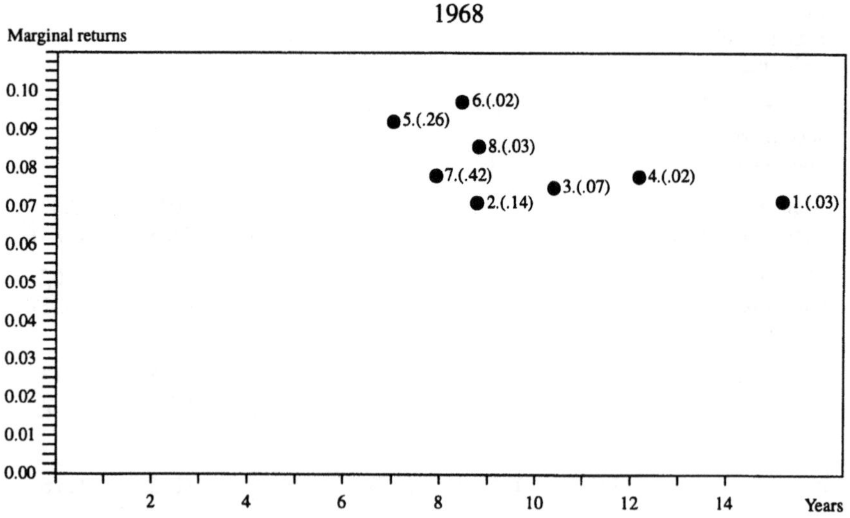

Fig. 4.2. Marginal returns to schooling and the average length of schooling for various social groups. Sample fractions within parenthesis.

Notes: 1 = Father social group 1 and high school or more.
2 = Social group 2 and compulsory school.
3 = Social group 2 and sec. or voc. school.
4 = Social group 2 and high school or more.
5 = Farmer and compulsory school.
6 = Farmer and sec. or voc. school.
7 = Social group 3 and compulsory school.
8 = Social group 3 and sec. or voc. school.

How can this result be interpreted within our analytical framework? One interpretation is that the marginal cost schedule is equal for all and completely flat. The existence of subsidized financial aid for students helps explain this interpretation. Another possibility is that family background affects both the costs and the returns so that the net effect on the marginal return is zero.

The quantity/quality trade-off hypothesis gets some (weak) support from the fact that the interaction variables for the number of siblings predominantly get negative coefficients. For men in 1968 this coefficient is around -.0023 with t-values around 1.7. A negative coefficient suggests that those with few siblings get more skills that are useful at school than other children with many siblings.

By comparing the results in columns 4, 5 and 6 one can see that there is some, but not very severe, multicollinearity between a father's social group and educational level.

4.5 Conclusions

Family background has a very strong impact on the length of schooling in Sweden; in 1981 men with a father from social group 1 had 15.8 years of schooling in contrast to 10.0 years for men with a father from social group 3. This suggests that there is considerable inequality of opportunity in Sweden.

Our analysis has revealed that the returns on schooling are higher for those with a strong family background; at least the educational level of the father seems to raise the returns. This finding helps explain the persistent intergenerational pattern of schooling choice; those with a strong family background invest more in schooling because they get more out of it!

We can not rule out, however, that a favourable family background also affects schooling choice via lower costs to finance schooling. We did find, though, that when we evaluated the *marginal* returns on schooling at the average length of schooling for various social groups they were quite equal (except for those with a farmer background who had a combination of low schooling and high marginal returns). This result is inconsistent with the notion that the intergenerational pattern of schooling choices represents a source of inefficiency.

One final caveat about the analysis is in order. We have treated years of schooling as homogeneous. Of course, it might be that those with strong family background have managed to get schooling of higher quality. We can not tell whether the higher returns are due to better schools or more appropriate investments by the parents. Whatever the reasons, however, our study suggests that those with a strong family background invest more in schooling because they get more out of it!

References

Becker, G. (1991), *A Treatise on the Family*. Cambridge: Harvard University Press.

Chiswick, B. (1988), "Differences in Education and Earnings Across Racial and Ethnic Groups: Tastes, Discrimination and Investments in Child Quality", *Quarterly Journal of Economics*, pp. 571–597.

Eriksson, R. and R. Åberg (eds.) (1987), *Welfare in Transition – Living Conditions in Sweden 1968–1981*. Oxford: Clarendon Press.

Willis, R. (1986), "Wage Determinants: A Survey and Reinterpretation of Human Capital Earnings Functions", in Ashenfelter, O. and R. Layard (eds.), *Handbook of Labor Economics*. Amsterdam: North Holland.

5 Regional and Occupational Wage Differences – Evidence from Workers in Norwegian Manufacturing Industries

Kristin Dale
Institute of Economics, Agder State College, Kristiansand, Norway[1]

5.1 Introduction

Wage differentials are closely related to cost differentials among firms and to differentials in the standard of living among individuals. Affirmative action (laws) against sex discrimination in hourly pay, and the close link between the Norwegian Federation of Trade Unions and the Norwegian Labour Party have impacts on the collective wage bargaining and may work in the interest of low-income groups. During the last two decades the petroleum sector has become a significant factor in the industrial development in Norway. The high wages in the petroleum sector have to some extent been carried over to the rest of the economy (Dyrstad 1987). Other factors, however, have also had an impact. Some industries, such as the printing and publishing industries and car repair, have experienced growing markets. Foundries and shipyards have experienced declining markets from the early 1970's till 1986. What are the resulting impacts of the factors influencing differentials on wage structures over time? In the present study the effects of these changes on the wage structure will be explored.

Since all the firms included in this study are members of the Norwegian Employers' Confederation, we can test the hypothesis that wage agreements within this confederation eliminate wage differences among member firms. The wage agreements between the Norwegian Employers' Confederation and the Norwegian Federation of Trade Unions imply that wage differences between lines of industries may exist because different agreements are signed by different trade unions covering different lines of industries. However, the agreement covers all member firms within a line of industry. Do these agreements eliminate regional wage differentials within an industry? The effects of local wage agreements at the firm level, and the fact that the agreements only regulate wage changes, and not

---

[1] Marjo-Riitta L. Rynnig has given very useful comments to a preliminary version.

wage levels, imply that the national wage agreements do not eliminate regional wage differentials.

Despite national wage agreements regional wage differentials may persist. The magnitudes of regional wage differences are of interest because the existence of lower wage levels in the rural districts increases the opportunities for regional firms to survive in competitive markets. Norway has an ambitious goal for regional policy: maintaining the present regional distribution of the population. This implies a need for governmental intervention through distributional measures or through subsidizing regional firms. The lower the wage levels in the rural districts, the smaller the needs for governmental intervention to keep up the regional income levels to sustain the population pattern.

5.2 Method

The changes in the wage structure over time are measured by comparing similar cross-sectional studies at three points in time (1973, 1982 and 1986). In each cross-sectional study we wanted to estimate the average hourly pay for different groups of workers in Norwegian industry. We used a log linear model and weighted multiple regression analysis.

5.2.1 Model

The model represents individual hourly pay as a function of personal characteristics, characteristics of the job and characteristics of the firm. Using the available group-level data for wage statistics, the number of available characteristics was seriously limited.

Of the many potentially relevant individual characteristics such as sex, education, on-the-job training, seniority, age, occupation, marital status, and dwelling area, we only had information on sex and occupational group. The occupational group partly reflects the person's overall "human capital", and partly characterizes the job. Classification as a skilled worker can be attained through a program of schooling and apprenticeship or through a less formal qualification scheme with more years of work experience. This also applies to jobs as semi-skilled workers. Classification as being a driver characterizes the job, but implicitly the job demands the appropriate kind of driving license.

Ideally one would like to have information on job-related characteristics of the different jobs. Different job-related characteristics could mean higher productivity or less pleasant jobs, thereby creating wage differentials of different magnitudes. As regards job-related characteristics for manual jobs, one would like to know whether the work is production work or maintenance work, whether it is overtime or not, whether the work is paid by piecework or by hour; after all, the former categories of work can be expected to be better paid than the latter. A study by Titlestad (1983) on wage differences among Norwegian industrial workers in three industries indicates that the most crucial missing characteristic may be that of piecework. Piecework is most frequent in certain industries and most frequent among female workers, and accounts for many more working hours than overtime work do for the groups studied.

As regards the characteristics of the firm, the line of industry and location district were available. Firm size could be generated by aggregating hours worked over all groups of workers within the firms. As all the firms in the study were members of the Norwegian Employers' Confederation we can not evaluate to which extent the wage structures differ between member firms and non-member firms. The importance of the wage policies practiced by individual firms and the impact of local wage agreements negotiated at the firm level were not taken explicitly into account as a characteristic of the firm. It is therefore possible that the observations within each firm are interdependent to a varying extent in the empirical analysis. Only a few studies of wage differentials have taken this factor into account.

5.2.2 Log Linear Form

We used the log linear model to facilitate comparisons over time. In a log linear model with series of dummy variables, the estimate of the coefficient can be interpreted as a crude approximation of the percentage deviation from the pay of a reference group. The increase in nominal hourly pay over time made the log linear model very attractive. As an example the hourly wage of the reference group was estimated to be about 19 NOK in 1973, 49 NOK in 1982 and 66 NOK in 1986. The log linear model, where effects are measured as constant percentages, also seems to fit the intuitive underlying structure of individual hourly pay better than the linear model, where coefficients represent constant amounts measured in NOK. However, both models are presented and estimated for the population and different sub-samples of observations in Dale (1988).

5.2.3 Weighted Analysis

Our units of observation are occupational groups within firms. For 1982 this means that the smallest group contained 1 hour worked and the largest group contained 55 000 hours worked. With no weighting, these two and all other observations will get equal weight in the analysis regardless of the number of hours the observation represents.

There are two reasons for weighting. The first is that we want to give each hour worked the same influence on the estimated values independent of how the information is grouped in the data. The second reason for weighting relates to the regression model we use in the calculations. If the hourly wage is a linear function of the independent variables, both weighted and non-weighted estimators are consistent and unbiased. The key to the weighting is the properties of the residual in the wage equation on the group level. Weighting is undertaken to correct for heteroskedasticity. If the variance of the residual, given the independent variables, decreases with the increasing size of the group, big groups ought to get greater weight than small. If the variance is inversely proportional to the size of the group, we get the best estimators if we use weights that are proportional to the size of the group. Examples include individual effects where the variation in the individual effects is independent of the size of the group, and group effects where the variance of the group effect is inversely proportional to the size of the group.

We chose to weight each observation with a weight that was the number of hours worked in the observation multiplied by a constant. This constant was the number of groups in the run divided by the sum of hours in the run. We used weights proportional to the number of hours in the observation because we thought that the residual might contain individual effects to a large extent. The division with the sum of hours in the run made the weights sum up to 1, and gave a correct size of the estimated standard deviation of the coefficients. The final multiplication by the number of groups in the run is a technicality in the SPSS 9 version of DEC 20 which signals to the program that we did not have one observation but rather thousands of them. It is hard to compare this weighting procedure with others, because weighting is still seldom used or discussed. For example, Dyrstad (1987) used the same 1982 data without discussing the need for weighting these group-level data.

5.3 Data

The data sets contained the grouped information on workers provided by member firms for the quarterly wage statistics published by the Norwegian Employers' Confederation. Included in the study were the data on the first quarter of each year: 1973, 1982 and 1986. The data for 1986 was prepared especially for this analysis. We chose the first quarter of the year to avoid periods of wage negotiations and delayed payments. The calculations presented below stem from data on more than 3500 anonymous firms, more than 14 000 worker groups and more than 79 million hours worked in the first quarter of each year. Table 5.1 contains the precise numbers.

5.4 Results

The results are shown in Table 5.1. The main report (Dale 1988) also contains results on analyses of subsets of the data. Some of these will be mentioned in the passing commenting on puzzling findings.

Table 5.1. Relative differences in wage rates among Norwegian workers in 1973, 1982 and 1986 by occupational group, gender, line of industry, firm size and region[1]

Variable	1973 weighted	1982 weighted	1986 weighted	1986 unweighted
Number of firms	3 576	4 179	3 972	3 972
Number of observations	14 283	17 389	16 292	16 292
Number of hours worked	91338040	88291394	79314575	79314575
R^2 adj.	0.71	0.70	0.68	0.54
Constant	2.940	3.884	4.1853	4.2262
Constant measured in NOK	18.92	48.63	65.71	68.46
Male occupational groups:				
Male, skilled (ref.gr.)	0	0	0	0
M. craftsmen, repairers	-0.0289	-0.0273	-0.0244	-0.0253
	(.0052)	(.0048)	(.0056)	(.0079)
M. production workers	-0.0492	-0.0693	-0.0708	-0.1018
	(.0037)	(.0038)	(.0044)	(.0059)
M. semi-skilled workers	-0.0540	-0.0615	-0.0686	-0.0829
	(.0044)	(.0049)	(.0052)	(.0091)
M. unskilled workers	-0.1324	-0.1022	-0.1026	-0.1412
	(.0042)	(.0041)	(.0050)	(.0061)
Male drivers	-0.0869	-0.0358	-0.0249	-0.0797
	(.0060)	(.0055)	(.0067)	(.0061)
Other m.w. above 18 years	-0.1042	-0.0876	-0.0806	-0.1030
	(.0040)	(.0037)	(.0044)	(.0055)
Male shift workers	0.0485	0.0756	0.0723	-0.0041**
	(.0045)	(.0035)	(.0041)	(.0072)
M.w. in oil activities	M	0.3590	0.3790	0.4202
		(.0101)	(.0086)	(.0176)
Working foremen	0.0820	0.0954	0.1062	0.1129
	(.0075)	(.0066)	(.0074)	(.0062)
Males < 18 years & apprentices	-0.4976	-0.4321	-0.4179	-0.4722
	(.0075)	(.0054)	(.0057)	(.0055)
Female occupational groups:				
Female w. above 18 years	-0.2363	-0.1747	-0.1198	-0.1744
	(.0048)	(.0059)	(.0098)	(.0097)
F. skilled workers	-0.1945	-0.0504**	-0.0185**	-0.0159**
	(.0618)	(.0405)	(.0167)	(.0130)
F. production workers	-0.2482	-0.1682	-0.1659	-0.1692
	(.0065)	(.0045)	(.0050)	(.0075)

Table 5.1. (cont.)

F. semi-skilled workers	-0.2554 (.0157)	-0.1877 (.0133)	-0.2107 (.0159)	-0.1766 (.0189)
F. unskilled workers	-0.3155 (.0230)	-0.2478 (.0265)	-0.2090 (.0119)	-0.1998 (.0134)
Other f.w. above 18 years	-0.2964 (.0087)	-0.1822 (.0076)	-0.1722 (.0079)	-0.2000 (.0086)
Female shift workers	-0.1949 (.0160)	-0.0647 (.0086)	-0.0558 (.0098)	-0.0748 (.0127)
Female, working foremen	-0.1334 (.0298)	0.0338** (.0349)	-0.0362** (.0378)	-0.0605 (.0194)
Females < 18 years & apprentices	-0.5715 (.0117)	-0.4741 (.0161)	-0.5166 (.0171)	-0.5219 (.0094)
Line of industry:				
Iron & metal ind. (ref.gr.)	0	0	0	0
Mining and sandpits	-0.0327 (.0089)	0.0001** (.0091)	0.0203** (.0110)	0.0255** (.0216)
Oil extraction	M	0.2177 (.0120)	0.1722 (.0106)	0.1839 (.0234)
Food and stimulants manuf.	-0.1416 (.0056)	-0.0970 (.0048)	-0.0639 (.0053)	-0.1026 (.0075)
Textile and clothing ind.	-0.1705 (.0068)	-0.1308 (.0062)	-0.1452 (.0075)	-0.1720 (.0091)
Wood industries	-0.0998 (.0062)	-0.0649 (.0055)	-0.0661 (.0062)	-0.0933 (.0087)
Paper mills etc.	-0.1644 (.0063)	-0.1123 (.0058)	-0.0857 (.0067)	-0.0785 (.0117)
Printing, publishing etc.	0.0542 (.0069)	0.1251 (.0064)	0.2349 (.0071)	0.1168 (.0089)
Chemical, technical ind.	-0.1287 (.0071)	-0.1143 (.0063)	-0.0943 (.0074)	-0.0964 (.0098)
Other chemical ind.	-0.1713 (.0082)	-0.1317 (.0094)	-0.0714 (.0104)	-0.0899 (.0173)
Manuf. of mineral products	-0.0931 (.0071)	-0.0291 (.0067)	-0.0207 (.0078)	-0.0067** (.0110)
Electrochemical ind.	-0.1107 (.0066)	-0.0433 (.0057)	0.0174 (.0065)	-0.0132** (.0129)
Petrochemical ind.	M	0.1399 (.0134)	0.1929 (.0152)	0.1726 (.0358)
Iron and metal goods ind.	-0.0258 (.0056)	-0.0617 (.0053)	-0.0618 (.0063)	-0.0732 (.0098)
Founding industries	0.0234 (.0081)	-0.0541 (.0089)	-0.0746 (.0112)	-0.0512 (.0180)

Table 5.1. (cont.)

Shipbuilding industry	0.0327	-0.0376	-0.0193	-0.0068**
	(.0052)	(.0048)	(.0059)	(.0133)
Electrotechnical ind.	-0.0077	-0.0455	-0.0195	-0.0352
	(.0072)	(.0062)	(.0070)	(.0127)
Other mechanics shops	-0.0408	-0.0209	-0.0262	-0.0208**
	(.0065)	(.0060)	(.0074)	(.0108)
Car repair shops	-0.0695	-0.0547	-0.0503	-0.0776
	(.0077)	(.0067)	(.0073)	(.0085)
Other manufacturing ind.	-0.0693	-0.0209	-0.0444	-0.0889
	(.0110)	(.0060)	(.0130)	(.0138)
Building and construction	0.0890	0.0818	0.0655	0.0140**
	(.0052)	(.0040)	(.0047)	(.0074)
Road transport	-0.1005	-0.0603	-0.0951	-0.0780
	(.0069)	(.0051)	(.0059)	(.0086)
Other businesses	-0.0753	0.0270	-0.0016**	-0.0446
	(.0085)	(.0076)	(.0086)	(.0120)
Region:				
1 Oslo (ref.gr.)	0	0	0	0
2 Østfold	-0.0528	-0.0763	-0.0772	-0.0637
	(.0039)	(.0039)	(.0047)	(.0067)
3 Asker and Bærum	0.0005**	-0.0127**	0.0207	-0.0236*
	(.0073)	(.0066)	(.0069)	(.0109)
4 Akershus - 3	-0.0462	-0.0561	-0.0474	-0.0531
	(.0058)	(.0056)	(.0065)	(.0082)
5 Hamar	-0.1343	-0.1098	-0.1106	-0.1043
	(.0068)	(.0063)	(.0077)	(.0103)
6 Hedmark - 5	-0.1535	-0.1315	-0.1351	-0.1243
	(.0076)	(.0070)	(.0094)	(.0102)
7 Oppland	-0.1401	-0.1285	-0.1340	-0.1328
	(.0058)	(.0058)	(.0063)	(.0080)
8 Drammen	-0.0434	-0.0333	-0.0373	-0.0430
	(.0051)	(.0053)	(.0064)	(.0087)
9 Buskerud - 8	-0.1049	-0.0667	-0.0921	-0.0760
	(.0084)	(.0062)	(.0063)	(.0091)
10 Vestfold	-0.0661	-0.0689	-0.0718	-0.0777
	(.0045)	(.0044)	(.0054)	(.0074)
11 Ø.Telem. + Setesdal	-0.0922	-0.0999	-0.1131	-0.0771
	(.0100)	(.0093)	(.0110)	(.0143)
12 Porsgrunn + Skien	-0.0781	-0.0714	-0.0482	-0.0604
	(.0056)	(.0052)	(.0061)	(.0097)
13 A.Agder + Kragerø-S.d.	-0.0852	-0.0923	-0.0984	-0.0946
	(.0076)	(.0067)	(.0078)	(.0109)
14 Kristiansand	-0.0824	-0.0578	-0.0790	-0.0792
	(.0060)	(.0056)	(.0071)	(.0100)

Table 5.1. (cont.)

15 Vest-Agder - 14	-0.1181 (.0101)	-0.1011 (.0078)	-0.0948 (.0089)	-0.0895 (.0125)
16 Rogaland syd	-0.1325 (.0078)	-0.0675 (.0070)	-0.0580 (.0080)	-0.0518 (.0124)
17 Stavanger + Sandnes	-0.1011 (.0044)	-0.0145 (.0045)	0.0334 (.0050)	0.0017** (.0074)
18 Haugesund + Sunnhordl.	-0.0824 (.0065)	-0.0626 (.0056)	-0.0202 (.0065)	-0.0410 (.0106)
19 Bergen	-0.1101 (.0040)	-0.1026 (.0038)	-0.1020 (.0046)	-0.0841 (.0065)
20 Hordaland, rest	-0.1099 (.0071)	-0.0976 (.0072)	-0.1041 (.0088)	-0.1004 (.0108)
21 Sogn and Fjordane	-0.1179 (.0094)	-0.1150 (.0071)	-0.1343 (.0089)	-0.1079 (.0108)
22 Møre and Romsdal	-0.1654 (.0058)	-0.1203 (.0048)	-0.0959 (.0056)	-0.0982 (.0070)
23 Trondheim	-0.1094 (.0046)	-0.0775 (.0045)	-0.0885 (.0056)	-0.0764 (.0077)
24 Sør - Trøndelag - 23	-0.1656 (.0105)	-0.1010 (.0086)	-0.1375 (.0106)	-0.1290 (.0117)
25 Nord - Trøndelag	-0.1572 (.0066)	-0.1114 (.0066)	-0.1034 (.0073)	-0.1282 (.0089)
26 Nordland	-0.1085 (.0057)	-0.0951 (.0053)	-0.0798 (.0058)	-0.0842 (.0072)
27 Tromsø	-0.1044 (.0097)	-0.1157 (.0101)	-0.1186 (.0109)	-0.0907 (.0119)
28 Troms + Finnmark - 27	-0.0802 (.0072)	-0.0523 (.0062)	-0.0831 (.0074)	-0.0694 (.0082)
Firm size:				
1 - 19 workers (ref.gr.)	0	0	0	0
20 - 44 workers	0.0506 (.0040)	0.0370 (.0034)	0.0463 (.0040)	0.0450 (.0037)
45 - 89 workers	0.0776 (.0039)	0.0737 (.0033)	0.0700 (.0039)	0.0662 (.0041)
90 - 179 workers	0.0906 (.0039)	0.0776 (.0035)	0.1003 (.0041)	0.1017 (.0053)
180 and more workers	0.1327 (.0038)	0.1275 (.0033)	0.1381 (.0038)	0.1479 (.0058)

[1] Estimated by natural logarithms. The coefficients approximate the percentage difference from the reference group: male, skilled workers, in engineering workshops, with less than 20 workers in Oslo. Estimated standard deviations in brackets.

* not significant on a 1 per cent level. ** not significant on a 5 per cent level. M = missing.

5.4.1 Comparing the Weighted and Unweighted Results

For 1986 both weighted and unweighted results are reported in Table 5.1. The table shows that weighting the observations increases the adjusted degree of explanation, and does not change the magnitude of the calculated estimates of the coefficients. However, we see that the estimates of the coefficients are different, and that the estimates of the standard deviations are systematically smaller in the weighted than in the unweighted results of 1986. For most variables the estimated coefficient is significantly different in the two analyses. This is the case also for 1973 and 1982 (see Dale 1988, Tables 21 and 22). Weighting is shown to influence the reported results significantly.

5.4.2 Occupational Differences

As expected, the results show that occupational groups with higher skill levels earn higher wage rates. The results reported in Table 5.1 show that working foremen were better paid than skilled workers, skilled workers were better paid than semi-skilled workers, and semi-skilled workers were better paid than unskilled. At all three points in time the difference was about 20 per cent between unskilled workers and working foremen. Wage differences among occupational groups are relative stable over time.

The group of workers under 18 years of age and apprentices attained about half the pay of skilled workers in 1973, but improved their relative wage level in the period up to 1986, as did the male drivers. There was a weak tendency towards diminishing relative differences between the "traditional" labour groups, while the differences increased sharply measured in nominal NOK. From these wage numbers it is hard to see any economic gain from choosing the career from apprentice to skilled worker instead of the "on-the-job training career" from unskilled through semi-skilled (and to skilled worker).

International comparison may show that wage differences to skill levels are small in Norway relative to other countries. One reason may be that the educational system is run almost exclusively by the government with no fees for pupils and students. This implies that the private returns on educational investments do not have to cover the costs of the educational system.

Data on male workers engaged in the oil industry were not grouped separately until the mid-1970's, thus accounting for the missing information for 1973. The off-shore workers engaged in the oil industry get the highest pay among Norwegian worker occupations. Taking into account the effect of occupational group compensating for working off-shore and the "line of industry" effect, we see that their hourly wage is about 50 per cent above that of the most skilled workers.

5.4.3 Regional Wage Differences

The division into regions is self-made. The reason why is that I could find no other satisfactory regional division. More than 400 communities was much too detailed.

A little more than 100 labour market regions meant too many (dummy) variables for the regression equation. The administrative division into 19 counties crosses natural labour market regions, but more importantly, a county hides the difference between the center and the periphery. Grouping counties into fewer groups, we get the regional division used by the Norwegian labour market statistics. However, this grouping increases the problem of putting cities and rural periphery into one group.

Norway was divided into 28 regions by aggregating the more than 100 labour market districts. Big city areas are grouped into separate groups. Knowledge of topography, communications and commuting have been taken into account in a less formal way. The approach takes account of the heterogeneity of Norwegian regional labour markets. Reported results of wage differentials between regions will indicate whether this regional division was useful. However, other divisions into regions might prove to be more efficient to bring forward regional wage dispersions.

The results show substantial regional variation in wage rates in 1973, 1982, and 1986. In 1973 the Oslo area had the top wage level. Little by little this top position has been overtaken by the Stavanger area. The low-wage regions are, according to Table 5.1, the middle of the country, except the Trondheim area. The region of the very lowest wage rates has shifted over time from the coast to the inland.

We found that the wage level in areas including big towns like Oslo, Drammen, Kristiansand and Trondheim were well above the regional wage level of the nearby rural areas. However, the wage level in town areas like Hamar, Bergen, and Tromsø did not surpass that of the nearby rural regions.

The region Rogaland and Agder is used in the labour market statistics. In our regionalization this covers all of regions 14, 15, 16, and 17 and parts of regions 11, 13, and 18. In 1986 the highest regional wage rates were estimated for region 17, some 3.3 per cent above Oslo, and the lowest for region 11, about 11.3 per cent less than Oslo. This spread of 15 percentage points within a region clearly indicates the heterogeneity within the region and the usefulnes of our division into more regions.

The northern part of Norway probably had the overall worst labour market situation. This does not show up in our results on the regional wage level in Table 5.1. One reason for this may be that the regional coefficient for Troms and Finnmark in Table 5.1 is heavily influenced by the missing information on piecework. Women in the manufacturing industry producing fish products in this region can earn fairly high wages via piecework. The fact that no correction is made for piecework may bias the regional effect. An indication that this explanation is correct comes from the separate estimations on women, and on the iron and metal industries. Separate estimations on women in 1982 showed that Troms and Finnmark were the top wage regions for women, followed by Oslo. However, separate estimations for the iron and metal industries showed that the regional wage level of Troms and Finnmark was 15 per cent below Oslo in 1973 and 1982, and 11 per cent below Oslo in 1986.

5.4.4 Differences Between Women and Men

Men earned more than women in the same occupation in 1973, 1982 and 1986. In 1973 the wage gap was substantial ranging from 19 to 24 per cent, the group of youngsters excluded. From 1973 to 1982 female occupational groups improved their positions relative to the corresponding male groups. From 1982 to 1986 the overall decrease in wage differences between women and men stopped, but there were some occupational groups with decreasing differences and others with increasing differences. We find a decreased wage gap between women and men among skilled workers, unskilled workers and shift workers, and an increased relative wage gap among semi-skilled workers, other workers, foremen and apprentices.

Because the female workers were grouped in fewer and more aggregated groups in the data set than men, women to a larger extent than men were grouped into "low" and general occupational groups. The lack of a separate group for "female workers in oil activities" is the most obvious example. This resulted in an estimate of 59 per cent for the coefficient of the oil extraction line of industry, when run on 1986 data for women only (Dale 1988). However, it leads to underestimation of wage differences attributable to sex because a few women with high wage rates are grouped in more general occupational groups, which violates the "same occupation" assumption.

This is a general problem with estimation of wage gaps between men and women in labour markets with unbalanced gender distribution. In our data set this problem is more substantial in 1973 than in 1982 or 1986. Therefore the relative improvement for women from 1973 to 1986 has probably been greater than shown by our Table 5.1. However, because the underlying occupational grouping is still less detailed for women than for men, this problem continues to exist in the 1986 data set. This indicates that the wage gap between the sexes is likely to be greater than shown by the 1986 figures.

Estimations on data for female workers only, and for male workers only, have shown that women get substantially less pay in industries like food and stimulants manufacturing, in printing, publishing etc., in the petrochemical industry, in car repair shops, in other industry and in other activities.

The results from the separate estimations on women and men indicate much smaller regional wage differences among women than among men. This contradicts the hypothesis that employers can use monopolistic discrimination more freely against women than against men. An alternative explanation is that men in certain central areas have been the ones to benefit in relative wage terms.

We also found that the regional carry-over effect from the oil sector only affected men. In 1986 the Stavanger area had the highest wage level for men, having passed all other regions including the Oslo area. In 1986 women in the Stavanger area still received 8 per cent less than women in Oslo, and the regional difference was the same as in 1973.

5.4.5 Wage Differences by Firm Size

Our results show that the bigger the firm, the better the pay. The coefficients for wage differences among firm sizes seem to be very stable over time.

Separate estimations for the total iron and metal industry show that wage differences by firm size were smaller in this industry than according to the results presented in Table 5.1.

5.4.6 Wage Differences by Line of Industry

The oil extraction and petrochemical industry, representing a new sector for which there are no 1973 statistics, exhibited the highest wages in 1986 along with printing and publishing. The textile and clothing industries paid the lowest wages.

In 1973 shipyards and foundries had the top wages, followed by building, construction and printing. From 1973 to 1986 no line of industry experienced a sharper decrease in the relative wage level than did foundries and shipbuilding. Declining markets are among the more visible explanations.

5.5 Conclusions

Time passes, but relative wage differences among Norwegian workers persist. That is the main finding of the reported study. This study also indicates that wage rates are better indicators of congestion problems in the labour market than problems of slackness. It shows that new industries may increase wage rates both directly and indirectly, and wage differences based on sex still exist among workers in Norway.

The study points to the necessity of taking proper account of the heterogeneity of regions and the heterogeneity of occupations by skills. The empirical results also show the importance of weighting the observations when grouped data sets are analyzed.

References

Dale, K. (1988), *Lønnsforskjeller i industrien.* Bergen: IØI-Arbeidsrapport nr. 85.

Dyrstad, J.M. (1987), "Resource Boom, Wages and Unemployment: Theory and Evidence from the Norwegian Petroleum Experience", *Scandinavian Journal of Economics,* Vol. 89, pp. 125–143.

Titlestad, K.D. (1983), *Lønnsforskjeller mellom kvinnelige og mannlige arbeidere i tre industrigrener.* Bergen: IØI-Arbeidsrapport nr. 53.

6 Workplace Skill Accumulation and its Impact on Earnings and Labor Mobility: The U.S. Experience

Lisa M. Lynch
MIT, Sloan School of Management, Cambridge MA, United States

6.1 Introduction

This paper shifts the discussion in this conference from issues related to human capital creation provided by formal education, to the determinants and outcomes of human capital accumulation that occurs in the workplace after formal schooling has been completed. In recent years this type of human capital creation has received an increasing amount of attention in the U.S. for three main reasons. First, growing international competition has forced firms around the world to identify ways in which they can increase the productivity of their labor inputs. Since labor productivity growth has been much slower in the U.S. than in other countries policies which might stimulate higher productivity growth in the U.S. are viewed as crucial for economic competitiveness. Second, rapid changes in technology, especially in the area of information technology, have resulted in the massive retraining of workers and substantial changes in the skill requirements of workers. This has been felt in all sectors but particularly in industries such as telecommunications. Finally, changing work organizations associated with the switch to "just-in-time" production from "just-in-case" production has resulted in workers rotating through a wider number of jobs. Consequently, they are being trained on-the-job in a wider set of skills. In addition, as firms decrease the number of layers within the organization and push more decisions down on to the line, workers need to have broader abilities to take on these new responsibilities.

The decision of whether or not to invest in post-school training is more complicated than the investment decision associated with schooling. In firm provided training there are two agents involved in the investment decision - the firm and the individual worker. These two agents may have very different levels of risk aversion, time horizons, information, access to capital markets, and preferences. In the standard human capital model proposed by Becker (1964) and later extended in Mincer (1974), workers have an incentive to invest in general training because this will raise their wages across all firms once the training is completed. This investment may be paid for either directly by the worker or indirectly through lower wages during general training spells. However, borrowing constraints or other constraints such as minimum wages may result in workers underinvesting in their own general training. On the other hand, firms are willing to invest in firm specific training because they can capture the returns to this training. They are not as willing to pay for the costs associated with general training because if they invest in externally recognizable general training they run the risk of their workers being "poached" or hired away by other firms. The end result is that there may be a market failure in the provision of general training. Therefore, if the demand for more generally trained workers is rising due to technological and organizational change, then those economies that have not been able to find a solution to this potential market failure may find themselves in a weaker competitive position.

There is growing consensus in the United States that firms (on average) underinvest in training compared to their international competitors – especially those in Europe and Japan. When one examines post-school training patterns across countries there seem to be four alternative training strategies followed by firms in North America, Europe and Japan (see Lynch (1992c) for a review of the outcomes across countries of these different training strategies). The first strategy, as exemplified by the German dual apprenticeship system, is characterized by coinvestment in training, codetermination of training, and certification of training. These three components of the training system result in both firm specific and general training being provided during an apprenticeship. There is coinvestment in training since employers and the government pay for the direct costs of training but workers receive much lower wages during their apprenticeship. The training program is codetermined by the unions and employers with unions pushing for more general training while employer associations bargain for more firm specific training. Finally, workers have an incentive to accept lower wages during their training because upon completion of their apprenticeship they can take an exam and receive a nationally recognized certificate for their training. This certificate acts as an insurance policy if they need to change employers and signals skills levels to potential employers.

The second strategy, followed by Japanese firms, is almost orthogonal to the German strategy. In Japan there are virtually no apprenticeships. Japanese firms are concerned with employees building up loyalty to the firm rather than to a specific occupation. Consequently, apprenticeship training is not viewed very favorably. In addition, employee turnover is much lower in Japan than in other countries (for the 40 percent of workers in the larger Japanese firms characterized by lifetime employment) since there are high costs associated with leaving an employer for the employee and for employers who are viewed as poaching workers. With lower worker turnover, firms are able to capture even the returns to investments in more general forms of training. The provision of training also differs from the German system in that it does not occur at the beginning of a worker's career but rather is embedded into the production system and occurs after workers join a firm. The ability of this system to sustain itself may be challenged as employee turnover increases in sectors such as financial services. It will be interesting to see what impact this has on the training strategies followed by Japanese firms in this sector.

A third strategy, followed in varying degrees by the Nordic countries, is a greater role of the government in the provision of skills training. In the U.S. government training programs are directed at those workers having the greatest difficulties in the labor market. However, in the Nordic countries, while it is still the case that workers experiencing unemployment are the most likely to receive training, this training is acquired by a broader cross-section of the workforce than in the United States. While this strategy may be useful in solving a market failure in the provision of more general training it can be quite costly if the government is also financing more firm specific training. In addition, in the Nordic countries, as in the U.S., there is a great deal of discussion over the actual returns associated with these government training programs. Therefore, more evaluation of government training programs needs to be done.

The fourth model of training provision is one that I will call the laissez-faire approach to training and this characterizes the provision of training in the United States. In the U.S. there are four possible sources of post-school training - formal and informal company provided training; off-the-job training obtained in "for-profit" proprietary institutions (business/vocational/technical institutes, barber and beauty schools, and correspondence courses); apprenticeships (primarily in construction); and government training programs such as the Job Training Partnership Act, JTPA. As mentioned earlier, the percentage of workers in government training programs is very small and these programs are targeted at those workers with the greatest difficulties in acquiring stable employment. The remainder of post-school training is provided by the private sector. While many have argued that we underinvest in training in the U.S. there are no systematic and representative surveys of training practices of firms in the U.S., and there is relatively little information on individuals' post-school training experiences. Nevertheless, the remainder of this paper will examine the characteristics of post-school training in the U.S. using one of the best sources of individual data on training.

6.2 Characteristics of Post-School Training in the U.S.

There are four types of workers who require training after the completion of formal schooling. These include new entrants into the labor market; workers who are being displaced by new technology and are being retrained for new jobs in their current firm or with another employer; employed workers who need training for career development and promotion within their current firm; and the unemployed. A thorough examination of training provisions for all of these types of workers is beyond the scope of this brief paper, therefore, I will focus my discussion on the skills development of new entrants into the labor market (see Lynch (1992d) for a more detailed discussion of the findings presented in this section). This is the group that typically experiences most of the post-school training and will be the workforce of the future. Hopefully, with this background information on the experience of new entrants it should be easier to contrast the U.S. experience with other countries.

While time series data can provide insight into changes in the patterns of education and labor market activity over time, and cross section studies can correlate patterns of training with personal characteristics at a point in time, longitudinal surveys of individuals allow an even more detailed and dynamic analysis of the patterns and consequences of post-school choices of young workers. One of the best sources of information on post-school training for new entrants into the labor market in the U.S. is the National Longitudinal Survey Youth Cohort (NLSY). This is a survey of a nationally representative sample of 12,686 males and females who were 14 to 21 years of age at the end of 1978. These youths have been interviewed in person every year since 1979 on all aspects of their lives. In particular, this survey contains detailed data on young people's education, jobs, military service, training programs, marital status, health, and attitudes on a wide range of issues.

In addition to asking about schooling, respondents in the NLSY were asked every year about the types of training they had received over the survey year (up to 3 spells), and the dates of training periods by source. Potential sources of training included business college, nurses programs, apprenticeships, vocational and technical institutes, barber and beauty schools, correspondence courses, and company training. Training received in formal regular schooling (including 2-year programs) is included in the schooling variables. The data on types of training received other than governmental training or schooling yield some of the most comprehensive information available in the U.S. on private-sector training. The training data are separated into three categories – company provided on-the-job training (ON-JT), off-the-job training from business courses, barber or beauty schools, nurses programs, technical and vocational institutions, or correspondence courses (OFF-JT), and apprenticeships.

Table 6.1 uses data from the NLSY to show by the age of 25 the patterns of human capital accumulation for youths in the U.S. in the 1980s. Almost 25 percent of males and 15 percent of females still have not completed a high school degree by the age of twentyfive. Approximately 22 percent of all 25 year olds have completed a four year university degree. The percentage of 25 year old males in 1988 who had received formal on-the-job training is 14 percent and the percentage of 25 year old females in 1988 who had received formal OJT is 8 percent. Females are more likely to receive off-the-job training than males. Finally, very few young workers in the United States participate in apprenticeship training. While a relatively high percentage of young workers in the U.S. go on to some form of further education after high school, approximately 60 percent of young workers receive no additional training after they complete their formal schooling. In contrast over 75 percent of German youths enter a formal apprenticeship and over 50 percent of British youths enter an apprenticeship or government training program.

It is possible to examine in even greater detail the patterns of post-school training in the NLSY than is presented in Table 6.1 using detailed information collected in the 1988 interview of the NLSY. The following discussion presents breakdowns on the incidence of post-school training in 1988 for the NLSY respondents who were aged 23-29 at the 1988 survey and in the labor force, by educational status, union status, industry, occupation, firm size, and the duration of training.

Table 6.1. Schooling and training in the United States by the age of 25

	Males	Females
High school graduates	76 %	86 %
4 year college graduates	22 %	22 %
2 year college	15 %	20 %
Formal company training	14 %	8 %
Off-the-job training	30 %	33 %
Apprenticeships	3 %	½ %
No post-school training	58 %	60 %

Incidence of training by schooling. There is a strong positive correlation between schooling and company provided training. Approximately 15 percent of all college graduates in 1988 participated in company provided training programs that year. Only 5 percent of males and 7 percent of females who were a high school graduate or dropout participated in formal on-the-job training. The relationship between schooling and off-the-job training is a bit different, especially for females. Female high school dropouts are much more likely to receive off-the-job training than female college graduates (10 percent vs. 9 percent). However, for males, the more schooling, the more likely an individual is to have participated in some off-the-job training.

Incidence of Training by Union Status. A higher percentage of union workers than nonunion workers are likely to receive on-the-job training, especially for women union members. However, this pattern reverses itself for off-the-job training with nonunion workers more likely to participate in off-the-job training programs than union workers. This differential pattern may be the result of union contracts containing specific policies on worker training while nonunion workers interested in acquiring additional skills must seek training outside the firm.

The Incidence of Training by Industry and Occupation. Almost one third of all young workers employed in finance, insurance and real estate, or in public administration received some form of training during 1988. That training was evenly divided between on-the-job training and off-the-job training. Males in finance, insurance, and real estate were more likely to receive training than females (32 percent vs. 25 percent). Other industries with higher than average training levels included transportation, communication and public utilities, wholesale trade, and business and repair services. In these industries 16–20 percent of the young employees had received either on-the-job or off-the-job training during 1988. The industries with the lowest amount of formal company provided training included retail trade and personal, professional and related services. Finally, apprenticeships were concentrated in the construction industry. Unfortunately, the industries where most young workers are employed are not the industries with the highest levels of training. For example, only 9 percent of young males and 15 percent of young females were employed in either finance, insurance and real estate, or public administration. Those industries with the lowest levels of training (retail trade, personal, professional and related services) accounted for 28 percent of young male employment and 54 percent of young female employment.

There are four main occupations in which over 20 percent of the young employees in 1988 had received some form of training – professional and technical workers, managers, clerical workers, and sales workers. In addition, over one fifth of women employed in crafts occupations had received some training (especially company provided training). Operatives and laborers were less likely to be engaged in any type of post-school training.

The Incidence of Training by Firm Size. When one examines the incidence of training by firm size one observes that the probability of receiving company training is influenced by both the plant size and whether or not there are more than one location in the firm. Small plants with less than fifty employees are quite likely to offer training but only if they have more than one plant. Otherwise there appears to be a linear relationship between training and firm size – the larger the firm the more likely it is that a young person will receive some training. The only other exception to this is large firms of 1000 or more employees with just one location. The probability of receiving training in these establishments is quite low.

The Average Duration and Hours of Each Training Spell. Most training spells, especially those provided by firms, last less than four weeks. The amount of time spent in the training programs seems to fall into two categories. Thirtyeight percent of all training spells for young males last 9 hours or less per week while over 50 percent of all female training spells last less than 9 hours per week. At the same time over 37 percent of male training spells last 40 hours or more per week and 22 percent of female spells last over 40 hours per week. On-the-job training is more likely to be more hours per week than off-the-job training. This suggests a pattern of short intensive employer provided training and less intensive but spread out over a longer period of time off-the-job training.

In summary, most company provided formal on-the-job training in the United States is acquired by college graduates who are employed in finance, insurance and real estate. Those who receive training are also more likely to be managers, professional or technical employees in these industries as well as working for larger firms. Black and Hispanic youth are much less likely to have received company provided training than white males and females. Unionized workers are more likely to have received company provided training while nonunion workers are more likely to have participated in off-the-job training.

One of the key differences in post-school training in the U.S. compared with training received by young workers in Europe is the lack of certificates or formal qualifications at the completion of training except for the minority who do an apprenticeship. As shown in Blanchflower and Lynch (1991) the certification of skills acquired by British youths in their post-school training is a major component in the return to training and raises the return relative to their U.S. counterparts. The certification improves the ability of employers to identify appropriate and qualified workers, and it provides an opportunity for young workers to carry their training from one firm to another.

6.3 The Impact of Training and Education on Wages

The previous section summarized the patterns of post-school training for all young workers. However, when we discuss deficiencies in the relative competitiveness and competence of the U.S. workforce, most attention of policy makers is focused on the majority of workers who are not college graduates. Therefore, this section concentrates primarily on the impact of post high school education and training on wages for non-college graduates.

For the analysis of the impact of education and training on the wages of young workers a subsample of the 12,686 NLSY respondents has been selected (see Lynch (1992a) for a more complete discussion of the results reported in this section). I have excluded the military subsample from the analysis (1280 respondents) and all college graduates. The final sample is composed of individuals who had completed their schooling by the 1980 interview date (where "completed" is defined as not returning to school by the 1983 interview date). The completion of schooling requirement reduces the sample size substantially given the age structure of the NLSY (4000 respondents are still 17 or less in 1980). In addition, these individuals had to have wage observations at both the 1980 and 1983 interview dates. These selection criteria yield a final sample of 3064 individuals that will be used in the empirical work. Using a constructed weekly event history of private-sector training, employment, and schooling for this subsample it is possible to examine the patterns and outcomes of training for non-college graduates.

The training data are separated into three categories – company training (ON-JT), apprenticeships (APPT), and training obtained outside the firm (OFF-JT). OFF-JT includes training obtained from business courses, barber or beauty schools, nurses programs, vocational and technical institutes and correspondence courses. Each of these three types of training is allowed to have different types of returns. Since the data are longitudinal it is possible to distinguish between spells of training in each of these categories received during employment with a previous employer and spells received during current employment. In addition, for training received on the current job, it is possible to identify both completed and uncompleted spells of training. However, the questions only refer to those spells of training that lasted 4 weeks or more (until 1988 when this restriction was finally relaxed). This suggests that the NLSY measure of training is more likely to capture formal training spells than informal on-the-job training.

In Lynch (1992a) the impact of these various types of training on the wages of non-college graduates is examined. Log wages of young workers are regressed on a function of tenure, work experience, schooling, training, and other factors. The additional factors in the wage equation include the local unemployment rate, the number of jobs held since finishing school, whether or not the respondent lives in an urban area, marital status, race, gender, coverage by a collective agreement, and health.

The results presented in Lynch (1992a) show the significant role that training plays in wage determination. Even after controlling for industry and occupation the various training measures have a significant impact on wages. Periods of off-the-job training and apprenticeship training acquired before the current employer raise wages significantly. Weeks of on-the-job training and apprenticeship with the current employer also raise wages. Other variables that significantly raise wages include total work experience, years of school, living in an urban area, male, white, married and coverage by a collective agreement. Being disabled or living in an area with high local unemployment depresses wages significantly. Adding industry and occupation dummies to the estimated wage equation slightly reduces the size of the effect of training on wages but the training variables that were significant without industry and occupation dummies remain significant when they are added. Workers employed in the mining, construction and transportation industries earn more relative to those in manufacturing while those in wholesale and retail trade, business, repair, personal and professional related services earn less. Professional, managerial and craft workers all earn a wage premium relative to laborers and farmers.

In order to have a better sense of how the different training variables affect wages relative to other factors such as tenure and schooling, Table 6.2 presents calculations of hourly wages for different characteristics of the sample. This table shows that training, especially company provided on-the-job training and apprenticeships, raises wages substantially. The impact of one more year of school or one more year of current tenure (keeping experience the same) raises wages to almost the same amount as 6 months of off-the-job training. The return to additional schooling and tenure is even smaller relative to the return to 6 months of on-the-job training from the current employer. The latter raises wages by almost ten percent while off-the-job training obtained before the current job raises wages by almost 5 percent. These findings on the role of training obtained from "for-profit" proprietary institutions are important for the current debate on whether or not Graduate Student Loans and Pell grants should be continued to be granted to students in these institutions. Some cities have expressed concern about the ability of these institutions (see INTERFACE 1989) to provide training to welfare recipients. However, this paper shows that on average for this sample of non-college graduates off-the-job training from proprietary institutions has a sizeable impact on wages.

Table 6.2. Predicted hourly wages by selected characteristics (1983 wages)

Average characteristics	White male	White female
No training	$5.47	$4.71
24 wks during previous job OFF-JT	5.74	4.94
24 wks current employer ON-JT	5.96	5.14
24 wks previous employer apprenticeship	6.17	5.31
24 wks current employer apprenticeship	5.74	4.94
1 additional year of school	5.64	4.85
1 additional year of tenure	5.65	4.88

Source: Using the estimated coefficients from estimated log wage equations in Lynch (1992a).
Note: Average characteristics are: single, high school graduate, 99 weeks of tenure on the job, 193 weeks of work experience, local unemployment rate of 10.01 percent, living in the inner city, healthy, not covered by a collective agreement, and 2 jobs since finishing school.

Some other interesting findings contained in Lynch (1992a) concern the variables that are not significant. For example, spells of on-the-job training acquired before the current job have no impact on current wages. This suggests that ON-JT is not portable from employer to employer for young workers who are not college graduates. This may be because formal ON-JT for these workers is more firm specific than general.

Off-the-job training acquired before current employment has a significant and positive impact on wages, while off-the-job training during current employment is not significant. This may be because young workers who are acquiring training from a proprietary institution are planning to use this training to move to another employer and career track, or the findings may reflect the sharing of costs of this training with the current employer through lower wages.

Before reaching any final conclusions on the basis of the results presented so far, it is necessary to discuss in more detail the possible sources of bias in the training estimates due to self-selection. Employers may only place employees in training programs who have some unobservable characteristic, "trainability", or individuals who are more motivated would be more likely to pursue off-the-job training. In either case the estimated coefficient on the various training measures will be biased upwards (i.e. the treatment selection problem).

A variety of ways to try to address this issue are described in Heckman (1979) and Heckman and Robb (1986). One method used in Lynch (1992) was a "standard" Heckman two-stage procedure that estimates a probit for the probability of receiving on-the-job training and a probit for the probability of receiving off-the-job training and then uses the appropriate inverse Mills ratios from these probits as regressors in the wage equation. None of the previous findings are altered with the inclusion of the inverse Mills ratios (the lambdas) as regressors in the wage equation.

A second approach to deal with sample selection assumes that self-selection varies only across individuals and not over time for the individual. An individual's wage at time t can be expressed as:

$$log\,(w_{it}) = Z_{it}\,d + f_i + e_{it}$$

where Z is a vector of variables affecting wages that vary for each individual over time, and f_i is all the characteristics which are individual specific but time invariant. The characteristics in f_i may be correlated with whether workers undergo training. Fitting equation while omitting f_i will lead to bias in estimates of d. By differencing individuals' wages between 1983 and 1980, all time invariant effects (both observed and unobserved) drop out, and the coefficients may be estimated without bias.

The results from this second approach to sample selection are presented in Lynch (1992a). A summary of these findings suggests that additional weeks of off-the-job training and apprenticeships significantly raise wage growth. Additional weeks of ON-JT, however, are never significant for the entire sample or for any demographic sub-group when the sample is divided by race, gender, or education. This suggests that there may be some problem of selection bias for those who have some ON-JT. It may also be the case that the cell sizes here are too small for a significant effect to be found.

In conclusion, private-sector training plays a significant role in the determination of wages and wage growth of the 75 percent of young workers in the U.S. who do not graduate from college. Specifically, when private-sector training is divided into different types (on-the-job training, off-the-job training, and apprenticeships) some very different patterns emerge. For example, the characteristics that appear to influence the probability of receiving training are primarily race and gender. Women and nonwhites are much less likely to receive training within a firm either through an apprenticeship or other forms of on-the-job training. This differential pattern in the acquisition of training by race and gender may be a partial explanation of the persistent wage gap between males and females and whites and nonwhites. Schooling raises the probability of receiving off-the-job training and apprenticeships but it had a smaller impact on the probability of receiving firm provided on-the-job training.

All types of training raise wages significantly. In particular, for this sample of non-college graduates, off-the-job training from proprietary institutions can be useful for increasing wages. The impact of these training variables also seems to be larger than the impact of tenure on wages. Finally, while on-the-job training with the current employer increases wages with the current employer, this type of training seems to be quite firm specific since on-the-job training from a previous employer is never significant for current wages. At the same time, there seems to be some evidence that if general training is being given to any group of workers on the job it is for those who have not completed high school. The finding that on-the-job training is primarily specific is consistent with recent findings from the Hudson Institute (Fowler 1990) which surveyed 645 firms in the U.S. and found that only 8 percent had any sort of general remedial on-the-job training programs. The fact that U.S. firms are more willing to invest in firm specific training than in general training is understandable given the inability to "capture" the returns on investments in general training. However, whether or not U.S. firms will be able to remain competitive with this strategy in the future, given the characteristics of the new entrants into the workforce and the skill demands of new technology, is questionable.

6.4 The Impact of Training and Education on Labor Mobility

The findings on the relationship between the various types of training and wages have several implications for the impact of training on mobility. One implication is that if company provided training is primarily firm specific then the probability of leaving an employer should decline if a young worker has experienced some on-the-job training. An additional implication is that if workers participate in off-the-job training programs they are more likely to leave the current employer. In this case, off-the-job training allows a young worker to change career paths and find a "better match". This part of the paper examines in detail the factors which influence the probability of new entrants leaving their first job, including the differential effects of company provided training, apprenticeships, and training from "for-profit" proprietary institutions.

For the analysis presented in this part of the paper a different sample is used to analyze mobility patterns than was used to examine the determinants of wages (for a more complete discussion see Lynch (1992b)). This sample uses more recent years of the NLSY. In Lynch (1992b) I have excluded the 1280 respondents in the military subsample from the analysis. However, I have also deleted any respondent who has completed school before the 1979 interview year. The final sample is a pooled sample of young workers who have left school and not returned to school for at least four years ("permanently" out of school). Therefore, this sample is made up of 5 waves of school leavers – those who left in 1979, 1980, 1981, 1982 and 1983. In addition, the respondents had to have obtained a job in the first year after "permanently" exiting school. This sample had many more college graduates in it given the age structure of the NLSY compared to the sample used for the wage study. However, it did not include anyone who completed school before 1979, which substantially reduced the sample size. In addition, there was no attempt to model the decision to leave school over the period (1979–1983). Obviously this was a period in which many young people may have delayed entry into the labor market given the high unemployment rate at that time. A dummy variable for year of entry into the labor market was included in the empirical analysis to capture part of this effect, but future theoretical and empirical work would benefit from a complete modeling of the schooling/employment/training decisions taken by young workers.

Table 6.3 presents results from Lynch (1992b) on the relationship between tenure on the job with the first employer, and the various types of training. The first panel shows that over 80 percent of the sample have left their first employer by the fourth year in the labor market. Those who left their employer relatively early were much less likely to have had any formal on-the-job training (only 1.3 percent) than those who stayed with their first employer 3 years or more (8.1 percent). The pattern is a bit different with participation in off-the-job training programs. Almost a quarter of those who left their first job between 2–3 years received off-the-job training. However, this percentage drops dramatically for those with 3 or more years on the job to only 11.7 percent.

Table 6.3. Characteristics of private-sector training and mobility of workers in the 4 years following school completion

Completed tenure by % with training by type				
Completed tenure	% of sample	ON-JT	OFF-JT	APT
1 - 26 weeks	33 %	1.3 %	10.6 %	0.7 %
27 - 52 weeks	20 %	1.5 %	11.8 %	0.9 %
1 - 2 years	19 %	2.6 %	15.6 %	2.4 %
2 - 3 years	7 %	6.6 %	23.6 %	0.5 %
3 - 4 years	21 %	8.1 %	11.7 %	0.8 %
Conditional on having training in 1st job – when did it begin?				
Year		ON-JT	OFF-JT	APT
During 1st year		39.8 %	57.2 %	69.4 %
1st - 2nd year		25.6 %	14.9 %	8.3 %
2nd - 3rd year		18.8 %	18.1 %	8.3 %
3rd - 4th year		15.8 %	9.7 %	13.9 %

Source: Lynch (1992b)

The second panel is perhaps even more interesting. This panel shows, conditional on having participated in one of the types of private training, when that training spell begins during the tenure with the employer. One view of training is that it is a "test" (Weiss and Wang 1990) of workers and does not really represent a productivity enhancing skills investment. Instead training allows the firm to obtain additional information on the suitability or match of recently hired workers for the firm. In other words, firms use formal training programs as a way to avail themselves of private information known only by the workers. Workers who fail the test leave the firms, and those who pass do not leave. This would imply that we should observe on-the-job training occurring early in a worker's tenure with the firm. However, in this second panel we see that 60 percent of on-the-job training spells begin after one year on the job at the firm. This seems to be more consistent with a job matching story where firms (workers) make a determination within the first 6–12 months on whether or not there is a match, and if yes, the firm then invests in more costly formal O-J-T. Since the measure of training used in this paper only captures spells that last 4 weeks it may be possible that shorter formal or informal training spells are used early in the career with an employer as an indication of match quality and longer training spells follow later.

Contrary to the timing of on-the-job training spells, almost 60 percent of spells of off-the-job training begin within the first year with an employer. This may be due to employees going outside the firm to obtain training that they need for their current job, or employees deciding that there is not a job match and seeking a training program that will allow them to leave their current employer and get a better job. Finally and not surprisingly, most apprenticeships begin very early in the tenure with an employer.

Lynch (1992b) presents estimates from a Cox proportional hazard with time varying and time invariant covariates. The time invariant intrinsic characteristics of the individuals/jobs in Lynch (1992b) that seemed to influence the probability of leaving an employer included being disabled, union status, race, and school level. Disabled respondents were more likely to leave their employer while being employed in a job covered by a collective agreement or being a college graduate significantly lowered the probability of leaving the first employer. Blacks were more likely to have shorter durations on their first job than whites and hispanics. There was no significant effect on the length of time with the first employer by gender. However, there were significant differences in expected length of employment by school attainment. Those with a high school degree or less were more likely to leave their employer, whereas those with a college degree were less likely to leave.

Of the time varying "exogenous" covariates the local unemployment rate was significant implying that those who lived in high unemployment areas were less likely to leave their employer. The hurdle for youths in high unemployment areas seems to be getting a job rather than keeping one. The number of children seemed to have no significant effect on the expected duration of the first job. Finally, those workers who were married were more likely to remain with their first employer.

With regards to the training variables, those young people who had some formal ON-JT were much less likely to leave their employer while those who participated in some form of OFF-JT were more likely to leave. This seems to suggest that

ON-JT is more firm specific while OFF-JT is more "general". These findings are consistent with the results on training and wages.

This section of the paper has summarized the findings in Lynch (1992b) on the link between training and the probability of leaving an employer. A high percentage of ON-JT spells begin after young workers have remained with their employer for at least one year. This seems to be consistent with a job matching story where firms (workers) make a determination within the first 6–12 months on whether or not there is a match, and if yes, the firm then invests in more costly formal ON-JT. In contrast to the pattern associated with ON-JT spells, almost 60 percent of spells of OFF-JT begin within the first year with an employer. This may be due to employees going outside the firm to obtain training that they need for their current job, or employees deciding that there is not a job match and seeking a training program that will allow them to leave their current employer and get a better job.

Evidence presented in the previous sections of this paper indicated that on-the-job training for young workers in the U.S. appeared to be quite firm specific whereas off-the-job training appeared more general. The results presented in Lynch (1992b) and summarized here seem to reinforce those conclusions. Those with on-the-job training are more likely to remain longer with their employer which would be consistent with firm specific training. Those who obtain off-the-job training are more likely to leave their employer and this would be consistent with off-the-job training being more general. However, when the sample is divided by race, gender and educational attainment it is shown in Lynch (1992b) that the training variables are only significant for females.

6.5 Summary and Conclusions

By the age of 25 only 22 percent of U.S. youths have completed a college degree and almost 60 percent have not received any form of post-school training even including very short training spells of less than four weeks. If they have received some form of post-school training, it is most likely to have been provided by a "for-profit" proprietary institution. Unfortunately, only 14 percent of employed males and 8 percent of employed females had received any formal company training by the age of 25.

Most company provided formal on-the-job training in the United States is acquired by college graduates who are employed in finance, insurance and real estate. Those who receive training are also more likely to be managers, professional or technical employees in these industries as well as working for larger firms. Black and Hispanic youth are much less likely to have received company provided training than white males and females. One of the key differences in post-school training in the U.S. compared with training received by young workers in Europe is the lack of certificates or formal qualifications at the completion of training except for the minority who do an apprenticeship. As shown in Blanchflower and Lynch (1991) the certification of skills acquired by British youths in apprenticeships, company provided training and off-the-job training is a major component in the return to training. The certification improves the ability of employers to identify appropriate and qualified workers, and it provides an opportunity for young workers to carry their training from one firm to another.

All types of post-school training raise wages significantly. In particular, for non-college graduates, off-the-job training from proprietary institutions can be useful for increasing wages. The impact of these training variables also seems to be larger than the impact of tenure on wages. Finally, while on-the-job training with the current employer increases wages with the current employer, this type of training seems to be quite firm specific since on-the-job training from a previous employer is never significant for current wages.

There are strong links between training and employment transitions of young workers. Those workers who are employed and receive company provided training are likely to remain longer with their employer. This suggests that most company provided training is firm specific training. Those who obtain off-the-job training are more likely to leave their employer and this would be consistent with off-the-job training being more general. It is interesting to note, however, that the effect of training on the employment and nonemployment transitions of young workers is only significant for females.

In general, the primary source of skill accumulation in the U.S. after individuals have completed formal schooling is concentrated among large firms and in narrow sectors and occupations. Those individuals who complete a university degree continue to acquire additional human capital in the workplace. However, those workers who have received the least amount of schooling, or are employed in smaller firms are also the least likely to receive additional skills training in the workplace. Yet it is these workers who are now expected to be involved in more tasks and take on additional responsibilities in the workplace. Policy makers interested in stimulating private-sector competitiveness should consider policies directed at improving the skills of these workers.

References

Becker, G. (1964), *Human Capital.* Chicago: University of Chicago Press.

Blanchflower, D. and L.M. Lynch (1991), "Training at Work: A Comparison of U.S. and British Youths", in Lynch, L.M. (ed.), *Private-Sector Training: International Comparisons.* Chicago: University of Chicago Press. (forthcoming)

Cameron, S. and J. Heckman (1991), *The Non-Equivalence of High School Equivalents.* University of Chicago. Mimeo.

Fowler, E. (1990), "Shortage of Skilled Workers Is Expected", *New York Times,* 31 July.

Heckman, J. (1979), "Sample Selection Bias as a Specification Error", *Econometrica,* Vol. 47, pp. 153–161.

Heckman, J. and R. Robb (1986), "Alternative Identifying Assumptions in Econometric Models of Selection Bias", in Slottje, D. (ed.), *Advances in Econometrics,* Vol. 5. Greenwich, CT: JAI Press.

Lynch, L.M. (1992a), "Private-Sector Training and the Earnings of Young Workers", *American Economic Review,* Vol. 82, pp. 299–312.

Lynch, L.M. (1992b), *Differential Effects of Post-School Training on Early Career Mobility.* NBER Working Paper No. 4034.

Lynch, L.M. (ed.) (1992c), *Private-Sector Training: International Comparisons.* Chicago: University of Chicago Press. (forthcoming)

Lynch, L.M. (1992d), *Young People's Pathways into Work: Utilization of Postsecondary Education and Training.* Report submitted to the National Academy of Sciences.

Mincer, J. (1974), *Schooling, Experience and Earnings.* New York: Columbia University Press.

Weiss, A. and R. Wang (1990), *A Sorting Model of Labor Contracts: Implications for Layoffs and Wage-Tenure Profiles.* Boston University. Mimeo.

7 Trends in Lifelong Learning in Europe

Leenamaija Otala
Pro Competence Inc., Helsinki, Finland, and Frankfurt, Germany

7.1 Competence as an Element of Competitiveness

The competitiveness of European industry is the key factor to Europe's future wealth. Industry is the only sector in society generating something that can be transformed into goods and services, into the wealth that society needs. There is a strong link between education and training systems and a country's level of industrial productivity and competitiveness. The Industrial Research and Development Advisory Committee of the European Commission (IRDAC) has stated: "The output of education and training systems in terms of both quantity and quality of skills at all levels, is the prime determinant of a country's level of industrial productivity and hence, competitiveness." The competitiveness of an industry depends more and more on the competence of its workforce (IRDAC 1991). Economists have also calculated that about 40 percent of competitive improvements for business come from the inputs businesses buy, including machines, buildings, and an educated workforce. The other 60 percent come from the way they use the resources they buy. In other words, a nation's businesses can buy 40 percent of their competitiveness, but the other 60 percent have to be generated from learning (Carnevale 1992).

Industry has realised that the educational level of the current workforce is not good enough. The competitiveness of Europe is at stake, and industry is slipping behind. The number of new jobs is growing much more slowly in Europe than in certain other competing nations (IRDAC 1991). The redistribution of the size and age groups in the population highlights the importance of maximising the use of human resources. Rapid advancements in knowledge require a recycling of human competence. There is now an increasing imbalance between the number of unemployed people and the labour shortages in key growing sectors of the economy. During 1987–1988, the European Round Table of Industrialists (ERT) surveyed the status of European education from the point of view of industry. The results of the survey were included in the ERT report Education and European Competence (ERT 1989). According to the report, the most serious educational problem facing Europe is how to update and upgrade the skills and competence of its working-age population in the rapidly advancing techno-economic environment.

7.2 Changing Business Environment – New Requirements on Lifelong Learning

There are many simultaneous changes in the working life and business environment that force us to re-think development of competence, e.g. employee training, adult education, Lifelong Learning. European integration with the Single Market is a major change for all European companies, industries, governments, and employees. Productivity, the yardstick of the economy for the past 300 years, is still a necessary condition for competitive success, but it is no longer enough to capture and keep market share. The game of economic competition has new rules, requiring great speed and flexibility on the part of business organisations. The new rules are changing the way work is done. They are changing the demands and ways of learning.

The new competitive standards are quality, variety, customisation, convenience, and timeliness (Carnevale 1991, Dertouzos et al. 1989, Evans et al. 1989). Success in the new economy depends on the ability to meet the new competitive standards – to run faster in the productivity race while simultaneously delivering to consumers quality, variety, customisation, convenience, and timeliness. Each of these new success factors depends on human competence. The competitive standards are continuously changing and making new requirements on organisations and employees. Those organisations whose employees learn fastest how to meet the new competitive standards will have the greatest competitive advantage (Senga 1992). Countries whose residents have the best possibilities to learn and develop their competence are going to be the nations of wealth.

The roles of people at work are changing. Capital-to-labour ratios are rising while direct labour participation in work is declining. People's responsibilities and skill requirements are becoming less job-specific, job assignments are becoming more flexible and overlapping, and employees are spending more time interacting with each other and with customers. The need to customise products and services also requires closely integrated work groups that can form and re-form in a fluid way. Members of such teams often have overlapping work assignments and skills because they share responsibilities. They also rely on shared information. Success becomes a collective activity of groups of people. Competitiveness depends on the collective competence of the work teams (Carnevale 1991).

7.2.1 Fast Developing Technology – Need for Continuous Competence Development

Technology has caused the major changes in industry and working life. The erosion of knowledge in many areas can be as high as 15–20 percent p.a. and 7 percent is about the lowest figure (1/2 life of 10 years). Product and production life cycles are shortening. Technology is not only related to technology-intensive products; instead, all products benefit from technology through process automation. People who develop and provide such technologies and products are obliged to upgrade their competence on par with product development. It is estimated that two thirds of Europe's technology in use by the year 2000 has not yet been invented; 3 out of 4 people working now will nevertheless still be active then. At a time when technologies are developing so rapidly, continuous updating and upgrading of working skills and competencies is crucial to our competitiveness (Telford 1992, EC SEC(92)1300 1992, Coates et al. 1991). Technical development also increases the knowledge base of all jobs. Many companies say that they have *no more jobs for unskilled employees.*

There is growing demand for higher technical skills (EC 1991). The information technology and telecommunications sectors, with an estimated future growth likely to be higher than that of GNP, are poised to be the most important manufacturing sectors by the beginning of the 21st century. These industries will also be the most pervasive, with 2 out of every 3 jobs using their products and services. Mastering these technologies will be an essential part of training for the future society. Japan has proved over the last 40 years that there is a direct correlation between the numbers of highly trained engineers and industrial productivity and competitiveness. The number of engineers in Japan is nearly twice the European or US levels in relative terms (Telford 1992 and Figure 7.1).

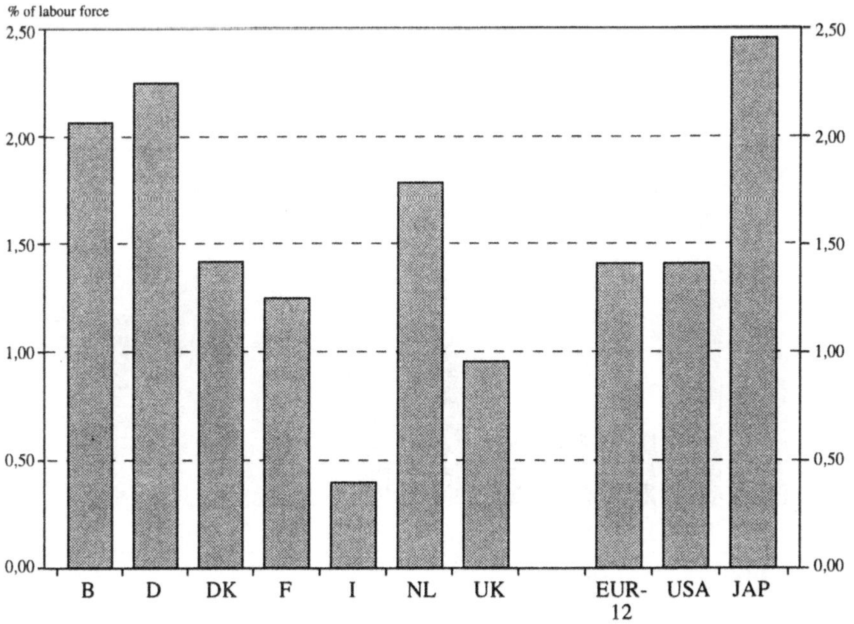

Fig. 7.1. Engineers as part of the labour force. Source: Telford (1992)

There is strong belief that the more young people pursue careers in science and engineering, the better the odds that society will develop technologies and products that fuel economic growth. One study, by Andrei Shleifer, Kevin M. Murphy and Robert W. Vishny, even estimates that if an extra 10 percent of university students went into engineering – a doubling of the current engineering enrollment – the growth rate of the economy would rise by 0.5 percent a year. By contrast, if law school enrollment doubled, the growth rate would fall by 0.3 percent annually (Business Week, April 6, 1992).

However, this potential engineering job market does not attract young people. The enrollment into technical studies has been decreasing in all industrialised countries. Even in Japan, which still has (in relation to population) almost double the number of enrollments in technical studies compared to the figures in Europe and the US, the government has launched a special programme to encourage young people to pursue studies in technology. If the UK represents the European figure and it is taken as 100 for Bachelor's Degrees in Engineering, then the US is 150 and Japan 250. For Engineering Master's Degrees and Doctorates the corresponding figures are UK 100, US 175 and Japan 310 (Telford 1992). When the trend of decreasing enrollment of technical studies is combined with the trend of a declining number of young people (age group 20–30 will reduce at 1.7 percent

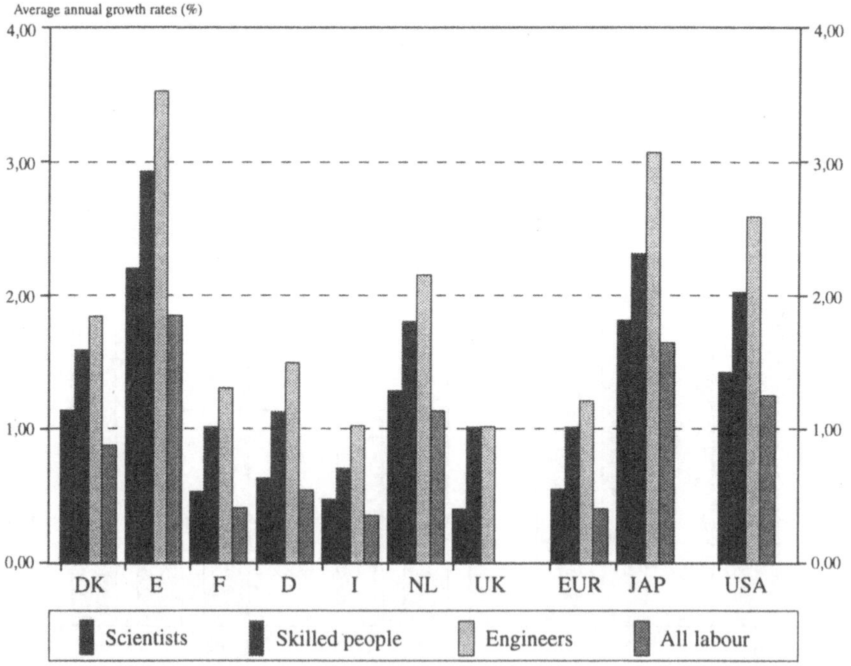

Fig. 7.2. Forecasted demand for educational categories in the 90's. Source: IRDAC (1991)

per annum in Europe, 1.3 percent in the US, however, still positive in Japan in the next decade), we have a shrinking engineering population.

Rapidly changing and newly emerging applications create new levels of technology. For example, the mobile telephones which have been based on analogue technology are becoming digital. This is a totally different technology from the previous one. If the same people who have been developing and producing mobile telephones want to continue their work, a totally new technology base or a new engineer's education is needed. Similarly, a plant manager who for the first time receives robots into his factory can no longer master the production process without upgrading his knowledge to the new level of technology.

To date job-related training has been available to help one do the current job better. Such training is organised by industry and is aimed at improving job skills and ultimately productivity. This kind of *training* provides the individual with *operational capabilities*. For many professions and jobs, this is no longer enough. In order to learn new tasks and new skills in tomorrow's workplace, individuals need continuous *education* to provide them with *strategic capabilities*, which can be gained through theoretical study, education, and the provision of tools to understand and learn new things. Education *for the future* requires a long-term commitment and a longer term goal than training.

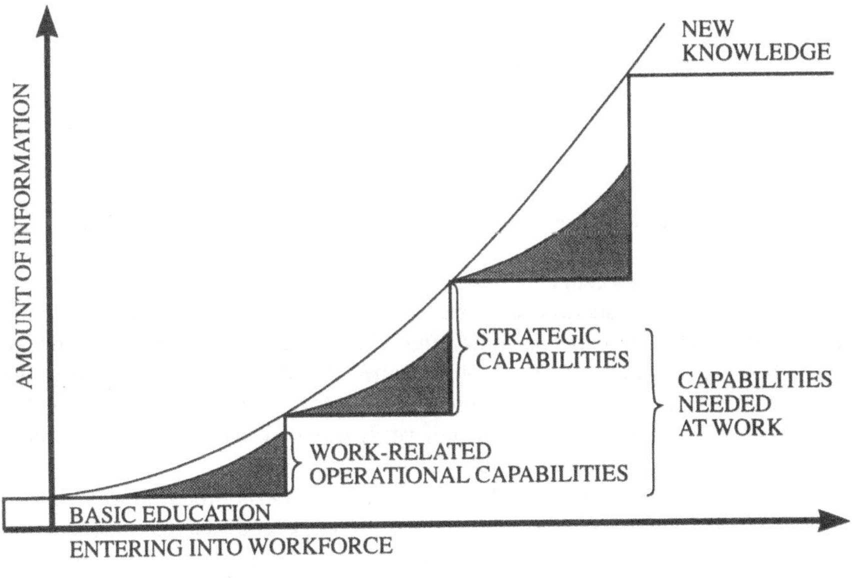

Fig. 7.3. Strategic and operational capabilities

7.2.2 Internationalisation of Business: New Demands on Human Resource Development

Companies and individuals find themselves in a new situation. An integrated Europe with open markets means new competition with new competitors. Simultaneously, the employment market is internationalising and, through mergers and acquisitions, many managers have to cope with an organisation encompassing various cultures and nationalities. This requires clear communication, which transforms the message over the cultural barriers. It requires language skills. Although English is today's "lingua franca", in many cases it is not enough. Effectiveness calls for business thinking, better management styles and reorganising of work. This is not only a challenge for the developing of management skills but also for human resource development policies and practices.

Many companies focus their training on management development. The main target is harmonising of management priorities and communicating the management cultures as well as providing executives with business and management skills. However, much of this business education is general without company-specific information. Business education as provided by business schools has been criticised for being too time-consuming and too general. Several British companies, Pilkington and Shell for example, have solved this by providing employees company-tailored MBA programmes jointly with business schools or universities. The studies are pursued alongside of work, mainly after working hours. The company pays for the courses but the individual gets the degree. Many of the course participants benefit from the company case studies, company lecturers and other company-specifics. Business schools control the total study and the level of courses and administrate the programme.

7.2.3 Ageing Population – Need for Training Programmes for All Ages

The need for new knowledge in industry formerly was supplied by recruiting new people with a fresh education. The demographic downturn has led to a prediction that by the year 2000 the net entry into the labour market in the European Community area will be negative, with some 300,000 more people leaving the labour force than entering it. The European workforce is becoming older. By the year 2000 it is going to be five to ten years older in many of the competing countries (IRDAC 1991 and Figure 7.4).

More than 80 percent of the workforce of the year 2000 is already at work. There will be an increasing number of changes in work and occupations, but the competence of this 80 percent should still be active in 2000. Europe's competitiveness depends on how effectively the skills and competencies of the existing workforce can be updated and upgraded, for example through adult education. Immigration from eastern Europe will not solve the problem of a shrinking workforce. In most cases, the educational level and working skills of the people moving to the western parts of Europe do not meet competence requirements. Instead, this increases the need for effective adult education at all levels.

Lifelong Learning of older employees involves the problem of motivation and requires a change of attitude. Only a few organisations are paying attention to the development needs of their older employees and responding to this new demand. Even management training in most companies is focused on young managers ("high flyers") and managers who have 10–15 years' experience. Nestlé is one of the first European companies to start a special in-house training programme for senior managers of around 50 years of age.

None of the European countries offer special subsidies or tax benefits for companies training older employees as is the case in Japan. The Japanese corporations get special government subsidies for training programmes targeted at older employees. Some Japanese companies, Fujitsu for example, organise a relatively lengthy retraining programme for all 45-year-old white-collar employees. The Fujitsu programme is of six to ten week's duration on three levels. The intensive programme is seven weeks for managers and four weeks for

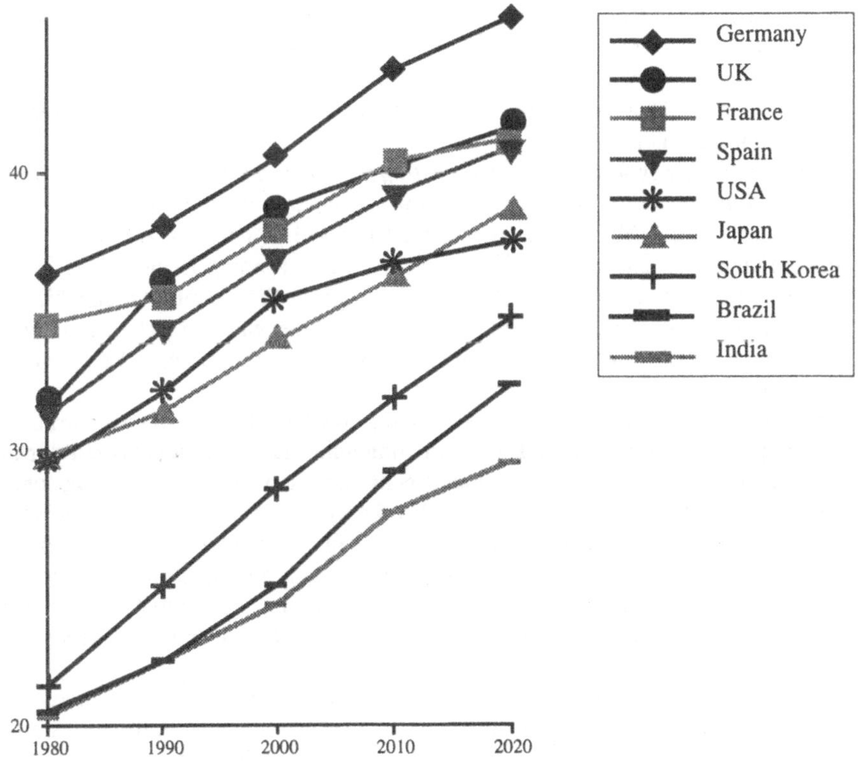

Fig. 7.4. The median age in various countries. Source: IRDAC (1991)

specialists. Half the programme is focused on technology update and management issues, the rest on culture and history. The cultural part includes writing poetry and listening to music. The total break is aimed at allowing employees to refresh their thinking. During training, they are totally released from duties and spend the time at the Fujitsu Institute of Management.

7.2.4 Decentralisation and Increasing Cost-Effectiveness – Training Becomes Better Focused but Only on Short-Term Issues

The changing environment requires companies to rethink their policies and practices. In order to flexibly meet the needs presented by continuous changes, companies are *decentralising* and *focus on short-term issues.* Large units are being pared and divided into small and relatively independent companies (Demmer et al. 1990). The organisation of big corporations has changed from functional organisations into strategic business units, which act "locally" in their own market area.

Previously centralised functions like human resource development have been downsized and the responsibility of personnel training is decentralised to operational units. Competencies needed by divisions are more operational than strategic as in the case of a corporation. Divisions and units invest in job-specific training but they are rarely motivated to invest in the development of strategic capabilities or education, the results of which can not be seen during the current or next accounting period.

Demands for cost-awareness and cost-effectiveness in training and education are also increasing. In reaction to this, *company training is focusing on short-term needs.* Training must be well-focused if benefits are to be seen immediately. Decentralisation improves the focus: training is integrated into a product, a process or a project. Its goal is to improve the operational capabilities of employees. During a recession, companies find it even more difficult to invest in strategic capabilities of employees, because the results can only be seen on a long-term basis.

Centralised training organisations are being downsized. Many of the centralised training departments of large European companies have totally vanished during the past couple of years. Training departments are often criticised for being costly and bureaucratic. Training is preferred to be closer to the business. However, there is a danger of losing the cumulative company know-how of human resource development, when the responsibility of training is too operational. Also the development of personnel training practices is no one's responsibility. Due to these continuous changes in business, competence development needs are changing, too.

Some of the large US companies, AT&T as an example, are already re-centralising their human resource development. The centralised training departments are responsible for the development and policy of training as well as providing the core curricula, which focuses on issues of the long-term corporate strategy.

7.2.5 New Values for Young Employees – New Demands on Employers

The short-term focus is strengthened by mergers and acquisitions, downsizing and even closings of businesses, which can suddenly change the corporate strategy and the role of an employee. An implication of the short-term focus in business is the reducing of the concept of lifetime involvement between employer and employee. A career in a single company is becoming more rare.

Employees under 30 have *new values* at work: they are aware of their own worth. They see their abilities as their capital, which they only "lend" to an employer. This is the "Inter-rail generation". With their education, technical skills and foreign language abilities, they think regionally rather than nationally and are not afraid to be mobile with their jobs and their families. They are ready to invest in themselves to stay in tune with the times. However, if they invest their time in education and training, they want a recognision of their new qualifications which they can pack into their curriculum vitae and take to their next job. A career in a company is changing into a career in a competency or a specific skill. Young people are looking for new challenges to develop a competency which they can sell to various employers or use in an entrepreneurial fashion in the free market.

The mobility of employees has made *degrees important* even in countries which have traditionally been non-degree-oriented, like the UK. In Germany, where degrees have always played an important role, higher degrees are becoming more and more important. For example, in 1990 seven out of ten new board members of the 20 biggest German companies held a Ph.D (Grätz 1991).

7.2.6 SMEs are Important – Competence Development is Still a Problem

Small and medium size enterprises (SMEs) play an important role in all European economies and in the creation of new jobs. Currently there are 7.5 million SMEs only in Italy. Over 94 percent of the Portugese companies are SMEs. Less than 1.8 percent of all industrial companies in Europe have more than 500 employees and about 90 percent of all companies have less than 100 employees (van der Brande 1992, Eurostat 1992 and Figure 7.5).

The number of SMEs can be expected to grow due to the rationalisation of large enterprises; many of the supporting functions will be purchased outside the company from a specialised SME. Much of the industrial competitiveness depends on the competence of SMEs. The development of competence in these companies is, however, a problem. Lifelong Learning in industry has mainly been developed by large enterprises. SMEs have a weak tradition in professional training and are faced with structural difficulties and a lack of skilled personnel. They need external help in determining employees' training needs. There is also a need for a mechanism delineating how SMEs can make their wishes and requirements known to the public authorities. Employees in SMEs need external opportunities and financial support to develop themselves.

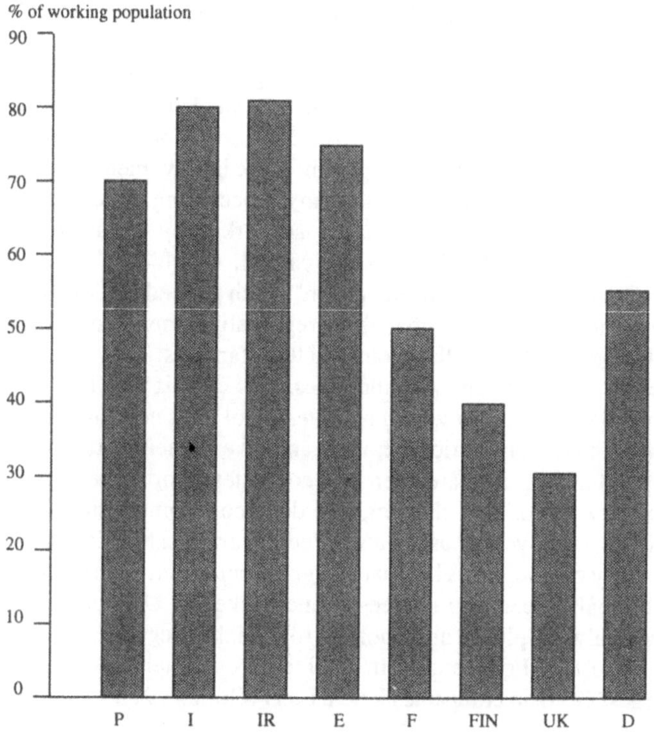

Fig. 7.5. SME employment. Source: van der Brande (1992)

The professional development of employees in SMEs has been one of the objectives of The European Commission programmes. One such programme known as COMETT (the programme for Community co-operation between universities and industry regarding initial and continuing training in the field of, in particular, advanced technology) has led to the establishment of a European-wide network of University-Enterprise Training Partnerships (UETPs) operating in both regional and sectoral bases. Many individual UETPs and COMETT activities have tried to meet the needs of SMEs. However, SMEs are not necessarily perceived as important partners or beneficiaries of COMETT by UETPs or university partners. There is also other criticism of COMETT for not being specific enough regarding the needs of SMEs. The competence needs of SMEs are often short-term and operational; they are difficult to be filled by an intermediary (EC SEC(92) 1300 1992). A good example of a private collaborative training programme of SMEs is the Mediatek-consortium of several companies, universities and polytechnics, and professional organisations in the region of Belgium, North of France and the Netherlands. It offers continuing education in advanced technology and technology management to industrial engineers and managers especially in SMEs, using distance education added to local elements and local tutorial support. Mediatek acts as an interface between the providers of education (universities) and SMEs.

The trends of building networking companies and closely integrating suppliers to large companies would require that the competence in SMEs develops on par with that in large companies. A survey carried out by the Harvard Business Review among 12,000 world business managers shows that about half the companies represented never offer their suppliers seminars or training programmes. Customer training is more common. According to the same survey, three out of four companies report offering seminars or training programmes for customers (Moss-Kanter 1991). The same answer is given by the large European companies. There is only little if any training collaboration with SMEs or with suppliers.

In order to encourage large companies to let small and medium size enterprises participate in their training programmes, the Spanish government started at the beginning of 1992 to subsidise up to 70 percent of the training budgets of large companies, given that the Ministry of Industry has approved the training plans with respect to content, practices, methods, investment etc., and *if the company allows SMEs to participate.*

7.2.7 Conclusions of Trends in Business Impacting Needs of Lifelong Learning

The *volatile business atmosphere*, partly created by a higher incidence of mergers and acquisitions, is changing the concept of loyalty for both the company and the employee. Flexibility is replacing loyalty. In this context, the interest of the company to provide training decreases, while the self-interest of the employee to keep up with the demands of the job increases. This means *shifting the responsibility for competence development towards the employee.*

The competitiveness of European industry now depends on simultaneously meeting two contradictory demands:

- a *short-term focus* to enable companies to adapt quickly to the changes in the immediate business environment
- a *long-term view* to develop the strategic capabilities to compete in the future.

7.3 New Approaches to Lifelong Learning are Needed

Companies have until now taken the main responsibility of adult education by providing work-related training, but they *can no longer bear the responsibility alone.* Companies are also recognising that their current training focusing on operational capabilities is not sufficient to maintain their core competence and increase competitiveness. They are seeking new approaches. The increasing need for updating and upgrading strategic capabilities has put more pressure on public education and on educational institutions. During recent history when vocational skills laid the groundwork for a nation's industrial success, industry and vocational schools developed a close co-operation in many countries. Now, most jobs have become more knowledge-intensive and require a continuously higher education. *The workplace has a growing need for competence development that can only be filled by institutions of higher education.* There is a need for the same kind of co-operation between industry and universities as has earlier been emerging on the vocational level. The universities are becoming important partners of industry because two out of every three graduates are today employed by the private sector (OECD 1989).

There are many examples of company-university partnerships in which the requirement of official accreditation is automatic. The companies' programmes include training and education which has a *formal status with public accreditation* by the universities, thereby offering possibilities for degree studies within the workplace. This type of education is often provided by universities or other public educational institutions, or is a combination of public university courses and company-specific training programmes accredited by a university. Companies pay for the education and the individuals contribute their own time and initiative. This model of integrating company training to public education is followed by technical training of engineers like in the case of the Finnish electronics company Nokia as well as by management training like in the case of the British glass manufacturer Pilkington. The German chemical company Hoechst offers an opportunity for university studies leading to a degree for both technically and economically oriented employees.

A good example of combining resources of industry and universities to serve the needs of a corporation and an individual is the EuroPRO programme. It is a continuing education programme for employees from several European companies with tailor-made curricula. The courses are provided by various European universities thus benefiting from the expertise throughout Europe. EuroPRO is an example of both industry-university cooperation as well as collaboration between enterprises and between universities from various European countries.

The Open University and distance learning approaches are making progress and have proven successful in educating adult students. They are becoming an integrated part of company training programmes. *New educational tools and methods* like video conferences and computer-based training are developing as well. Computer-based training can improve the effective training by allowing every student to learn and study according to his/her own capabilities. Video conferences can multiply a good tutor by distributing the lectures to several locations. Video conference also facilitates the development of a common corporate culture in an international organisation.

7.4 Increasing Need for European-Wide Policies

Education has been a very national issue in Europe. The practices and policies vary a lot from country to country. Company-based training follows the rules and circumstances of national and local educational systems. This has resulted in a large variety of company training models and practices, and a variety of possible approaches to adult education. However, companies today operate European-wide. Certain generalities in the adult education infrastructure would support a European-wide personnel policy. European employees have a European-wide job market, and they should be able to benefit from continuing education opportunities in all countries. There is a growing need for generalities in developing competence throughout Europe.

At the national level, there is a variety of initiatives to develop policies for adult education. The collaboration between national governments as well as between individual companies to enhance competence on the international level is minimal. The EC Commission has played a key role in introducing the European-wide policies and in encouraging the industry-university co-operation in continuing education.

The Commission has also enhanced the European-wide accreditation system. The European credit transfer system ECTS is already used by over 200 universities and discussions are taking place about how to apply it to the company programmes. Europe lacks an organisation that can assess the company courses and credit them like PONSI (Program on Noncollegiate Sponsored Instruction), a programme of the American Council on Education which aims to recognise high quality, academically sound workplace training and to provide a mechanism for employees to receive college credit for that training. Somewhat similar is the Irish application of the European-wide credit transfer system of the National Council for Educational Awards (NCEA).

So far an official policy and framework are lacking in Europe. They should include at least *the following features*:

- intense collaboration between companies and educational institutions
- individual study plans
- modularity of studies
- multiple sources and providers of education
- universities used as gateways to various sources of education
- accreditation of studies and transfer of credits throughout Europe
- work-related studies supported by enough continuing education
- benefits from the new distribution media and new educational technologies.

Because adult education is developing, it can adopt new principles without being in conflict with any of the national educational traditions. It can be a forerunner of a European-wide educational tradition that, after all, is not only the generator of competence but also the creator of our culture.

Europeanism means a variety of cultures and the ability to cope with cultural differences. This should also provide us with competitive advantages. Besides transferability and comparability, Europeanism in education should result in a higher standard of competence than any of the national standards in Europe.

References

van der Brande (1993), *Flexible and Distance Learning*. UK: The Commission of European Communities and John Wiley & Sons Ltd.

Carnevale, A.P. (1990), *America and the New Economy. How New Competitive Standards are Radically Changing American Workplaces*. San Francisco: Jossey-Bass Publishers.

Coates, J.K., J. Jarrat and J.B. Mahaffie (1991), *Future Work*. US: World Future Society.

Commission of European Communities Council Decision of 29 May 1990 establishing an action programme for the development of continuing vocational training in the European Community (Force). Brussels: Official Journal of the European Communities 21.6.1990 E.E.C./267/90, pp. L 156/1–7.

Commission of European Communities Memorandum on Rationalisation and Co-ordination of Vocational Training Programmes at Community Level. Brussels: COM(90) 334, Task Force Human Resources, Education, Training and Youth, 1990.

Commission of European Communities Memorandum on Higher Education in the European Community. Brussels: COM(91) 349 final, Task Force Human Resources, Education, Training and Youth, 1991.

Commission of European Communities Memorandum on Open Distance Learning in the European Community. Brussels: COM(91) 388 final, Task Force Human Resources, Education, Training and Youth, 1991.

Commission of European Communities Memorandum on Vocational Training in the European Community in the 1990s. Brussels: Task Force Human Resources, Education, Training and Youth, 1992.

Commission of European Communities Report: COMETT Programme Report of 1991 Activities. Brussels: SEC(92) 1299 final, 1992.

Commission of European Communities Report: Transnational Training for Technology in Europe – The COMETT Experience. COMETT II interim evaluation report 1990-1992. Brussels: SEC(92) 1300 final, 1992.

Davies, W.K. (1991), *The European Lifelong Learning Initiative*. Brussels: Working Paper at the ELLI Workshop.

Demmer, C., J. Saltz and H-P. Scherer (1991), "Grenzen überschreitend", *Management Wissen* 1/1991, pp. 16–35.

Dertouzos, M.L., R.K. Lester and R.M. Solow (1989), *Made in America. Regaining the Productive Edge*. Cambridge, MA: The MIT Press.

Education and European Competence: ERT study on education and training in Europe. Brussels: European Roundtable of Industrialists, 1989.

Eurostat: Enterprises in Europe. Luxembourg: Commission of the European Communities and Eurostat, Second Report, 1992.

Evan, O., Y. Doz and A. Laurent (ed.) (1989), *Human Resource Management in International Firms, Change, Globalization, Innovation. An INSEAD report by leading management scholars, based on the best-in-practice in fifty multinational companies.* London: The Macmillan Press Ltd.

Grätz, F. (1991), "Der Königsweg zum begehrten Doktorhut", *Weiterbildung* 1/91, pp. 36–38.

"Industrial Policy. Call it what you will, the nation needs a plan to nurture growth", *Business Week*, April 6, 1992, pp. 44–50.

IRDAC opinion: Skills shortages in Europe. Brussels: Industrial Research and Development Advisory Committee of the Commission of the European Communities, 1991.

Moss-Kanter, R. (1991), "Transcending business boundaries: 12,000 world managers view change", *Harvard Business Review*, pp. 151–164.

OECD (1989), *Country Statistics 1989.* Paris.

Otala, L. (1992), *European Approaches to Lifelong Learning. Trends in industry practices and industry-university co-operation in adult education and training.* Geneva: CRE-ERT The European University-Industry Forum.

Senge, P. (1990), *The Fifth Discipline. The Art & Practice of the Learning Organization.* New York: Doubleday/Currency.

Telford, R. (1992), *Demography, Education and European Competitiveness.* London: Proceedings of EIRMA Conference on Industrial R&D and the Human Resource.

8 Continuing Education and Schumpeterian Competition: Elements for a Theoretical Framework

Gérard Ballot
E.R.M.E.S., Université Panthéon-Assas (Paris-II), France[1]

8.1 Introductory Remarks

Human capital accumulation has been studied in an essentially static theoretical framework until recent models of endogenous growth (e.g. Romer 1990, Azariadis and Drazen 1990). These models have the scope but also the limitations of aggregate models. There remains a need for a careful analysis of the accumulation processes at the microeconomic level of the individual and the firm. Such an analysis can develop our understanding of the timing of education over the life cycle, the distribution of education among heterogeneous individuals, the links between education and performance of the firms, and the identification of the payers. This is not a closed list and both the positive and the normative levels are implied. Such microeconomic research need not, however, be contrasted with the standard human capital theory which has been developed at that level.

The present paper tackles the task of looking at the role of continuing education in an economy characterized by competition à la Schumpeter – *creative destruction.*[2] Innovation in goods and processes as well as competition via prices are central to the competition between firms and between countries. It is therefore the framework into which education processes and normative decisions on continuing education should be modelled and discussed.

Specialists of the economics of technical change have mentioned its evident impact on the demand for higher skills, yet no or very little theoretical work seems

[1] I gratefully acknowledge the financial support of the Direction de l'Evaluation et de la Prospective, Ministère de l'Education Nationale, Paris, for the present phase of the E.R.M.E.S. project on "continuing education, performance and growth". I am grateful to Philippe Cazenave and the participants in the Helsinki seminar for many remarks which have improved this manuscript. All errors remain mine.

[2] Eliasson in Chapter 9 of this book offers parallel and complementary foundations for a micro-macro analysis of the effects of education on growth.

to have been done.[3] This may be because it is a rather formidable task for the theorist, since very few models capture the essential features of Schumpeterian competition.[4] Most of those which do are microanalytic simulation models such as those of Nelson and Winter (1982) and Eliasson (1985). Yet some well-defined problems may be addressed with mathematical tools that give more general answers. Setting first a general theoretical framework then seems a prerequisite to model building.

We will start by tackling a specific topic, the challenge to Becker's theorem on the financing of general human capital investments. This will allow us to point out important features of the economy which are invoked when one wants to criticize that theorem. It will lead us to sketch some elements of a Schumpeterian economy with human capital.

The paper will be divided as follows. First we will try to summarize very briefly the state of the debate on Becker's theorem (8.2). Then we will present our own exposition that aims to prove that firms should share the costs of general training, a thesis based on Schumpeterian competition (8.3). Finally we will use the paradigmatic framework to describe some of the important features of human capital creation and the allocation of workers which cannot be dealt with adequately in a static framework (8.4). Some final notes (8.5) will look at the consequences for the competitiveness of the economies.

8.2 The Debate on Becker's Theorem

Becker's theorem, as set out in Becker (1975), states that employees should pay for the accumulation of *general* human capital because it is embodied in themselves and they may leave with it so that the firms will not get the returns in competitive markets. Employees may pay directly or by getting wages lower than their marginal product (the market wage) while being trained.

The argument has a strong logical appeal and has gone almost unchallenged until recently.[5] Yet it is well documented that firms spend important resources on

---

[3] For instance Stoneman (1983, p. 159). Katsoulacos (1986) offers a detailed study of the effect of innovation on aggregate employment, yet it takes labour as an homogeneous factor (except in chap. 8, but he does not consider the problem of training).

[4] See Gaffard (1990) for a detailed review of some models and Aghion and Howitt (1990) for a recent endogenous growth model.

[5] For instance, the otherwise useful review of the literature on the role of firms in training by Parsons (1990) does not question Becker's framework. However, Stern and Ritzen (1991) offer a collection of contributions generally critical of Becker's theorem which have fed this section. Bishop (1991b) supplies an extended review of the state of knowledge on employer's training.

training. This is interpreted as expenses on the creation of specific human capital (which should be shared), or as expenses on general human capital paid back by the lower wages.

However, Bishop (1991a) uses detailed data on OJT (on-the-job training) for newly hired employees and shows that productivity rises much faster than wages, contrary to the prediction of general human capital theory. Moreover, this training is considered by the employers as useful in other firms and therefore general. Feuer et al. (1991) find no evidence that the employees whose employers paid for some of their formal schooling have obtained lower wages.

Uncontroversial evidence will always be difficult to obtain, notably because of the impossibility to control completely for the differences of ability between workers. There is, therefore, an urgent need for alternative theories to support the recent results.

The normative question of who should pay for the accumulation of general human capital is, nevertheless, of the highest social and economic importance. It is a widely held view that lack of competitiveness and unemployment, on the one hand, and training, on the other, are negatively correlated, both at the level of the individual and the nation. The high unemployment rate in France and continuous complaints about insufficient and inadequate training urge discussion on the possibility of underprovision of training.

One should, however, distinguish explanations of the low expenses of workers on general human capital creation from the theories that explain that firms should (or do) share the costs. The former explanations are well known. First, the *minimum wage* acts as an upper boundary on the worker's contribution. This is not very convincing because of the possibility of offering a part-time job and payment, with the worker being trained during unpaid hours. Brown (1990) reviews the evidence on this subject and finds it inconclusive. Secondly, the *liquidity constraints* caused by limitations on borrowing in the absence of collateral and the presence of uncertainty (future demand for the human capital of the employee and moral hazard on his part) prevent an important direct or indirect contribution. Thirdly, *risk aversion* lowers the expected utility from uncertain returns to training, even though this is not an argument as convincing for continuing education of an employee as for formal schooling (initial or subsequent entry for an unemployed person or non-participant).

These explanations of low provision of training may call for government intervention, but *per se*, do not imply that firms should pay for general training. We have found three different theories for the sharing of the general investment costs, but there may be more.

The first two imply the association of general and specific human investment, which has the important advantage of providing a fairly general *viability condition* for the sharing by the firm of the costs of general human capital investment. This viability condition developed by Glick and Feuer (1984, p. 123) states that firm-sponsored training is not vulnerable to poaching risks *if the sum of the worker's return on his specific training investment plus his share of the returns from his firm's general training investment exceeds the market value of that general training.*

Complementarity of general and specific human capital acquisition is an explanation for the sharing of the costs by the firm provided the viability condition is fulfilled.[6] If it is not, the firm will simply have a larger number of less skilled employees do the work. If it is not and there is complementarity in use as well, which is likely in the case of joint production of the two types of human capital, the level of production will be constrained by the investment of the employees.

Another explanation is the *exchange of hostages* theory developed by Feuer et al. (1987). They argue that there is an asymmetric bargaining situation between the firm and the employee in the bilateral monopoly over specific human capital returns. The employee then needs insurance to be willing to pay a share of the specific investment. The firm can provide general training as a *hostage* offered to the employee who offers his own investment in specific human capital as a hostage. This exchange of hostages enhances the actual value of the contract, because it will increase its expected duration. It is a very economical hostage since the firm benefits from part of the returns on the general training, under the viability constraint.

While these two theories are intellectually appealing, they rely on the statement that the employees pay for part of the specific training, which is also a theorem of human capital theory. This might need a closer look, however, because the explanations for underprovision of competence by the employees apply here also.

A third explanation is the *accreditation theory*. The general human capital acquired outside the *formal schooling system* may not be easy to signal to a firm other than the firm in which it is acquired. Hence it has no or little market value. From the point of view of the workers, it looks like specific human capital. Firms should then be willing to pay part of the costs, and the workers will in any case not be willing to pay all of them, since they may be fired by the firm. This is certainly an important explanation of the actual sharing of the costs, but it is partial. Part of the general experience acquired by workers is acknowledged by the external labour market.

These theories have somewhat extended the environment in which human capital accumulation is discussed, notably by assuming away the transparency of information or honesty of the parties. However, we think that a more fruitful study of the role and accumulation of human capital requires a new framework based on Schumpeterian theory, with new goods and new processes, and the corresponding exit of the old goods and processes. This framework at the same time offers compelling arguments for the firms to invest in general as well as specific human capital. Furthermore, it justifies sophisticated human resource policies by firms.

---

[6] See Stern and Ritzen (1991, p. 5) for some complementary discussion of that case.

8.3 Innovation and the Sharing of General Training Expenses

We offer here in six steps a proof that Becker's theorem does not hold in a Schumpeterian framework.[7] A seventh point deals with the determinants of the relative shares of the firm and the employee.

1. A firm that introduces a new good and/or a new process which is viable earns a quasi-rent.

2. This quasi-rent will be eroded away by the entry of competitors, but empirical studies show that this takes time, notably because the necessary building of the competencies (human capital) is a time consuming process. It will also be eroded away by later inventors with new goods (having some better characteristics in the sense of Lancaster (1966) or higher quality).[8] Some day the quasi-rent might become zero or negative. The firm will have to divert its resources from that good and/or process. There is creative destruction.

3. The firm must use new processes or technology. A strong case can be made for a production function which, at a certain date, involves almost fixed proportions in the inputs. Changing the proportions is costly. Furthermore, these inputs are many, and among them, there is a vector of competencies (or human capital types). These can be ranked from the totally general to the totally specific (to the technology).

This characterization of the technology remains very rough, but seems enough for our reasoning. However, a richer view below enables us to describe more carefully the demand for continuing education and its supply.

From the technology, one obtains a derived demand for competencies. One has to translate it into a demand for workers, which is no easy task if workers have several competencies and are heterogeneous. However, it is simpler and more realistic to consider the problem of adjustment at the time of introduction of a new process. The labour force has a certain endowment of competencies. Some competencies are no longer in demand or their level is too high, some are missing or their level is too low.

The change of the derived demand is on average biased towards a larger number of competencies, and higher levels in more general competencies. The argument is not empirical, but can be made theoretically in a Schumpeterian environment. It is based on the notion that many of the new goods must be of better quality to take a share of the market, and the new processes have higher requirements (at least but

[7] A mathematical model does not seem to be necessary for our present purpose, but is on our agenda to derive partial and general equilibrium results.

[8] See Beath and Katsopoulos (1991) for a detailed analysis of product differentiation.

not only through servicing). This should be possible to document with the example of the quest for zero default. However, it is sufficient for the argument that some new type of general competence or some higher level in the existing general competencies is required.[9]

4. Employees invest in too low levels of general competencies. The reasons for this underprovision have been exposed. The liquidity constraint is the first. Risk aversion and accreditation are the others. They should lead to a lower level of investment than in a risky but static environment. The creative destruction assigns a zero value to many competencies for the rest of the life cycle. It lowers the expected return for the employee, because it lowers the expected length of the period of return.

Therefore, the introduction of a new process involves in the firm an excess demand for some of the more general competencies.[10] Some other general competencies are now in excess supply.

5. The firm must allocate funds out of the quasi-rent for the R&D expenditures or patents to obtain innovations in the future. *The crux of our argument is that some of the remaining quasi-rent should optimally be devoted to the investment in general human capital which is necessary to obtain a renewed quasi-rent.*[11] If the shareholders or the managers refuse to do so, for instance because of a high preference for short-term profits (high dividends, profit-based earnings), then there will be no future quasi-rent because the competencies will be too low to produce the good efficiently even if the firm has a monopoly on the exploitation of the innovation.

6. The firm can pay the market wage and prevent poaching as long as the innovation yields a quasi-rent high enough relatively to the other firms.[12] This contrasts with the pure competition case, which supports Becker's theorem. When the quasi-rent gets low, some firms that have an excess demand for some general competencies held by some employees of the firm may poach.

As far as non-wage induced quits are concerned, they reduce the profits, but do not imply the losses that justify Becker's theorem as in perfect competition.

---

[9] Bishop (1991b, p. 21) mentions some studies which show a positive correlation between the rate of technological progress in an industry and the intensity of training of the workers.

[10] There might as well be an excess demand for some competencies which are process-specific and complementary to the general competencies.

[11] If borrowing takes place, the quasi-rent pays for the investment. If the investment is paid out of non-distributed profits, the quasi-rent pays for the investment which will yield the future quasi-rent. This does not seem essential to the argument.

[12] If this makes sense in the economy we describe, it implies that firms set their own wages for incentive reasons (see Section 8.3. below).

7. How are the shares of the employees and the firm in general training investment determined?

It depends logically on the bargaining powers of the two parties between the threat points. The threat point of the individual employee is determined by the minimum of the liquidity constraint and the other uses of his wealth. Unions will have better bargaining positions. The threat point of the firm is the minimum of the quasi-rent (after provision for the R&D expenditures) and a wage sufficient to poach outsiders with the required competencies.[13]

8.4 Continuing Education in a Schumpeterian Framework – Some Preliminary Ideas

The Schumpeterian framework is not only helpful to challenge Becker's theorem, but rather it can be integrated with other recent theoretical ideas to study carefully the demand and financing of continuing education, both from a positive and negative point of view. We will therefore introduce the organization of work in more detail with the tool of the hierarchical production function. Then we will have a look at general human capital as an input in the production of specific human capital in a dynamic framework. Finally, we will consider briefly the path dependency of technology on the accumulation of competencies.

8.4.1 Hierarchical Production Functions

The production and sale of a good require, besides physical capital and intermediary inputs, different types of functions exerted by the labour force.[14] If one leaves aside finance, marketing etc. and considers production only, it should be recognized that the division of labour entails a hierarchy of employees and that those above the bottom level *manage and supervize* rather than produce. The production function is hierarchical (Rosen 1982).

The efficiency of employees at the different levels depends on their competencies, their *effort*, the quality of the supervisors' management and the hours. This corresponds to the case where their result is separable from the result

[13] The latter may not exist, however, notably because some competencies may be acquired by learning by doing in the new process.

[14] Functions correspond better to the work done by a large fraction of the employees of a firm nowadays as opposed to tasks. A function can be defined by an objective or a set of objectives whereas tasks are precisely defined. Functions are more difficult to monitor.

of the other employees at the same level.[15] If they work in teams, it also depends on the efforts of their colleagues. Their effort depends on the efficiency of their supervisor, and so on up to the top.

This means that even if some minimum levels in the competencies are required for each position in the hierarchy, some substitutability between competencies and effort exists. Effort – which has disutility, at least above some level – nevertheless depends on incentives, as agency theory has shown. Hence the costs must be weighted, all the more that fairness considerations limit the changes in relative wages inside a firm.

Another consequence is that wages are set by the employer under an incentive compatibility constraint, and they will therefore differ between firms. There will be no market wage, but a participation constraint endogenous to the market, which will be defined in terms of discounted life cycle utility.

If production is not separable at some level of the hierarchy, employees work in teams and can probably combine their competencies more easily and complement one another. However, teams lead to incentive (free rider) problems which are different from those applicable to the separability case and not easy to solve.

The point we want to argue on the base of this description of the organization of work is that when a new technology replaces an old one, the firm must modify the organization of work to some extent. In some extreme cases, the length of the hierarchy line must be changed (there is a tendency to shorten it), while in some cases the number of jobs in each position (or hierarchical level) is changed. In all cases some changes in competencies are necessary.

This leads to another crucial statement, i.e. that the structure of the hierarchy influences the creation of the new competencies. This can be illustrated by studying specific topics.

Teamwork and Training. If employees work in teams, it is easier to replace an employee in production to give him some formal training than when the employees have jobs with a definite set of functions to fill alone. First, the effort of the other members may be stimulated, and second, some employees may have the assignment of replacing employees who are trained. This also facilitates mutual teaching as Aoki (1988) has shown.

Rotation on Jobs and Training. The rotation of workers on jobs at some level in the firm, but with different functions, leads to an accumulation of different types of specific human capital through learning by doing. Such a wide array of specific competencies enables the employee to deal with unpredictable situations, and this capability can be labelled to some degree a *general competence or human capital*, since it can be transfered to another function or firm.

A rotation policy is a policy decided upon by the firm. It has a cost, temporary lower productivity. Part of this cost is paid by the firm since the latter is not

[15] An indirect marginal productivity can be defined for the supervisors.

committed to carry it to the point where it becomes general human capital. This is therefore a supplementary argument for the firms to pay for general human capital creation.

Promotions and the Allocation of Training. If the positions are filled from lower positions in the firm, this practice has a considerable influence on the continuing education/training policy of the firm. The argument is by no means new, yet it must be mentioned because it takes its significance in a hierarchical production function framework.

The supervisor observes the abilities and effort of an employee in a certain position over a substantial period of time.[16] He selects the most able and motivated and invests in their education.[17] This investment is justified by the competencies required by the functions in the higher position. It is probably shared, but one wonders if the investment in effort and the hours necessary to assimilate the training do not constitute the employee's share. In that case, no reduction of wage can be observed.

The employer will promote the selected employee when the higher position becomes vacant. This system, widely observed, yields a very efficient allocation of the resources devoted to human capital accumulation by the firm.

8.4.2 General Human Capital as an Input in the Production of Specific Human Capital in a Schumpeterian World

General human capital improves the efficiency of the production of specific human capital, the other factors being given. It is a different argument from the complementarity assumption. The accumulation of the two types is sequential and the argument is stronger. In a world with a flow of new goods/processes, a specific competence or type of human capital becomes obsolete fairly quickly and another type must be created. General human capital is therefore intensively used to produce new specific human capital. It should have higher returns on average in a Schumpeterian world than in a static world and there is a stronger case for the firms to finance it.[18]

---

[16] Even in teams some evaluation is sometimes possible. Otherwise, some internal competition/exam may be organized as in the French mail company.

[17] The selection process may feed back in the effort as stated by tournament theory. This leads to an extremely selective human capital creation investment by the firm.

[18] Lynch (1992) offers empirical evidence that individuals with more schooling have a higher probability of obtaining OJT and more off-the-job continuing education. Schooling can be considered as a proxy of general human capital. Of course, this is not direct evidence that firms offer more general training.

8.4.3 Human Resources as a Determinant of Future Technology and Performance

The endowment of competencies at some date acts as a determinant of the future quasi-rent: it influences the *technological trajectory* because the competencies-technology complementarity at some date will determine the learning by doing and the costs of training.[19] A high endowment in general competencies appears very efficient because it enables the making of choices using a larger set of technologies, through innovation or imitation. The firm can seize better profit opportunities.

A dynamic argument can be made, however, for the voluntary specialization in some specific competencies.[20] There may be increasing returns to training in some competencies. The employees able to teach the competencies are numerous in the firm when the average level of the competencies is high. One sometimes speaks of the competence of the firm. The firm will then specialize and be very successful. On the other hand a narrow specialization of competencies may lead to failure if demand shocks at the microeconomic level are important.

These remarks should show that within the broad framework of a Schumpeterian economy, there are many arguments for the firms to sponsor some of the expenditures on continuing education, and that far-sighted strategies can be a key to performance. Modelling some of these arguments is on our agenda for research.

8.5 Some Notes on the Consequences for the Competitiveness of the Economies

Firms are innovators or imitators. An economy will be composed of many innovating firms and also many more firms which will adopt progressively the innovations and drive the quasi-rents to zero. To do comparative statics and study the effects of some variables, we can conceive the notion of a flow equilibrium level of the quasi-rent. The microeconomic quasi-rents disappear and are replaced by others. Some firms disappear and are replaced by others.

High aggregate investment in the competencies required to renew the quasi-rents should yield high competitiveness for a nation in the world economy, provided that the firms in the other nations invest less, or have some other

[19] See Dosi (1984) on this notion.

[20] There is also an involuntary specialization by a natural tendency to forget the unused competencies.

unfavourable factors (low capital stock, low natural resources, etc.). Leaving aside these other factors, firms in other nations should, however, provide also optimally for human capital creation and the nations should be equally competitive.

Various reasons may be singled out to explain differences in the rates of investment in human capital by firms between nations, and we will review briefly some of them.

Financial constraints are one of them. R&D has a highly variable and unpredictable economic outcome. The quasi-rent is a highly stochastic variable. Even at the level of a nation, the quasi-rent may fluctuate at some date. Not enough funds may then be available for general training. Governments should be aware that there may be an irreversible effect on the future accumulation of competencies.

The rate of preference for short-run profits and the dividends policy, on the one hand, and the cost of labour, on the other, may vary from nation to nation and act as constraints on the funds available for training in firms, in the context of severe international price competition.

Finally, firms underinvest in general human capital when there is no co-operation to overcome the free-rider problem. From a social point of view, the poaching of workers with general training is not a social loss, but rather a social gain (because of better matching). Countries where the institutions or the cultural environment favour co-operation of firms in the provision of continuing education may have an advantage in the accumulation of general education and competitiveness.

The role of the government in a Schumpeterian framework may then be to set the incentives for the firms to invest in general training, rather than only act as a substitute for a worker unable to finance an investment for which he should pay, as is the case in Becker's framework. Such incentives may, for instance, take the form of setting a minimum rate of investment by firms, subsidizing firms which lose from mobility, and improving the information on competencies held by workers.

References

Adnett, N. (1989), *Labour Market Policy*. Longman.

Aghion, P. and P. Howitt (1990), *A Model of Growth Through Creative Destruction*. Colloque "Instability and persistence", Palais du Luxembourg, Paris, 4–6 January. Mimeo.

Aoki, M. (1988), *Information, Incentives and Bargaining in the Japanese Economy*. Cambridge U.P.

Azariadis, C. and A. Drazen (1990), "Threshold Externalities in Economic Development", *Quarterly Journal of Economics*, Vol. 105, pp. 501–526.

Beath, J. and Y. Katsoulacos (1991), *The Economic Theory of Product Differentiation.* Cambridge U.P.

Becker, G. (1975), *Human Capital.* New York: National Bureau of Economic Research, 2nd edition.

Bishop, J.H. (1991a), "On-the-job Training of New Hires", in Stern, D. and J.M. Ritzen (eds.), *Market Failure in Training?* Springer-Verlag.

Bishop, J.H. (1991b), *Employer Training and Skill Shortages: A Review of the State of Knowledge.* Cornell University: Center for Advanced Human Resource Studies, Working Paper 32/91.

Brown, C. (1990), "Empirical Evidence on Private Training", in Ehrenberg, R. (ed.), *Research in Labor Economics,* Vol. 11. JAI Press.

Dosi, G. (1984), *Technical Change and Industrial Transformation.* Macmillan.

Eliasson, G. (1985), *The Firm and Financial Markets in the Swedish Micro to Macro Model.* Stockholm: IUI.

Feuer, M.J., H.A. Glick and A. Desai (1987), "Is Firm-Sponsored Education Viable", *Journal of Economic Behavior and Organization,* Vol. 8, pp. 121–136.

Feuer, M.J., H.A. Glick and A. Desai (1991), "Firm-Financed Education and Specific Human Capital: A Test of the Insurance Hypothesis", in Stern, D. and J.M. Ritzen (eds.), *Market Failure in Training?* Springer-Verlag.

Gaffard, J.-L. (1990), *Economie Industrielle et de l'innovation.* Dalloz.

Glick, H.A. and M.J. Feuer (1984), "Employer-Sponsored Training and the Governance of Specific Human Capital Investments", *Quarterly Review of Economics and Business,* Vol. 24, pp. 91–103.

Katsoulacos, Y. (1986), *The Employment Effect of Technical Change.* Wheatsheaf Books.

Lancaster, K.J. (1966), "A New Approach to Consumer Theory", *Journal of Political Economy,* Vol. 74, pp. 132–157.

Lynch, L. (1992), "Private-Sector Training and the Earnings of Young Workers", *American Economic Review,* Vol. 82, pp. 299–312.

Nelson, R. and S. Winter (1982), *An Evolutionary Theory of Economic Change.* Cambridge, MA: Bellrap Press, Harvard University.

Parsons, D.O. (1990), "The Firm's Decision to Train", in Ehrenberg, R. (ed.), *Research in Labor Economics,* Vol. 11. JAI Press.

Romer, P.M. (1990), "Endogenous Technological Change", *Journal of Political Economy,* Vol. 98, pp. S71–S102.

Rosen, S. (1982), "Authority, Control, and the Distribution of Earnings", *Bell Journal of Economics,* Vol. 13, pp. 311–321.

Schumpeter, J. (1943), *Capitalism, Socialism and Democracy.* London: Unwin University Books.

Stern, D. and J.M.M. Ritzen (eds.) (1991), *Market Failure in Training? New Economic Analysis and Evidence on Training of Adult Employees.* Springer-Verlag.

Stoneman, P. (1983), *The Economic Analysis of Technological Change.* Oxford: Oxford University Press.

9 Education, Competence Development and Economic Growth – A Microeconomic Explanation to Macroeconomic Growth

Gunnar Eliasson
IUI, Stockholm, Sweden

9.1 Introduction

In this paper I define education broadly and indirectly as the investment activity that produces the kind of competence capital that contributes to economic growth, as measured. Hence, this essay is partly a study of proper economic measurement. I am concerned both with the particular educational activity that occurs in educational institutions, separated from the job context, and learning in a broader sense, on-the-job or in the context of the job. I ask:

1. Why is *education* in a narrow and a broad sense important for economic growth?
2. What do we know about the quantitative relationships involved, and the incentives that promote development of competence?
3. What can governments do? Are there well defined parameters? What knowledge is required to achieve political ambitions?

With the growth objective in focus the knowledge capital that drives economic growth will necessarily be broadly defined. This is one important point. Above all we cannot restrict ourselves to competence embodied in individuals. Competence embodied in teams, in the organization of firms, of markets and the entire economic system will have to be accounted for.

Once the incentive problem is allowed in, and the imperfections of markets for competence accepted, the analysis is taken down to the micro-level. The argument will be that the dynamics of agent behavior and markets matter at the macro-level. More specifically, the benefit of efficient markets will be the capacity of the economic system to take decisions down to locations where the appropriate competence resides.

Hence, the problem addressed in this paper includes three tasks. *First*, identify the educational factor that contributes to economic growth. *Second*, learn how the markets for education should be organized for incentives to develop competence to be strong. *Third*, once this has been done, study how educational production can be efficiently organized. This paper is mainly concerned with the first task.[1]

One "magic" variable will run through the entire analysis: the rate of return to invested capital over the interest rate, the temporary monopoly rent that the firm captures. I will call it $\hat{\varepsilon}$, and define it precisely in Section 9.5. It can be measured ex post as in Figure 9.1. It can be interpreted as a rent or a profit generated from an invisible stock of competence residing in the firm (Knight 1944, McKenzie 1959, Eliasson 1990b). This variable is an important incentive variable in the capital market. Firms strive to keep it high. The expected $\bar{\varepsilon}$ drives investment behavior in

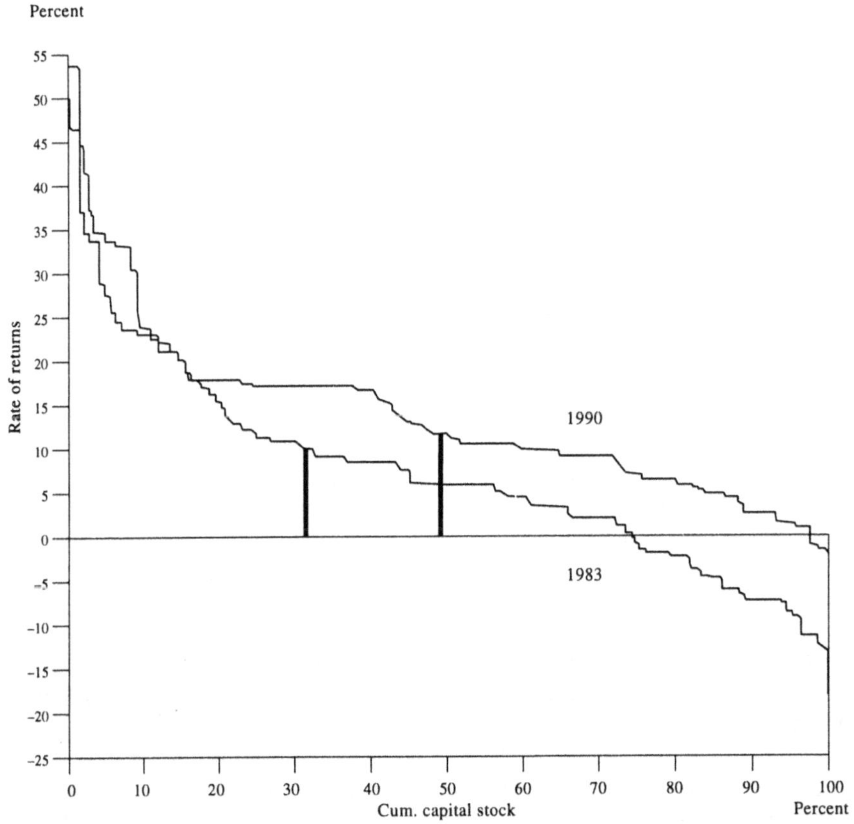

Fig. 9.1. Epsilon distributions (Salter curves). Excess rates of return ($\hat{\varepsilon}$) distributions 1983 and 1990. Source: Eliasson (1991c, p. 164)

[1] In a parallel paper, prepared for the OECD: *The Markets for Educational Services*, all three tasks are undertaken.

firms. The present value of future expected rents of the firm is evaluated all the time in the stock market. In finance theory this rent is labelled the risk premium. Most important of all, as I will demonstrate in the concluding section, there is a direct relationship between the measured change in this competence rent and the rate of total factor productivity change, or the shifting of the macroeconomic production function. With the help of this magic variable we will be able to tie the growth, the incentive and the educational problems together.

9.2 Growth Explanation or Accounting?

The importance of knowledge for the economic wealth of a nation has been discussed in the literature for centuries. To connect education with growth, and to define the content of knowledge contributing to growth – which is the main purpose of this paper – we need a theory. It is convenient to keep four different theoretical approaches apart: pre-quantitative times, neoclassical analyses, the "new" growth theory, and micro-based macro-analyses.

9.2.1 Early Thinking About Education – Pre-quantitative Times

Most early treatises in economics recognized the importance of knowledge, competence and skills. Such recognition was not so demanding in times when quantification was not required for "proper" analysis. In fact, already in 1768 before *The Wealth of Nations* the Swedish economist Johan Westerman was very clear about the importance of skills and knowledge for the international competitiveness of Swedish production. He traveled to England and to Holland to learn about superior production techniques, and he observed that labor productivity in the British shipyards was twice that in the Swedish shipyards. He concluded (already in 1768!!!) that the new machines were good to have, but what really mattered was the know-how to use them and knowledge about how to organize work around them.

Awareness of the nature and importance of education and of production organization was by no means as explicit among the academic economists of these days, but it was there at least until John Stuart Mill (1848). But then it mysteriously disappeared, a disappearance in the literature for about 100 years (Abramovitz 1988).

The reason should be sought in the nature of this particular capital item. It is not only difficult to measure, but also difficult to represent analytically in the kind of mathematical models that began to appear with the marginalist revolution. Knowledge is vested in human beings and acquired through the educational process (broadly defined). It applies very flexibly, and differently, depending upon use. It cannot be analytically disentangled from its carrier, and it does not wear out from use as does ordinary capital.[2] The easiest way was to disregard it. Heterogeneity is the frustration of capital theory. The most heterogeneous capital item one can think of is knowledge (Ysander 1978b).

9.2.2 Neoclassical Analysis

Neoclassical analysis is a natural extension of classical Ricardian analysis of the late 19th century. In the immediate postwar period it took on a very concrete shape, as more and more statistical data were brought together. Input/output analysis picked up the notion of a macroeconomic production function which was ultimately refined by Solow and his followers.

As macroeconomic development of the postwar western economies surpassed past benchmarks, the profession began to worry whether they had gotten their numbers properly organized. Above all, the Ricardian-Marxian notion of a production system fed with machines and manual labor hours, and possibly land, was not sufficient to explain observed, rapid productivity growth. Many researchers (Denison 1967, Jorgenson and Griliches 1967 etc.) began to look for *quality* dimensions of factor inputs that could explain measured productivity growth. They all, however, more or less stayed within the equilibrium framework of neoclassical economics, and notably Jorgenson and Griliches (1967), who designed a sophisticated method of correcting factor inputs one by one for quality change, using the implicit price structure of an equilibrium system. In doing so they more or less removed the residual, the unexplained technical or productivity factor. This, however, has to be the result by virtue of the method used. It can be demonstrated (see Eliasson 1987, 1990c, and below) that unaccounted for factor inputs, or factor inputs not paid the equilibrium price, will nevertheless contribute to the market value of production, and hence, instead contribute a residual value to the owner of capital. Since this residual profit has been created by factor inputs not measured, or measured, but not properly paid for, it will exhibit itself as an unexplained residual growth factor in macroeconomic production function analysis. If you correct factor inputs for errors of measurement in price statistics, you remove the corresponding unexplained production factor by definition. Jorgenson (1984) and Jorgenson and Fraumeni (1989, 1990) and others have used that method recently to demonstrate the importance of education in macroeconomic growth. In doing this they find that education matters economically very much, since pay differences, whether being the result of education, original underlying talent or some market imperfection, explain a large part of total factor productivity growth.

---

[2] The literature, until now, does not recognize depreciation of knowledge capital (see e.g. von Weizsäcker (1986) and Romer (1986)).

As a consequence they also find that the decline in relative compensation for education since the middle of the 1970s, and the strong increase in relative compensation for education thereafter (Blackburn et al. 1990), also goes a long way in explaining the disappearance in the 1970s, and "the return" in the 1980s of total factor productivity growth. The method guarantees such results, and even though they are plausible, they have to be more carefully studied before any firm conclusions on educational policy can be drawn.

It is important to keep in mind that if Jorgenson's method were applied to Swedish data, with more compressed wage differences than in the U.S. and longer lasting, large divergencies between marginal productivity and compensation because of Swedish distributional policies, the result technically would be that slow production growth, if it correlates well with the factor inputs corrected in this manner, could be explained in terms of these corrections, i.e., by the egalitarian wage policies pursued in Sweden. Also this is a very plausible explanation, but much more analysis than such correlations is required for policy advice. To this I return in the micro section below.

The macroeconomic production function approach establishes one-to-one links between labor qualities and the corresponding output. It, however, misses important characteristics associated with imperfect markets and changes in the organization of production within firms and in markets. Such arrangements encompass technology of various kinds within firms and in the organization of the institutions of markets, notably contract technology (see Eliasson 1992b). Changes in such technology normally violate standard aggregation assumptions of macroeconomic production function analysis. If the contribution of organizational change to economic growth is disregarded, too much weight will be given to individual factor quality change and education. Hence, such change has to be made explicit. Thus, it becomes natural to discuss what changes in *industrial structure* mean for the demand for particular labor qualities. It also becomes natural to discuss what more education at different levels will mean for output growth. As I will argue later this is, however, the wrong way to ask the question.

A recent "puzzle" has been the increased demand for highly educated labor in the U.S. (Blackburn et al. 1990, Kosters 1990, Bishop and Carter 1990) being accompanied by a matching increase in the return to education. On this, Berndt et al. (1992) find that these increases are related to growth in highly technical (office and information technology) capital. There is, however, no reported positive relationship between growth in such competence or in highly educated labor, on the one hand, and labor productivity, on the other. The problem is to capture the nature of technology change and the interaction of supply and demand of human capital. As we will see, such answers require that we step down to the microeconomic level. First, however, a few additional variations on the macroeconomic theme.

9.2.3 The "New" Growth Theory

The so-called "new" growth theory originated in Lucas (1988) and Romer (1986) has generated a cascade of variations on the theme. The reason for its popularity probably is its close mathematical connections with the above standard neoclassical production theory. The mathematics is the same, and some members of the old neoclassical school, like Dale Jorgenson, would argue that the "new" is no more than a modification of the "old" macroeconomic growth theory.

The idea is simple. Romer (1986) introduces an "infrastructure" knowledge competence as an externality in his model economy. This knowledge factor confers scale economies to all other factors of production. Since Romer's model is essentially the old static general equilibrium model, his problem is to obtain an internal solution, despite the existence of increasing returns. His trick is to assume strongly diminishing returns to knowledge accumulation ("education"). The only difference between Romer's model and the classical (or neoclassical) model, hence, is that he has shifted the exogenous productivity or trend assumption of macroeconomic production function analysis backward in the investment production chain, from the exogenous total factor productivity assumption to the productivity assumption associated with the educational process that shifts the production function. The new growth theory also makes it more natural to introduce all kinds of externalities in the analysis of productivity advances, notably know-how created in other sectors. Thus, for instance, government sponsored education, health care and insurance carry spill-over effects for private firms.

Suppose, following Romer (1986, p. 1015) and Eliasson (1989), that the production function

$$Q = F(k_i, K, x_i) \tag{9.1}$$

is concave as a function of measured factor inputs k_i and x_i for any fixed value of K. The term K is the *level of general knowledge,* which improves the productivity of all other factors. K is a capital good with an increasing marginal product. As long as there are diminishing returns in the activities that create K, the static general equilibrium model will have a finite solution.

I will now translate Romer's model for the general equilibrium setting of an entire economy to a firm model.

Let me assume that measured factor inputs are:
k_1 = machinery and equipment capital,
k_2 = product-oriented R&D capital,
k_3 = marketing capital,
x_i = labor input, standard hours, allocated to the various capital items,
i = 1, 2, 3.

K is the general, unmeasured knowledge base *of the firm* that is accumulated as part of the ongoing production process. In so far as some "tacit knowledge" has been compensated in the form of wages to other factors X_i, the term K incorporates the general organizing knowledge needed to organize all other factors into a team, a firm (Eliasson 1990b). K has thereby been defined as the recipient of residual profits when all other factors have been paid. This is a capital input traditionally associated with the risk taking of owners, but it can as well be associated with all knowledge (competence) inputs of the owners (Eliasson 1988b). In so far as top-level managers hold stock in the company, they get paid two ways for their competence input: in the form of salaries and in the form of dividends and capital gains on company stock if their competence contributions generate excess profits.

The main point here is that the competence capital K generates increasing returns to all other factors of production of the company, but that it is a scarce resource whose production occurs at diminishing returns. The K factor input is assumed not to wear out from use, as do other factor inputs.

It now only remains to show that K in fact has the "scale" or "leverage" properties we have postulated. To do that – following Romer (1986) – assume $F()$ to be homogeneous of degree one as a function of (k_i, x_i) when K is constant. This is an insignificant further restriction. Given that, for any $\phi > 1$.

$$Q = F(\phi k_i, \phi K, \phi x_i) > F(\phi k_i, K, \phi x_i) = \phi F(). \tag{9.2}$$

F now exhibits increasing returns to scale in K. In the growth process of the firm, K is the know-how created, say from organizational learning that can be exploited by increasing the size of the firm.

The proof I have given has been in terms of the traditional, static production function. We can then use the term economies of scale, although economies of scope may be more appropriate. However, even this term is not the right one, since we are talking about an *organizational learning process* that creates tacit competence embodied in the organization and its people.

If both traditional economies of scale and unspecified embodied knowledge are present, the two cannot be econometrically separated. And if the tacit knowledge capital – whatever it is – is perfectly correlated with "scale", a prior scale formulation will reinterpret improvements in organizational competence as originating because of scale and vice versa. The acquisitions of Zanussi (Italy) and White Consolidated Industries (U.S.) by Swedish Electrolux provide a good illustration. Obviously the acquisitions enlarged the scale of Electrolux in physical terms. There should be mechanical scale economies to exploit. However, the success of Electrolux over the years has to do with more than that. Top management in other firms doing exactly the same thing would not necessarily have achieved the same successful results, because they lacked the particular experience the Electrolux management team had obtained over the years.

Even though one can give several examples of pure, physical economies of scale with economic implications (e.g. the natural laws controlling electricity transmission, see Smith 1966), the notion of scale becomes the wrong concept if the exploitation of economies of scale requires technology, i.e., knowledge. The question, then, is how to represent the dominant competence input in the production process mathematically. The above production function representation, borrowed from Romer (1986), is a step in the right direction, but it does not take us out of the static neoclassical world, since it does not explain the accumulation of competence. This has to be done simultaneously with the explanation of production, if competence, or knowledge capital, is "tacit" and "learned" through participation in production. Then dynamics are created in the form of a "path-dependent" economic process, to which we now turn.

9.3 Micro-Based Growth Analysis

There are two problems to deal with. *First*, neoclassical or the "new" growth theory are no theories of growth. They describe measured economic growth, but the growth engine is essentially exogenous. In particular, they do not capture the macroeconomic importance of agent behavior in dynamic, "imperfect" markets, and of organizational change within firms and between firms. And these factors matter significantly.

Second, knowledge and competence are human embodied "factors" that occur as microeconomic phenomena. To understand them, one has to begin with the behavior of micro-level agents. Once we have accepted economic growth as the policy objective, and defined the circumstances of the production system that contribute positively to growth, we can derive certain tangible (definable) characteristics of the competence capital that we want to increase. It is necessary to say something on the organization of educational production. To identify the knowledge factor behind microeconomic growth at the macro-level it is necessary to begin with each of the three different agents involved:

- the *firm*, the employer
- the *individual*, the employee (incentives)
- the *policy maker* (macroeconomic policy and distribution).

Each of these agents operates in an economic environment called:

- the *market*.

It is obvious from this presentation that the ways microeconomic behavior is combined (aggregated) to macroeconomic behavior matter for economic growth. The way individual behavior results in macroeconomic output then depends upon how individuals team up in firms, how competition in markets affects firms and how rules imposed by the policy maker affect competition. Hence, there are two aggregation problems to recognize; *within* the hierarchies of the firm and *through* markets.

Since competence and knowledge are inherently heterogeneous (this proposition will be elaborated upon in the next section) and since knowledge can confer strong economies of scale (here I buy the idea of the "new" growth theory) it matters very much for growth whether knowledge is efficiently allocated. The combined proposition of this paper (to be stated already here, see also Eliasson 1992b) is that macroeconomic growth critically depends on *the capacity of the economic system to take decisions down to the levels where the appropriate competence resides*. This means that relevant growth theory *has* to be micro-based (firm, individual) and that the competence or knowledge endowment of a nation includes the particular organizational knowledge that makes this allocation possible.

9.3.1 The Firm, Employer

To identify the nature of the competence capital at work in a business firm the firm has to be characterized in terms of its market environments. As will become clear from what I say, the mainstream economic model will take us along the wrong track, since it does not allow for the relevant characteristics of the firm.

The business firm organizes people with competence to satisfy financial (profit) targets. This involves recruiting people, coordinating people and upgrading their competence. This process is controlled by a top level *organizational competence* (vested with the top competent team (Eliasson 1990b)) that also has to learn to make superior organizational decisions.

The firm of the mainstream model makes no mistakes. All *information* is available (in principle, at a cost) for the market or the auctioneer to arrange an equilibrium, full information solution. Conditions have to be *assumed* to be such for the aggregation assumptions of the above macroeconomic approaches to human capital-based growth theory to be upheld. Modern IO theory, allowing for asymmetric and costly information, arrives at the same result, provided the market is free from various kinds of selection problems, notably the lemons problem (Akerlof 1970, Greenwald 1986). I will demonstrate below that these problems are typical of markets, notably the labor market, and hence necessitate the micro-based macroeconomic analysis that I attempt here. The lemons problem is also the key troublemaker of the incentive system (see next section).

9.3.2 The Individual

The firm looks for competence in the labor market, not for labor hours. The individual supplies the same qualities.

The individual is, however, at a disadvantage. It is risk avert by mental design (and assumption) and it commands no resources, except its talent and knowledge (= competence), which is difficult, however, perhaps impossible, to assess prior to inspection. *A certain market or contract technology is needed to establish the trade in human competence that eventually drives economic growth.*

There is a market for educational services, for intermediation services, in the labor market (search) and for insurance for the income risks over the individual's life cycle in the labor market. The absence of, or the failure of, the market system to create viable such markets, or the political destruction of already functioning such markets through regulation, are sufficient causes for reducing the efficiency of the allocation of competence in the economy, and hence macroeconomic growth.

9.3.3 The Market

The nature of the firm or the individual as appearing in economic theory depends on the theory of the markets in which they are supposed to operate. The classical model offers little help here, since it is totally silent on the dynamics of competition and of firms as well as on the significance of knowledge, except as it appeared in the macroeconomic production function analysis above.

This is not a particularly promising foundation for an inquiry into the nature of the knowledge base that contributes to economic growth. For this we need an alternative to the classical model, a model of dynamic markets which never clear, but are characterized by an evolutionary ongoing economic process, moved by ex ante unpredictable entrepreneurial initiatives, some generating success stories but also a steady flow of incorrect decisions. I have called this the *experimentally organized economy*[3], since this economy thrives on a certain amount of local uncertainty caused by individual agent behavior, and loses performance from the imposition of too much order.

Hence, the experimentally organized economy is not merely a means of allocating given resources for given uses. It is also – and more importantly – part of the creation (entry) and the allocation of new resources, and of forcing obsolete resources to move, or to exit. In the labor market such innovative activity takes on particular forms since it concerns human beings that are both creative and capable of upgrading and changing their ability characteristics. Education and experience accumulation in a broad sense is part of this selection and allocation process.

Economics and pedagogics have been caught, over a couple of decades, in a long winding controversy over the relative importance (for economic growth and individual proficiency) of this selection, on the one hand, and educational investment, on the other. The classical economic model which reallocates given resources to given and known uses is, by its very assumptions limited to the analysis of the educational investment decision (human capital theory), disregarding more or less the selection effects. Its representatives tend to push this particular view hard as an empirical phenomenon, by assumption.

It is obvious that the theory of the experimentally organized economy allows a much broader view of the educational process, allowing explicitly for both the educational investment process and selection phenomena. In fact, studies on the Swedish micro-to-macro model – an approximation of the experimentally organized economy (Eliasson 1990c, 1991b,c) – suggest that the selection

---

[3] For a presentation of the distinguishing characteristics of the experimentally organized economy, see Eliasson (1987, 1988a,b, 1990b, 1991c). It is obtained by a seemingly innocent modification of the assumptions of the classical, static equilibrium model, forcing bounded rationality on the agents of the economy, namely a sufficient expansion of the state space (called the opportunity set) of the economy and a provision for free innovative entry. All conclusions in favor of a centrally planned order have been achieved by assuming a sufficiently small or transparent (at no cost) state space in models with no entry.

component of total factor productivity growth may be by far the most important one (Eliasson 1991a, Carlsson 1991).

The ability of the individuals of the economy to cope with the unexpected change of the selection-dominated experimentally organized economy constitutes part of the human capital of the economy. As will become apparent as I go on this ability depends on the capacity of the economic system to provide adequate *insurance* (see further Eliasson 1992a) in an economy where risk-averse individuals are subjected to rather rough treatment as a consequence of business mistakes, being in turn a normal cost of economic growth.

9.4 Organizational Learning and Competition Drive Economic Growth

Once we have left the accounting framework of macroeconomic theory and taken the growth explanation down to the level where agents operate in dynamic markets organizational learning, knowledge and technological competition become the mechanisms behind a viable growth explanation.

9.4.1 The Limits to Learning

New competence can be acquired through internal education, or in the market through recruitment and through the acquisition of competent firms or parts of firms (Eliasson 1991d). At some rate such acquisition of new competence is perfectly reliable, but the economic value of the competence is reduced to the extent that competitors acquire the same or better competence faster. If, on the other hand, the firm tries to acquire competence very rapidly, it normally incurs a higher cost in the form of a higher rate of business failure. When seen at the aggregate level of a sector or the entire industry, business mistakes constitute a standard cost of economic development. The more rapid (everything else the same) the competence accumulation of a firm, a group of firms or a whole industry, the higher the incidence of failure, but also the higher the probability of a major business success.

Since the economic value of acquired know-how depends on what other competitor firms do, *strongly diminishing returns to learning* or the acquisition of knowledge should be exhibited because of the rapidly increasing rate of business failure (Eliasson 1990c). This means that no individual firm will be able to raise K in (9.1) through allocating *all* its resources on learning and thus, forever outcompete its competitors through the consequent gains in economies of scale. The same results should hold for a country.

9.4.2 The Content of Economically Valuable Knowledge

Apparently, the content of economically valuable knowledge is a quite complex blend, that has to be defined at different levels of aggregation. It is multidimensional beyond comprehension from one point of assessment and only parts of it are applied on each occasion. Individuals also embody human capital of different quality. Firms organize individuals into competent teams, contributing through their organizational technology something in addition to the component individual qualities. The economy as a whole merges – through its organization (the economic system) – individuals and firms to generate economic values (output).

The number of possible combinations, if we start from the level of the individual and move up, is enormous and beyond everybody's understanding. This is the "basic fact" of the experimentally organized economy. Each "merge" has been achieved through experimentation in markets and hierarchies, not through careful analysis and explicit decisions. The key to macroeconomic performance, hence, is to organize the economy so that the mass of heterogeneous human and firm-based competence residing in an industrial economy is optimally exploited. This, first of all, means organizing the economy in such a way that decisions are taken down to levels where the appropriate competence resides, i.e., in general at the level of firms and individuals, and away from central hierarchies.

But this is only part of the organizational, "tacit" knowledge capital of a national economy. The enormous complexity of this organization means that there exists no simple optimal point. There are several "high levels" and even though the economy may be temporarily close to one optimum, nobody in the system will be aware of it. The economy, hence, is in a state of constant flux, being moved by agents striving to reach better positions, pushing other agents out of their established positions (Eliasson 1991c).

The ability of the agents to compete successfully through innovation is in principle a "learning" phenomenon, as is the ability of agents to cope with unexpected change.

The continuing flux of the competitive market process also means that the exact nature of firm or individual competence required for success will also constantly change. There is no stable specification of the characteristics of the optimal knowledge at each allocation (organization). Since requisite knowledge is not a well defined item that can be replaced when necessary, knowledge capital as all other capital has to be depreciated and increased through new investment (education).

The complex nature of such knowledge makes it more or less unmeasurable, except indirectly in terms of the present value of future expected returns of firms as assessed in the stock market, or directly in terms of the cumulative value of investments in "education" of a firm or an individual. The reader should take notice of a particular distinction here. Human capital theory assumes the existence of stable earnings functions, implying the existence of perfect markets, being perfect in terms of their capacity to evaluate perfectly the human capital embodied in an individual. Such measures will always be biased by the imperfections of the labor market.

At the same time the standard method in capital theory is to accumulate investments in machines, buildings and inventories, assuming a certain depreciation rate, thus obtaining a measure of the capital stock. Even though I say that competence capital, due to its complex and varying specification, is not directly measurable, what I propose to do is to apply the standard capital measurement method in economics to measure competence. The only distinction to add, however, is that it may be possible to measure certain simple capital items, like machines directly through explicit specification of performance characteristics, which is done in engineering contexts, but rarely in economics.

The firm of my market reference model, *the experimentally organized economy* (see Eliasson 1991c), makes plenty of mistakes, because of the general non-transparency of its local market environment and the unpredictability of the responses of its competitors. The firms are, however, supposed to be capable of coping with such a competitive market environment, or go bankrupt and exit, even though firms frequently try to protect themselves from market competition, thus creating market imperfections. Hence, unique but transient knowledge and the competence to identify and correct decision errors early dominate firm success (Eliasson 1990b). *Individuals,* on the other hand, being assumed to be normally risk averse, cannot be expected to be able to cope with their experimentally organized market environment alone and, hence, have to be treated specially.

Since the unique knowledge base of the firm is constantly exposed to competitive peril threatening the firm with sudden obsolescence, coping with change, forgetting and organizational learning are critical competence characteristics that also dominate firms' recruiting.

The recruitment problem of the firm is, hence, schizophrenic. At each point in time the firm needs a particular package of competence characteristics. But firm management does not know and will not be able to predict with any accuracy the nature of that package. It will have to develop the required characteristics through experimentation, and suffer from repeated failure along the way.

This means that a firm will be as concerned with getting rid of people with the wrong competence, as it is with acquiring people with the right competence (in expectation) provided internal retraining programs, that are also profitable, cannot be organized.

This behavior on the part of the firm also determines the local environment of its employees. Employees, typically characterized as being *risk averse* do not like this environment. As a consequence, labor directly and indirectly through unions or through the political process has exercised a demand on the firm for *insurance* for the vagaries of market life.

Even though knowledge capital cannot be directly measured and its content still remains more or less a mystery, we can say that besides *education* broadly defined, individuals as well as firms require the *additional ability to cope with unexpected change*. This is partly a capacity acquired through experience in the market. For individuals this means that a *functioning labor market* is part of their educational experience. It also requires that appropriate and efficient *insurance* markets exist to make individuals overcome their innate risk aversion that is otherwise detrimental to their human capital accumulation.

9.4.3 Technical Change Creates More Competition

At this juncture we may make a choice. We can tell (1) a *neoclassical* story about exogenous technical change, which will be partly untrue and misleading, or (2) we can do micro-macro analysis and also explain technical change. I will do both, and begin with the micro-macro analysis and then simplify it in the next section through imposing some strong aggregation assumptions, such that the outcome looks very neoclassical and devoid of the important and interesting economic knowledge content.

The micro-macro analysis will be done verbally in terms of what may be called a Salter curve analysis.

In this section the magic variable $\bar{\varepsilon}$ will be defined. Its presence in my story – besides being a useful tool to derive neoclassical macroeconomic analysis as a distilled version of dynamic micro-macro analysis – becomes a natural part of a nice chronology of economic doctrines.

Since the marginalist revolution, diminishing returns have been needed to secure internal solutions in economic models. But diminishing returns have consistently failed to show up in empirical studies, which has been a source of constant concern. Knight (1944) suggested that observed increasing returns must be the result of an unmeasured knowledge input.

McKenzie (1959) came back to the same problem, observing that measured factor payments constantly failed to exhaust total production value. This difference, again, when divided through by employed capital, constitutes – as we shall see – the epsilon value. And McKenzie suggested that this difference must be the return of (the rents from) some unmeasured knowledge capital that can be associated with individuals or firms.

At the micro-level such rents are both positive and negative signifying business success or failure. Hence, in the computable risk environment of modern finance theory the epsilon constitutes a risk premium only, since finance theory, being shaped in the classical model without selection, does not recognize the presence of unmeasured competence capital (Eliasson 1988b).

In the experimentally organized economy of our analysis, uncertainty as distinct from risks prevails (Eliasson 1990b). Already Knight (1921) suggested that the competence to convert uncertainty into ex ante computable risks constituted the rational foundation of a firm. So the two devices come together naturally in a world where both uncertainty and risk prevail, and then allow an empirically better founded explanation than that of finance theory alone.

The story can therefore be nicely concluded if the competence rent, that I have called $\hat{\varepsilon}$, can be demonstrated to be related to the shift factor in production function analysis.

With competence being the ultimate, dominant capital input of a firm, its incentive system has to be organized such that returns to the competence to coordinate inputs to the benefit of the owners of the firm are satisfactory. At the firm level, however, such competence has to be much more broadly defined than technological competence. It resides in the people of the organization and how they have learned to work together in teams. And the top competent team of the firm is instrumental in achieving this coordination through integrating the three dimensions. Exploiting market imperfections is an important business activity. Competence is, however, human or team embodied and not subject to the same contractual property rights as physical goods. It is acquired through experimental learning in the market. It is not easily tradable and difficult to learn or imitate by simply observing outsiders if they lack the requisite receiver competence. Failures are hence frequent, both when learning is through imitation and when innovative and bold. It follows that "lost competence" or "obsolescent competence" can rarely be replaced by crash learning or innovation programs, especially on a broad industry-wide basis. Strongly diminishing returns to learning rapidly set in, due to frequent failures.

The dynamic competition story on the allocation of educational knowledge services can be nicely expressed in terms of so-called Salter distributions of epsila ($\hat{\varepsilon}$), or the rents from competence (see Figure 9.1). I will discuss this market in terms of competing firms, but it is equally valid for competition among individuals in the labor market.

9.4.4 Competition Creates Technical Change

Firms in Figure 9.1 are lined up from the left in terms of their ability to generate rents, or a return above the market interest rate ($\hat{\varepsilon}$). The size of the rent is measured vertically and the size of the firm (its capital in per cent of total capital of all firms) is measured horizontally. There is a layer of such ex ante distributions at each moment of time, depicting the ex ante perceived rents of all existing firms, of all firms including entering firms and excluding exiting firms, and (very important) the corresponding expected distributions as anticipated by each firm. All these distributions change as decisions taken are ultimately realized ex post, reflecting over time the dynamics of competition in financial markets, being driven by the organizational competence of firms.

Let me briefly go through the dynamics of competition in the capital market as it occurs in the Swedish micro-to-macro model (Eliasson 1991c). Each firm in the model is represented in each market by a ranking on the vertical axis or the epsilon distribution, the width of the column measuring the size of the firm in percent of all other firms. (Fig. 9.1 shows that even though the firm indicated has increased its rate of return between 1982 and 1992 it has lost in ranking.)

Each firm also has its own potential productivity frontier, under which it is operating to position itself on the productivity and rate of return rankings. This is still actual ex post performance. The market dynamics on the other hand is controlled by a *second* set of *potential ex ante* distributions that capture the planned actions of all other firms, including new entries.

There is a *third* set of Salter curves that tell how *each firm sees itself positioned relative to other firms*. The real world of the experimentally organized economy, and its model approximation, the Swedish micro-to-macro model both show large *divergencies between actual and perceived positions*. Those ex ante distributions indicate the potential for a given firm to outbid all other firms in wages, or in paying a higher interest rate.

The firm learns directly if competitors can do better. Management then knows that it had better improve in order not to be pushed down along the Salter distribution, and, perhaps, out. Similarly, when the firm finds itself close to the top, it knows that close competitors are taking actions to better their positions through innovation or imitation. If potential Salter distributions are sufficiently steep in the top left-hand group, firms attempt to improve their positions on the Salter curve through innovative activity, or through entry. No firm is ever safe under these market circumstances, and constantly has to take action to better its position. This moves the entire economy through a selfperpetuated, growth creating, competitive process.

The other side of this growth process that concerns us, is the steady change in the environment of the employees, as each firm tries to outcompete its competitors. Large opportunities are created for everyone capable of capturing them. In doing so they push their competitors down and right on the curve. However, in the process, people lose their jobs and are forced to move elsewhere and retrain to get a new job.

This turnover in the labor market increased during the rapid growth years of the 1960s. Even though people rapidly found new jobs and unemployment was kept low, political resistance to a dynamic labor market increased. Thus, during the 1960s and part of the 1970s it was thought among policy makers in Europe that better planning would replace this experimentally organized competitive process and reduce the social adjustment costs. Measures were taken that slowed down the process, lowering exits and as a consequence the competitiveness of firms. Economic growth slowed down, eventually causing even more hardship on the people.

This policy of the 1970s in particular was based on a fundamental misunderstanding of the functioning of dynamic markets. The adjustment costs were mistakenly looked at as waste instead of a cost for reallocation of resources and economic development. It was mistakenly thought that an improved overview would make central policy makers more competent to make local decisions from the agents in the market. Such an overview is not possible in the experimentally organized economy (Eliasson 1991c) and this fact significantly lowers the ability of the central government to do good for its citizens (Eliasson and Taymaz 1992, Eliasson 1993). This is gradually being understood.

Currently economic political sentiment seems to be moving in the contrary direction, as more and more sectors are deregulated and even the most hard core of all protected production, the public sector, is gradually opened up to competition. Decisions and responsibilities are increasingly moved back and down to where the appropriate local competence resides.

My a priori position (also expressed in an earlier book, Eliasson 1992a) is that the preferred policy is to make people accept and learn to cope with the volatile environment of the experimentally organized economy. This is essentially an argument for improved insurance in the labor market. In this insurance, education plays a fundamental role in the sense of raising the competence to cope with market change.

The story will therefore be nicely concluded if the competence rent, that I have called $\hat{\varepsilon}$, can be demonstrated to be related to the shift factor in production function analysis.

9.5 Connecting Organizational Competence Back to Competition and Economic Growth

Competence coordination and monitoring is a matter of managing people with competence. It involves not only incentives to contribute but also to stay with the team. In this section I link the "unmeasurable knowledge" or innovative competence function to firm objectives (profits) and the creation of economic value over and above the value of resources put in (total factor productivity growth = *DTFP*).[4] I will do this mathematically in terms of the information and monitoring system of a firm as it appears in the Swedish Micro-to-Macro (M-M) model. The task is to establish a relation between the competence rents $(\bar{\varepsilon})$, firm total productivity change *(DTFP)* and growth in output *(DQ)*.

In doing so I cut right through the dynamics of competition discussed in the previous section. I thus exclude the endogenous growth drive of the macro-economy by assuming price taking behavior of firms (exogenous prices), thus making ex ante equal to ex post and removing business mistakes by assumption. In doing so I remove the endogenous explanation to economic growth and take the model back to the neoclassical accounting format.

Let me assume for simplicity that the only measured inputs needed to produce output *(Q)* are labor *(L)* and capital *(K)*. *DX* stands for the rate of change in *X*.

Define:

$$\varepsilon = pQ - TC \tag{9.3}$$

$$\bar{\varepsilon} = \frac{\varepsilon}{K} \tag{9.4}$$

[4] The mathematical derivation has been taken directly from Eliasson (1990c).

$$TC = wL + (r + \rho - \frac{\Delta p^K}{p^K})K \tag{9.5}$$

$$R^{NE} = R^N + (R^N - r)\Phi \tag{9.6}$$

$$R^N = M\alpha - \rho + \frac{\Delta p^K}{p^K} \tag{9.7}$$

$$M = 1 - \frac{w}{p}\frac{1}{\beta} \tag{9.8}$$

It follows immediately that:

$$\bar{\varepsilon} = R^N - r \tag{9.9}$$

$$pQ = TC + \bar{\varepsilon}K \tag{9.10}$$

R^N = nominal rate of return to total assets K
R^{NE} = nominal rate of return to net worth $(E = K - D)$
ρ = rate of depreciation
M = operating surplus per unit value
D = nominal debt
w = cost per unit of labor input (L)
r = interest rate
p^K = capital goods deflator
p = value added (Q) deflator
Φ = D/E
α = pQ/K (capital productivity, uncorrected for relative (p, p^K) price change)
β = Q/L (labor productivity).

The term $\bar{\varepsilon}$ is the difference between the rate of return on total assets (R^N) and the interest rate (r) paid by the firm. It can be positive or negative. But a firm will not survive forever with a negative $\bar{\varepsilon}$. Compare (9.3) and (9.8) and you will see that $(r + \bar{\varepsilon})$ is the equilibrium price for capital services that exhausts total value (pQ) product when $R^N = r$ and $\bar{\varepsilon} = 0$.

It is evident that $\bar{\varepsilon} > 0$ arises – as suggested by McKenzie (1959) – as a consequence of unmeasured (or not measurable) capital, not included in K. This asset has a time dimension in the sense that returns may come with a lag. Even if $\bar{\varepsilon}$ is negative the corresponding asset, hence, might very well have a large positive present value. Part of this time dimension can be interpreted as a risk factor that demands a reward (a risk premium).

To explain growth, however, you have to explain the way $\hat{\varepsilon}$ arise (innovation) and are competed away. This is done in the micro-based macroeconomic model or in the theory of the experimentally organized economy. In neoclassical macroeconomic growth analysis aggregate $\check{\varepsilon}$ are assumed or measured, but not explained. To the extent one $\bar{\varepsilon}$ measures value created by an unmeasured capital input in a firm it must have something to do with economic growth. I therefore prove (see appendix where the critical price taking assumption is sneaked in) the following relationship:

$$DQ = s_1 DL + s_2 D\bar{K} + \frac{\Delta\varepsilon}{pQ} \tag{9.11}$$

where s_l and s_2 measure labor and capital income shares respectively. Apparently $\Delta\varepsilon = 0$ when these shares exhaust total value added.

Many technologies are compatible with constant income shares, s_l and s_2, the most well-known being the power function (so-called Cobb-Douglas) specification.

After differentiation the entire class of functions:

$$Q = CL^{s_1} K^{s_2} T \tag{9.12}$$

becomes (9.11), where T is a shift factor, usually assumed to represent exogenous disembodied technical change.

As is evident from (9.11) and (9.12) the total factor productivity change becomes:

$$DTFP = DT = \frac{\Delta\varepsilon}{pQ} \tag{9.13}$$

under the assumption of Cobb-Douglas technology. This is enough for my purpose. I have demonstrated – for one particular production technology – that the estimated (on specification (9.11)) shift factor *(DTFP)* picks up a host of economic influences related to the allocation of resources and the exercising of competence within the firm. As a consequence the return to that unmeasured capital – that I have labeled – also shows up in the "technical shift factor". This competence input – by definition – also includes the ability to deal with uncertainty (successfully taking on business risks). Hence, the interpretation of $\bar{\varepsilon}$ in the modern theory of finance becomes part of this more general formulation.

The technology factor, however, also picks up the contribution of the entrepreneur, or trader, from exploiting market imperfections, for instance to successfully hire talented people at lower wages or salaries than their marginal productivities. Also capital gains will appear in ε. Since capital gains are also the result of trading in imperfect markets, they reflect the competence of the entrepreneur to trade successfully. They represent value added and should not be deflated away in productivity measurements. This competence can be seen to be exercised through the formation of synergistic teams, in which individual contributions are magnified through the exercising of top entrepreneurial competence.

Scale effects originating in the application of top entrepreneurial knowledge by definition make markets imperfect. Whether the firm operates as a Kirznerian (1973) equilibrator or trader or imitator, making money from moving the economy closer to equilibrium, or as a Schumpeterian entrepreneur, enhancing the productivity of the system through changing its parameters and disturbing the equilibrium, it creates (in both cases) positive value additions to output.

It is not, however, universally accepted to allow such improvements in allocational efficiency to appear as technical change in macroeconomic production function analysis, and much work has been devoted to correct price indexes for the effects of such market imperfections. (For a discussion see Dargay 1988, Färe and Grosskopf 1990, and Morrison 1990.)

If, for instance, prices used are equilibrium prices – corrected or not – a new competitive situation is reflected in a new set of equilibrium prices, and all quantities adjust to this new price configuration along the production frontiers. This is the method of computable equilibrium modeling. The a priori production technology chosen usually demands a particular price index to leave the shift factor *(DTFP)* invariant to such adjustments.

The preceding discussion, however, raises a much more profound question. If imperfections in markets are fundamentally due, not to asymmetrically distributed information or slow learning or adjustment behavior, but rather to fundamental inconsistencies in beliefs, competence endowments or the formation of business judgements, actions taken on the basis of such inconsistent opinions will constantly reshape the structures that at each point in time represent the productivity characteristics of the firm or the economic system, that in turn shape future ex ante perceptions of what is to come and so on. The path the economy takes will spin off ex ante/ex post realizations that will be reflected in the shift factor *DTFP* in (9.13) since they represent positive or negative value contributions to output.

This paper has been devoted to showing that the use of economic knowledge embodied in the organization of the firm or the economy, notably the organization of human talent, determines the character of the value added contributions that appear as total factor productivity changes in macroeconomic production function analysis. The ultimate organizational policy technology of a nation then becomes the art of organizing itself – through experimental learning – such that these value added contributions are steadily positive. Then economic growth occurs. Hence, an analysis of the macroeconomic effects of competence also requires (1) an analysis of the capacity of markets to stimulate (reward) competence development and allocate competence, and (2) the capacity of firms and schools to organize learning efficiently.

9.6 Summing up

I have shown in this paper that the returns to some unmeasured capital input that I call knowledge or competence by definition makes up the excess returns or rents on measured capital in firms, while the change in these excess returns figures importantly in total factor productivity change in macroeconomic production function analysis.

I have presented no explanation per se of economic growth, only measurement or growth accounting. Growth theory or a growth explanation demands that the dynamics of rent creation and destruction through competition in markets also be explained at the micro-level. In such a model of what I call the experimentally organized economy, the creation of new knowledge (innovation) in firms and the destruction of old knowledge capital through technological competition through the use of such new knowledge become the driving forces behind macroeconomic growth. I also argue that the competition to create such new knowledge and rents is as much a matter of how people with competence are allocated in the market or team up in firms as it is the result of well defined educational investments in people. Since this allocation is very much a matter of how the institutions of markets for educational services and competence are organized, this organization of markets in turn becomes a major explanation of economic growth. As a consequence, any educational policy to become effective has to be supported by policies aimed at improving the allocative functions of markets, notably the labor market.

Appendix

Proof of (9.10). From (9.1) and (9.3):

$$pQ \;=\; wL + (r + \rho - \frac{\Delta p^K}{p^K})\, K + \varepsilon$$

Take differences, assuming exogenous prices (p, w, r, p^K) to be fixed:

$$p \cdot \Delta Q \equiv w\Delta L + [\;]\, p^K \Delta \bar{K} + \Delta\varepsilon$$

Thus,

$$\frac{\Delta Q}{Q} = DQ \equiv \frac{wL}{pQ} DL + \frac{[\;]\Delta p^K \bar{K}}{pQ} \cdot D\bar{K} + \frac{\Delta\varepsilon}{pQ}$$

$$DQ = s_1 DL + s_2 D\bar{K} + \frac{\Delta\varepsilon}{pQ}$$

$$s_1 = \frac{wL}{pQ}$$

$$s_2 = \frac{[r + \rho - \frac{\Delta p^K}{pK}]p^K}{pQ}$$

$\frac{\Delta \varepsilon}{pQ}$ is, by definition *DTFP*. QED.

References

Abramovitz, M. (1988), "Thinking about Growth", in Abramovitz, M. (ed.), *Thinking about Growth.* Cambridge: Cambridge University Press.

Akerlof, G.A. (1970), "The Market for "Lemons": Qualitative Uncertainty and the Market Mechanism", *Quarterly Journal of Economics,* Vol. 84, pp. 488–500.

Berndt, E.R., Ch.J. Morrison and L.S. Rosenblum (1992), *High Tech Capital Formation and Labor Composition in the US Manufacturing Industries; an exploratory analysis.* NBER Working Paper No. 4010.

Bishop, J. and S. Carter (1990), *The Worsening Shortage of College Graduate Workers.* University of Pennsylvania and Cornell University, Ithaca, NY: Center on the Educational Quality of the Work Force, Working Paper No. 90–15.

Blackburn, N.L., D.E. Bloom and R.B. Freeman (1990), "The Declining Economic Position of Less Skilled American Men", in Burtless (ed.), *A Future of Lousy Jobs? The Changing Structure of U.S. Wages.* Washington, DC: The Brookings Institution.

Carlsson, B. (1991), "Productivity Analysis: A Micro-to-Macro Perspective", in Deiaco, E., E. Hörnell and G. Vickery (eds.), *Technology and Investment – Crucial Issues for the 1990s.* London: Pinter Publishers.

Dargay, J. (1988), *Factor Demand in Swedish Manufacturing: Econometric Analyses.* Stockholm: IUI Research Report No. 34.

Denison, E.F. (1967), *Why Growth Rates Differ.* Washington, DC: The Brookings Institution.

Eliasson, G. (1987), *Technological Competition and Trade in the Experimentally Organized Economy.* Stockholm: IUI Research Report No. 32.

Eliasson, G. (1988a), "Schumpeterian Innovation, Market Structure and the Stability of Industrial Development", in Hanusch, H. (ed.), *Evolutionary Economics. Applications of Schumpeter's Ideas.* Cambridge, MA: Cambridge University Press.

Eliasson, G. (1988b), "Ägare, entreprenörer och kapitalmarknadens organisation – en teoretisk presentation och översikt", in Örtengren, J. et al. (eds.), *Expansion, avveckling och företagsvärdering i svensk industri.* Stockholm: IUI.

Eliasson, G. (1989), "The Dynamics of Supply and Economic Growth – how industrial knowledge accumulation drives a path-dependent economic process", in Carlsson, B. (ed.), *Industrial Dynamics.* Boston/Dordrecht/London: Kluwer Academic Publishers.

Eliasson, G. (1990a), "The Knowledge Based Information Economy", in Eliasson-Fölster-Lindberg-Pousette-Taymaz (eds.), *The Knowledge Based Information Economy.* Stockholm: IUI.

Eliasson, G. (1990b), "The Firm as a Competent Team", *Journal of Economic Behavior and Organization,* Vol. 13, pp. 275–298.

Eliasson, G. (1990c), "Business Competence, Organizational Learning and Economic Growth – Establishing the Smith-Schumpeter-Wicksell (SSW) Connection", in Scherer, F.M. and M. Perlman (eds.), *Entrepreneurship, Technological Innovation, and Economic Growth: Studies in the Schumpeterian Tradition.* University of Michigan Press.

Eliasson, G. (1991a), "Deregulation, Innovative Entry and Structural Diversity as a Source of Stable and Rapid Economic Growth", *Journal of Evolutionary Economics*, No. 1, pp. 40–63.

Eliasson, G. (1991b), "Modeling Economic Change and Restructuring. The Micro Foundations of Economic Expansion", in de Wolf, P. (ed.), *Competition in Europe. Essays in Honor of Henk de Jong.* Dordrecht/Boston/London: Kluwer Academic Publishers.

Eliasson, G. (1991c), "Modeling the Experimentally Organized Economy: Complex Dynamics in an Empirical Micro-Macro Model of Endogenous Economic Growth", *Journal of Economic Behavior and Organization,* Vol. 16, pp. 153–182.

Eliasson, G. (1991d), "Financial Institutions in a European Market for Executive Competence", in Wihlborg-Pianigiani-Willet (eds.), *Financial Regulation and Monetary Arrangements after 1992.* Elsevier Science Publishers.

Eliasson, G. (1991e), *Produktivitet, vinster och ekonomisk välfärd – hur ser sambanden ut?* Stockholm: IUI.

Eliasson, G. (1992a), *Arbetet – dess betydelse, dess innehåll, dess kvalitet och dess ersättning.* Stockholm: IUI.

Eliasson, G. (1992b), *The Markets for Educational Services.* Stockholm: IUI Working Paper.

Eliasson, G. (1993), "Den ekonomiska politikens gränser och möjligheter", in *Den långa vägen (The Long Road).* Stockholm: IUI.

Eliasson, G. and E. Taymaz (1992), *The Limits of Policy Making: An analysis of the consequences of boundedly rational Government using the Swedish micro-to-macro model (MOSES).* Stockholm: IUI Working Paper No. 333.

Färe, R. and S. Grosskopf (1990), "A Distance Function Approach to Measuring Price Efficiency", *Journal of Public Economics*, Vol. 43, pp. 123–126.

Jorgenson, D.W. (1984), "The Contribution of Education to U.S. Economic Growth, 1948–73" in Dean, E. (ed.), *Education and Economic Productivity.* Cambridge, MA: Ballinger.

Jorgenson, D.W. and B.M. Fraumeni (1989), "The Accumulation of Human and Non-Human Capital 1848–1984", in Lipsey-Tice (eds.), *The Measurement of Saving, Investment and Wealth.* Chicago University Press.

Jorgenson, D.W. and B.M. Fraumeni (1990), "Investment in Education and U.S. Economic Growth", in Walker-Bloomfield-Thorning (eds.), *The U.S. Savings Challenge; Policy Options for Productivity and Growth.* Westview Press.

Jorgenson, D.W. and Z. Griliches (1967), "The Explanation of Productivity Change", *Review of Economic Studies,* Vol. XXXIV, pp. 249–283.

Kirzner, I. (1973), *Competition and Entrepreneurship.* Chicago: University of Chicago Press.

Knight, F. (1921), *Risk, Uncertainty and Profit.* Boston: Houghton-Mifflin.

Knight, F.H. (1944), "Diminishing Returns from Investment", *Journal of Political Economy,* Vol. LII, pp. 26–47.

Kosters, M.H. (1990), "Schooling, Work Experience and Wage Trends", *American Economic Review, Papers and Proceedings,* Vol. 80, pp. 308–312.

Lucas, R.E., Jr. (1988), "On the Mechanics of Economic Development", *Journal of Monetary Economics*, Vol. 22, pp. 3–41.

McKenzie, L.N. (1959), "On the Existence of General Equilibrium for a Competitive Market", *Econometrica,* Vol. 27, pp. 30–53.

Mill, J.S. (1848), *Principles of Political Economy with Some of Their Applications to Social Philosophy.* London.

Morrison, C.J. (1990), *Market Power, Economic Profitability and Productivity Growth Measurement: An Integrated Structural Approach.* NBER Working Paper No. 3355.

Romer, P.M. (1986), "Increasing Returns and Long-Run Growth", *Journal of Political Economy,* Vol. 94, pp. 1002–1037.

Smith, V.L. (1966), *Investment and Production – a Study in the Theory of the Capital-Using Enterprise.* Cambridge, MA: Harvard University Press.

Westerman, J. (1768), *Svenska Näringarnes Undervigt emot de Utländske förmedelst en trögare Arbets-drift* (On the inferiority of the Swedish compared to foreign manufacturers because of a slower work organization). Stockholm.

von Weizsäcker, Ch. (1986), "Rights and Relations in Modern Economic Theory", in Day, R. and G. Eliasson, (eds.), *The Dynamics of Market Economies.* Stockholm: IUI and Amsterdam: North-Holland.

Ysander, B.-C. (1978a), "Homogeneity in Education – a comment on economic theories of education", in Bowman, M.J., Å. Sohlman and B.-C. Ysander (eds.), *Learning and Earning.* Stockholm: National Board of University and Colleges, Liber Tryck; also reprinted in Ysander, B.-C. (ed.), *Truth and Meaning in Economics – Selected Essays on Economic Theory and Policy.* Stockholm: IUI, 1991.

Ysander, B.-C. (1978b), "Homogeneity in Education. Appendix (The meaning of human capital)", in Bowman, M.J., Å. Sohlman and B.-C. Ysander (ibid); also reprinted in Ysander, B.-C. (ed.), *Truth and Meaning in Economics – Selected Essays on Economic Theory and Policy.* Stockholm: IUI, 1991.

10 Uncertainty, Multivalence and Growth

Kim Huynh and Marie-Pierre Merlateau
E.R.M.E.S., Université Panthéon-Assas (Paris II), France[1]

10.1 Introduction

The purpose of this paper is to study the impact of investment in different kinds of human capital in an endogenous growth model. It focuses on the role of the agents' specialization in one type of capital versus the multivalence in terms of growth. This analysis is made under a certain world and a stochastic world.

Several recent papers have explored mechanisms through which growth rates are endogenously determined and the role of investment in human capital. Thus, Lucas (1988) and Azariadis and Drazen (1990) analyze the impact of investment in human capital and externalities on the long-run growth rate of the economy.

The first contribution of this paper is to consider human capital as heterogeneous. Indeed, it seems realistic to distinguish general education from vocational training. General education gives a background allowing an agent to be efficient in many areas. By contrast, an agent who has invested in vocational training becomes specialized in one area. His specific knowledge allows him to be very efficient, but only in the corresponding area. Note that several types of vocational training may exist, but the agent is said to have "specialized" if he has invested in only one of them. The concern of the paper is at first to determine the agent's behavior. The agent has to choose between investing either in general education, in vocational training, or in both.

The advantages of specialization are well known since the times of Smith and Ricardo. More recently, the theory of economic organizations has the objective to explain and to describe the structure of organizations. Most of the theories developed in this tradition hinge on information problems and bounded rationality. Thus, Williamson (1989) considers that the organizational structure of

[1] We gratefully acknowledge the financial support of the Direction de l'Evaluation et de la Prospective, Ministère de l'Education Nationale, Paris, for the E.R.M.E.S. Project on "Continuing Education, Performance and Growth".

a firm rises as a result of the distribution of information and the inability of agents to capture all of the information. Therefore, specialization allows a decrease in uncertainty with respect to information. Along the same lines, Heiner (1988) achieves very close results by assuming the information imperfect and its use imperfect too. Thus he shows that specialization allows to reduce the focus of an agent, so that his reliability to take the best decision is raised.

By contrast, this paper aims to show that it may be optimal for the agent to invest not only in vocational training but also in general education. The main contribution of this article is to introduce uncertainty with respect to the human capital returns. The results achieved are compared with the ones under certainty. Starting with the certainty case, the article emphasizes the choice of the agent's specialization in vocational training as a result of a learning effect. Then the article investigates the impact in terms of growth. Several cases which highlight that specialization does not always provide growth are reviewed. In contrast, under uncertainty, the agent may prefer to diversify his investment between general education and several types of vocational training to adapt quickly to economic fluctuations that affect human capital returns. The idea is based on the same argument that the portfolio choice theory introduced in 1952 by Markovitz and applied to monetary analysis by Tobin (1958).

The paper is organized as follows. In the next section, the model is set up under a world of certainty. It is an overlapping generation model where agents live for two periods. During the first period, the agent can invest in heterogeneous human capital. The heterogeneity comes from the existence of several kinds of activities requiring different knowledge, general knowledge acquired by education, and specific knowledge, namely vocational training such as traditional or high technological know-how. The agent earns the benefits of his investment during the second period when he has a full-time job. Each type of human capital has a specific return which may differ in the short and in the long run. The analysis shows the tendency of specialization in vocational training and focuses on the consequences in terms of growth.

The third section introduces uncertainty in an identical setting through the fluctuations of human capital returns. This section emphasizes the role of general education compared to vocational training. Indeed the agent may be often induced to multivalence, which may benefit growth. There is a brief concluding comment in the last section.

10.2 The Model Under Certainty

The purpose of this section is to study the behavior of individuals who are faced with a choice of investing in heterogeneous types of human capital. During the first period of their life, the agents have to choose between investment in general education and in several types of specific vocational training relative to ability in new or in old technologies. General education is characterized by a low immediate return but a potentially high one in the long run. The agents' choice is determined by the returns of the different types of human capital. The analysis emphasizes the tendency of specialization in old specific vocational training due to a learning effect.

10.2.1 Assumptions

We consider an overlapping generation model à la Allais (1947) – Diamond (1965). Time is discrete, and the identical agents live for two periods. At time t N_t individuals are born and the population grows at a rate n, so that:

$$N_t = (1+n)\,N_{t-1} \tag{10.1}$$

An individual born at time t is young at t and old at $t+1$. Each agent works for two periods and has the following utility function:

$$U(c_t, d_{t+1}) \tag{10.2}$$

where c_t and d_{t+1} stand for the consumption of the agent respectively in period t and $t+1$. Consumption depends on the human capital stock owned by the agent in each period. Consumption in each period is equal to:

$$c_t = (1 - g_v - g_y)\, w_t\, x_t \tag{10.3a}$$

$$d_{t+1} = w_{t+1}\, x_{t+1} \tag{10.3b}$$

The variable x_t denotes the stock of human capital inherited by young agents in terms of efficiency units of labor services by unit of time. It stands also for the average quality of labor of both young and old agents at period t. This stock is increased in the second period according to the investment realized in the first period.

Human capital is heterogeneous so that a young agent has to choose the fraction of time he wants to devote in attaining each kind of human capital. His decision will directly determine his consumption in the next period. Here, for simplicity, we consider only two kinds of human capital denoted by v and y. However, the analysis can easily be extended to several kinds of human capital. The symbols g_v and g_y stand for the investments, in terms of time, respectively in general training (education) v and in training in a specific activity y.

The sum of the investments in the two kinds of human capital is bounded by one, so that the agent can still consume in the first period:

$$g_v + g_y < 1 \tag{10.4}$$

$$0 \le g_v < 1 \tag{10.5a}$$

$$0 \le g_y < 1 \tag{10.5b}$$

For simplicity, we assume that there is no physical capital. Agents do not save and then consume their whole income in each period. Since there is no physical capital dynamics, the variable w_t, which stands for the wage rate for an efficiency unit of labor supplied, can be normalized to one: $w_t = 1$. Equations (10.3a) and (10.3b) can then be written as:

$$c_t = (1 - g_v - g_y)\, x_t \tag{10.6a}$$

$$d_{t+1} = x_{t+1} \tag{10.6b}$$

10.2.2 The Model

The Basic Model. We consider that both the investments in general training and in a vocational training increase the whole human capital stock in the following period as follows:

$$x_{t+1} = [1 + h_v(g_v) + h_y(g_y)]\, x_t \tag{10.7}$$

where $h_v(g_v)$ and $h_y(g_y)$ denote respectively each return on investment in each type of human capital. Formally, the derivatives of these functions are linear and positive in g_v and g_y:

$$h'_{g_v} > 0$$

$$h'_{g_y} > 0$$

As an example, we can consider that:

$$h_v(g_v) = a\, g_v \qquad a > 0 \tag{10.8a}$$

$$h_y(g_y) = b\, g_y \qquad b > 0 \tag{10.8b}$$

In a very standard way, an agent born in t seeks to maximize his utility (10.2) subject to (10.6a) and (10.6b) in order to settle the optimal investment rate for each human capital. The agent's program can be written as:

$$\begin{cases} \underset{g_v,\, g_y}{Max}\ U(c_t, d_{t+1}) \\ s.t.\ \ c_t = (1 - g_v - g_y)\, x_t \\ \qquad d_{t+1} = x_{t+1} \end{cases} \tag{10.9}$$

The first order conditions lead to:

$$\begin{cases} \dfrac{\delta L}{\delta g_v} = -u'_1\, x_t + u'_2\, h'_{g_v}\, x_{t+1} & = 0 \text{ if } g_v > 0 \\ & < 0 \text{ if } g_v = 0 \\ \dfrac{\delta L}{\delta g_y} = -u'_1\, x_t + u'_2\, h'_{g_y}\, x_{t+1} & = 0 \text{ if } g_y > 0 \\ & < 0 \text{ if } g_y = 0 \end{cases} \tag{10.10}$$

The agent invests in the two kinds of human capital only if:

$$h'_v(g_v) = h'_y(g_y) \tag{10.11a}$$

He invests only in general training v if:

$$h'_v(g_v) > h'_y(g_y) \tag{10.11b}$$

He gets specialized in vocational training y if:

$$h'_v(g_v) < h'_y(g_y) \tag{10.11c}$$

The agent's behavior depends on the marginal returns on each type of human capital. The agent chooses multivalence only when the marginal returns are equal. If they differ, the agent tends to specialize in the asset the return of which is the highest.

The human capital dynamics is determined by the following equations:

$$x_{t+1} = [1 + g(N_t)\, h_v(g_v)]\, x_t \quad \text{if} \quad h'_v(g_v) > h'_y(g_y) \tag{10.12a}$$

$$x_{t+1} = [1 + g(N_t)\, h_y(g_y)]\, x_t \quad \text{if} \quad h'_v(g_v) < h'_y(g_y) \tag{10.12b}$$

Since growth is run by these dynamics, the growth rate of the economy can be inferred: it is equal to the highest human capital rate of return and takes into account the number of people who invest in it, through the function $g(N_t)$. This function is increasing in N_t and is bounded by one.

Coming back to the example $h_v(g_v) = ag_v$ and $h_y(g_y) = bg_y$, growth converges to a balanced growth path. The growth rate is $g(N_t)a$ if $a > b$ and $g(N_t)b$ if $b > a$.

Growth is higher under specialization than under multivalence. If $\bar{u}$ denotes the sum $(g_v + g_y)$, it is clear that:

$$a\bar{u} > ag_v + bg_y \quad \text{if} \quad a > b \tag{10.13}$$

Since general education may present an immediate low return compared to that of specific types of knowledge, the agents never invest in it and always specialize in vocational training. This specialization in vocational training provides growth. The result is well known in the literature.

However, cases may exist under which growth would have been increased with an investment in general training even if its return is lower than the one of vocational training.

First Case: We can consider that general training is the only human capital that can be inherited by young agents from their parents. Human capital accumulation is, for instance, the following:

$$x_{t+1} = [1 + g(N_t)\, g_v]\, x_t \tag{10.14}$$

In this case, investment in vocational training reduces growth.

Second Case: Existence of Returns to Scale. An additional gain may appear if individuals invest in both types of human capital. The idea is straightforward. The investment in general training may facilitate the learning derived from vocational training. As a result, an agent who has invested in both may be more efficient at work than agents who have invested in either vocational training or general training only. Hence, if the whole population invests in the two kinds of human capital, the human capital accumulation assumes the following form:

$$x_{t+1} = [1 + g(N_t)\, h_v(g_v) + g(N_t)\, h_y(g_y) + g(N_t)\, h_v(g_v)\, h_y(g_y)]\, x_t \qquad (10.15)$$

Diversification increases growth compared to multivalence if the return on general training is not too small with respect to vocational training.

The problem is that the positive return to scale due to the investment in both types of human capital may be unknown to the agent before any investment. The connection between general training and specialization appears only when the agent is familiar with both types of human capital. Then, it appears as an externality and is not taken into account in the agent's program. As a result, the agents always specialize in vocational training even if this choice does not provide the highest growth.

Third Case: Existence of a Lock-in Effect. Another case where investment in general training would have increased growth can be highlighted. We consider now that human capital increases in each period with characteristics specific to the kind of human capital that has been invested in during the previous period. Activities increase in pay-off the more they are undertaken due to a learning effect. Therefore, two separate human capital dynamics exist.

The general training dynamics is given by the following equation:

$$v_{t+1} = h_v(g_v, v_t)\, v_t \qquad (10.16a)$$

The vocational training dynamics is as follows:

$$y_{t+1} = h_y(g_y, y_t)\, y_t \qquad (10.16b)$$

At each period, the total human capital is still given by the sum of these two quantities:

$$x_t = v_t + y_t \qquad (10.17)$$

When he is young, the agent can still devote the fractions of time g_v and g_y to the activities v and y, respectively. The sum of these investments is still bounded by one:

$$g_v + g_y < 1 \qquad (10.18)$$

The agent's program can now be written as:

$$\begin{cases} \underset{g_v,\, g_y}{Max} \; U(c_t, d_{t+1}) \\ s.t. \quad c_t = (1 - g_v - g_y)\, x_t \\ \qquad d_{t+1} = h_v(g_v, v_t)\, v_t + h_y(g_y, y_t)\, y_t = x_{t+1} \end{cases} \qquad (10.19)$$

First order conditions lead to:

$$\begin{cases} \dfrac{\delta L}{\delta g_v} = -u'_1\, x_t + u'_2\, h'_{g_v} v & = 0 \text{ if } g_v > 0 \\ & < 0 \text{ if } g_v = 0 \\ \dfrac{\delta L}{\delta g_y} = -u'_1\, x_t + u'_2\, h'_{g_y} y & = 0 \text{ if } g_y > 0 \\ & < 0 \text{ if } g_y = 0 \end{cases} \tag{10.20}$$

where u'_1 and u'_2 denote respectively the utility derivatives with respect to consumption in the first and in the second period.

The agent invests in the two kinds of human capital until:

$$h'_{g_v} v = h'_{g_y} y \tag{10.21a}$$

He invests only in general training v if:

$$h'_{g_v} v > h'_{g_y} y \tag{10.21b}$$

He invests only in vocational training y if:

$$h'_{g_v} v < h'_{g_y} y \tag{10.21c}$$

A lock-in effect can be characterized if, for instance, the return of an investment in vocational training grows at a decreasing rate at each period, while that of an investment in general training increases at a constant rate. This can be explained by technical progress that makes investment in one specific vocational training progressively less and less profitable. By contrast, general training always yields the same rate of return.

As an example, we can have:

$$y_{t+1} = \left(1 + \frac{a\, g_y}{1 + y_t^2}\right) y_t \tag{10.22a}$$

$$v_{t+1} = (1 + b\, g_v)\, v_t \tag{10.22b}$$

If we consider that in period t individuals inherit a considerable amount of human capital in vocational training v from their parents, but a very low amount of human capital in general training y ($y_t \approx 0$), the inequality (10.21b) becomes pertinent, that is to say:

$$h'_{g_v} v > h'_{g_y} y$$

with, in our example:

$$h'_{g_v} = \frac{a v_t}{1 + v_t^3} \tag{10.22c}$$

$$h'_{g_y} = b y_t \tag{10.22d}$$

As a result, in period t, the agents invest only in vocational training v since it yields the highest return. Due to the learning effect, they will always keep to this choice. The activity that is chosen the first continues to be chosen thereafter, even if it is not necessarily an efficient choice in the long run. Therefore, the optimal initial choice leads the rational agent to be locked in, through a self-reinforcing mechanism.

As a consequence, the dynamics are based only on the accumulation of vocational training v. Considering equation (10.22a), the equilibrium is then a steady state. However, if the agent has invested in general training y, the dynamics would have converged to a balanced growth path at the constant rate b (see equation (10.22b)). Hence, the lock-in effect results in the specialization of individuals and leads to reduced growth.

Note, the same interpretation can be made in terms of human capital associated either to an old activity y or to a high technology v. Agents inherit from their parents more human capital in the old activity y than in the new, since their parents were not used to working in the new activity at the previous period. The model shows that individuals never choose to invest in new human capital because it has the lowest short-run return, even if it has the highest long-run return.

10.3 The Model Under Uncertainty

10.3.1 Introduction and Assumptions

For exogenous motives (development of new technologies, for instance), some human capital returns may become uncertain and risky. This is typically the case for vocational training returns that can fluctuate in each period depending on the state of the technology. However, general education is needed in each period, regardless of the prevailing technology. Therefore, its return remains always certain.

Our analysis demonstrates that the agent can be induced to choose multivalence, in contrast with the case of certainty. This behavior is adopted in order to reduce the whole risk. The intuition hinges on the same basis that the portfolio choices theory used by Tobin (1958). The application to a growth model leads to an interesting result: the variance of each human capital and their correlation coefficient act directly upon growth.

Until here, the model dealt with only two types of human capital. Another one is now introduced since the environment is uncertain. The three assets differ by their expected return and their variance.

We distinguish now between two different types of human capital derived from vocational training denoted respectively by m and n. Their returns are $\tilde{r}_m$ and $\tilde{r}_n$. They are random variables, normally distributed according to the following parameters: $N(r_m; V_{mm})$ and $N(r_n; V_{nn})$. The symbols V_{mm} and V_{nn} stand for their respective variances. The terms V_{mn} and ρ_{mn} denote their covariance and their correlation coefficient, respectively. The combination of assets m and n yields a return $\overline{r}_p$ randomly and normally distributed according to $N(r_p; V_{pp})$.

General training z has a certain return r_z. This return may be lower than the others in the short run. However, the certainty of its return counteracts its low level. This contributes to explain the choice of investment in this type of human capital when the world is stochastic. Education has some properties identical to the asset money in the portfolio theory. Both have a certain return and both can have an indirect utility since they may increase the other risky assets' returns.

The determination of the agent's behavior involves the application of portfolio theory and the separation theorem. The analysis is performed in two steps. At first, the agent must determine the parts of investment allocated to each kind of vocational training. Then, he decides the part to allocate to vocational training, on the one hand, and to general training, on the other. Then the consequences in terms of growth can be analyzed.

10.3.2 The First Step

This first step consists of determining the optimal combination of investment in vocational training. The individual seeks to minimize the variance of these human capital returns, given their expected rate of return. The program is equivalent to the maximization of the expected rate of return for a given variance.

The Program. The agent who has invested in both forms of vocational training has the following expected human capital rate of return:

$$r_p = g_m r_m + g_n r_n \tag{10.23}$$

where g_m and g_n denote respectively the investment in vocational training m and n of the total investments allocated to human capital with risky returns.

Hence, the variance of the risky human capital, V_{pp}, can be written as:

$$V_{pp} = V(r_p) = g_m^2 V_{mm} + g_n^2 V_{nn} + 2 g_m g_n V_{mn} \tag{10.24}$$

So the agent's program is:

$$\begin{cases} \underset{g_m,\, g_n}{Min} \; V_{pp} = g_m^2 V_{mm} + g_n^2 V_{nn} + 2 g_m g_n V_{mn} \\ s.t. \quad r_p = g_m r_m + g_n r_n \end{cases} \tag{10.25}$$

with $0 < g_m \leq 1$ and $0 < g_n \leq 1$.

The Lagrangian is:

$$L = g_m^2 V_{mm} + g_n^2 V_{nn} + 2 g_m g_n V_{mn} + \lambda (r_p - g_m r_m - g_n r_n) \tag{10.26}$$

The first order conditions lead to:

$$\begin{cases} \dfrac{\delta L}{\delta g_m} = 2g_m V_{mm} + 2g_n V_{mn} - \lambda r_m & \begin{array}{l} = 0 \text{ if } g_m > 0 \\ \geq 0 \text{ if } g_m = 0 \end{array} \\ \dfrac{\delta L}{\delta g_n} = 2g_n V_{nn} + 2g_m V_{mn} - \lambda r_n & \begin{array}{l} = 0 \text{ if } g_n > 0 \\ \geq 0 \text{ if } g_n = 0 \end{array} \\ \dfrac{\delta L}{\delta \lambda} = r_p - g_m r_m - g_n r_n & = 0 \end{cases} \tag{10.27}$$

Resolution. Three cases can occur mathematically for a strictly positive expected rate of return.

In the first case, the agent invests in both forms of human capital and becomes multivalent, i.e. $g_m > 0$ and $g_n > 0$, and we obtain:

$$\begin{cases} g_m = \dfrac{r_p (r_m V_{nn} - r_n V_{mn})}{r_n^2 V_{mm} - 2r_n r_m V_{mn} + r_m^2 V_{nn}} > 0 \\ g_n = \dfrac{r_p (r_n V_{mm} - r_m V_{mn})}{r_n^2 V_{mm} - 2r_n r_m V_{mn} + r_m^2 V_{nn}} > 0 \end{cases} \tag{10.28}$$

The denominator Δ of these two expressions is always positive as can easily be demonstrated. More precisely, Δ can also be written as:

$$\Delta = r_n^2 V_{mm} - 2r_n r_m V_{mn} + r_m^2 V_{nn} \tag{10.29a}$$

$$\Delta = r_n^2 V_{mm} - 2r_n r_m V_m V_n \rho_{mn} + r_m^2 V_{nn} \tag{10.29b}$$

with $-1 \leq \rho_{mn} \leq 1$.

For the upper bound, $\rho_{mn} = 1$, Δ becomes:

$$\Delta = r_n^2 V_{mm} - 2r_n r_m V_m V_n + r_m^2 V_{nn} = (r_n V_m - r_m V_n)^2 \tag{10.29c}$$

So Δ is always positive for the upper bound of ρ_{mn}. Therefore, Δ is a fortiori positive for $\rho_{mn} < 1$. Since Δ is always positive, the conditions under which g_m and g_n are positive are given by their numerator:

$$\begin{cases} r_n V_{mm} - r_m V_{mn} > 0 \\ r_m V_{nn} - r_n V_{mn} > 0 \end{cases} \tag{10.30a}$$

Rearranging those inequalities, we obtain:

$$\begin{cases} r_n V_m > r_m V_n \rho_{mn} \\ r_m V_n > r_n V_m \rho_{mn} \end{cases} \tag{10.30b}$$

These inequalities allow us to find the conditions under which the agent becomes multivalent with respect to both types of vocational training. If the returns to human capital m and n are perfectly and positively correlated, say $\rho_{mn} = 1$, then the two previous conditions cannot be respected simultaneously. In this case, diversification is not chosen by the agent because the risk of the whole human capital is equal to the linear combination of both types of human capital:

$$V_p = g_m V_m + g_n V_n \tag{10.31}$$

In contrast, if $\rho_{mn} \leq 0$, these conditions are always satisfied, so that diversification is always an optimal choice. Between these two cases, if $0 < \rho_{mn} < 1$, the choice of diversification or specialization will depend on the return on each type of human capital and their variances.

In the second case, the agent specializes only in vocational training n. Formally, $g_m = 0$ and $g_n > 0$ occurs under the following conditions:

$$\begin{cases} g_n = \dfrac{r_p}{r_n} > 0 \\ \rho_{mn} \geq \dfrac{V_n r_m}{V_m r_n} \end{cases} \tag{10.32}$$

The first condition is always respected. If $\rho_{mn} = 1$, the second condition becomes:

$$V_m r_n > V_n r_m$$

Specialization in human capital n is chosen when its expected return is high and its variance is low, related to those of human capital m.

In the third case, by symmetry with the second case, the agent specializes only in human capital m when its expected return is high and its variance is low compared to those of n. This case where $g_m > 0$ and $g_n = 0$ occurs under the following conditions:

$$\begin{cases} g_m = \dfrac{r_p}{r_m} > 0 \\ \rho_{mn} \geq \dfrac{V_m r_n}{V_n r_m} \end{cases} \tag{10.33}$$

Proposition. The resolution of the first step of the program leads to the description of the agent's behavior concerning his investments in vocational training. It appears that the optimal choice depends not only on returns and variances but also on the correlation coefficient ρ_{mn}. The agent's preferences do not matter at this stage. If the returns on both forms of human capital are perfectly and positively correlated, then the agent never chooses to diversify, because there is no gain from doing so.

In contrast, if $\rho_{mn} < 1$, there is always an additional gain coming from multivalence. Furthermore, if $\rho_{mn} \leq 0$, this gain is sufficiently high to induce the agent to choose diversification, irrespective of the returns and variances.

Otherwise, if $0 < \rho_{mn} < 1$, the agent's choice depends on the returns on both forms of human capital and their standard deviations. Of course, if one of them gives back a higher return than the other, at a simultaneously lower level of risk, the agent specializes in this type of human capital. The problem arises when an asset provides a higher return with a higher risk than the other one. In that case, the choice is then based upon ρ_{mn} and their relative returns and risks.

10.3.3 The Second Step

The Program. After having decided his investments in each type of vocational training, the agent aims now to settle the respective parts to invest in vocational training and in general education, according to his preferences. The variance and the expected rate of return on his vocational training investment are now given. We consider a utility function defined on mean and variance. This assumption is justified if the random return process follows a normal distribution or if the von Neumann and Morgernstern utility function is as follows:

$$U(x) = ax^2 + bx \qquad a < 0$$

The concavity of the function illustrates the fact that the agent is risk averse. The parameter a expresses the role of risk aversion in the utility function.

Therefore, the expected utility has the following shape:

$$E[U(x)] = bE(x) + a\,[Var(x) + E(x)^2]$$

Hence, the agent seeks to maximize his expected utility, depending on the consumption of the first and the second period. So his program is:

$$\begin{cases} \underset{c_t,\, d_{t+1}}{Max} \; E[U(c_t) + \beta U(d_{t+1})] \\ s.t.\; c_t \;\; = (1 - g_z - g_p)\, x_t \\ \quad\;\; d_{t+1} = (1 + r_z g_z + r_p g_p)\, x_t = x_{t+1} \end{cases} \tag{10.34}$$

with $r_p = mr_m + nr_n$ and $x_t = z_t + p_t$.

The agent's program can be turned into the maximization of the following simpler function of two variables:

$$\begin{aligned} E[U(g_z, g_p)] = {} & a(1 - g_z - g_p)^2 x_t^2 + b(1 - g_z - g_p)x_t \\ & + a\beta x_t^2 (1 + r_z^2 g_z^2 + r_p^2 g_p^2 + V_{pp} g_p^2 + 2r_z g_z + 2r_p g_p + 2r_z r_p g_z g_p) \\ & + b\beta x_t (1 + r_z g_z + r_p g_p) \end{aligned} \tag{10.35}$$

with g_z and g_p positive. Note that g_p stands for the investment in both types of vocational training.

Resolution. The first order conditions lead to:

$$\begin{cases} 2ax_t(1+\beta r_z^2)g_z + 2ax_t(1+\beta r_z r_p)g_p - (2ax_t+b)(1-\beta r_z) & =0 \text{ if } g_z>0 \\ & <0 \text{ if } g_z=0 \\ 2ax_t(1+\beta r_z r_p)g_z + 2ax_t(1+\beta r_p^2+\beta V_{pp})g_p - (2ax_t+b)(1-\beta r_p) & =0 \text{ if } g_p>0 \\ & <0 \text{ if } g_p=0 \end{cases} \quad (10.36)$$

The first case to study is the case of diversification between the various types of human capital, that is to say $g_z > 0$ and $g_p > 0$. We obtain by a Cramer resolution:

$$\begin{cases} g_z = \dfrac{(2ax_t+b)\,[(r_p+1)(r_p-r_z)+V_{pp}(1-\beta r_z)]}{2ax_t\,[(r_p-r_z)^2+V_{pp}(1+\beta r_z^2)]} > 0 \\ \\ g_p = \dfrac{(2ax_t+b)(r_z+1)(r_z-r_p)}{2ax_t\,[(r_p-r_z)^2+V_{pp}(1+\beta r_z^2)]} > 0 \end{cases} \quad (10.37)$$

Since a is negative and very small, if we consider that $2ax_t + b > 0$, then the conditions under which g_p and g_z are positive are the following:

$$\begin{cases} (r_p+1)(r_z-r_p)+V_{pp}(\beta r_z-1) > 0 \\ \\ (r_z+1)(r_p-r_z) > 0 \end{cases} \quad (10.38)$$

If those inequalities are verified, then the agent diversifies between risky vocational training with high variance and education which yields a low but a certain return. From (10.37), the investments in the two kinds of human capital are positively correlated with their respective returns. The higher the variance is, the more the agent is induced to invest in general training z.

The second case to be considered is: $g_z > 0$ and $g_p = 0$. The agent specializes in general training under the following conditions:

$$\begin{cases} g_z = \dfrac{(2ax_t+b)(1-\beta r_z)}{2ax_t(1+\beta r_z^2)} > 0 \\ \\ \dfrac{\beta(2ax_t+b)(r_p-r_z)(1+r_z)}{1+\beta r_z^2} < 0 \end{cases} \quad (10.39)$$

The agent invests only in general training z if its return is sufficiently higher than the risky asset's global expected return.

The third case is: $g_z = 0$ and $g_p > 0$. By symmetry, the resolution leads to the following conditions:

$$\begin{cases} g_p = \dfrac{(2ax_t+b)(1-\beta r_p)}{2ax_t(1+\beta r_p^2+\beta V_{pp})} > 0 \\ \\ \dfrac{\beta(2ax_t+b)\,[(r_p+1)(r_z-r_p)+V_{pp}(\beta r_z-1)]}{1+\beta r_p^2+\beta V_{pp}} < 0 \end{cases} \quad (10.40)$$

The individual invests only in vocational training if its expected return is sufficiently high relative to the return on general training z for a low variance.

Proposition. Vocational training is assumed to have a higher expected rate of return than general training. Then the agent specializes in vocational training for a low variance. He invests only in general training for a high variance. For other values of the variance, the individual diversifies.

10.3.4 Consequences in Terms of Growth

Under certainty, the agent specialized in vocational training even if it reduced growth in the long run. He was not induced to invest in general training.

Under uncertainty, his investments depend mainly on the correlation coefficient and on the variance. The lower the correlation coefficient is, the more the agent diversifies between the two specific types of training. The higher the variance is, the more the agent tends to invest in general training. Therefore, these two variables have a direct impact on growth as can be easily shown by studying the cases viewed in the previous section.

First Case. If general training is the only asset that can be inherited from parents, it is straightforward that a rise in the variance, which increases investment in general training, improves growth.

Second Case: Existence of Returns to Scale. Here, we consider (see Second Case, p. 200) that specific training can be inherited too and that an unknown gain exists, coming from diversification. Therefore, the lower the correlation coefficient is, the more the agent diversifies in vocational training and growth is increased. The higher the variance is, the more he invests in general training and diversifies his investments. This behavior increases growth.

Third Case: Existence of a Lock-in Effect. In the context presented in the Third Case (p. 201), each type of human capital increases in accordance with its own characteristics, not globally. We consider the same three types of human capital comprising vocational training m and n, which are risky, and general training z, which is risk-free. Again, the resolution is performed in two steps. Firstly, the agent determines the respective parts of each risky asset relative to his whole risky investment, given the amount of each asset inherited from his parents. Then, the second step consists of determining the respective parts of vocational and general training.

The First Step: Given the expected portfolio return, the agent seeks to minimize its variance. However, the expected return and its variance are modified since they must take into account the amount of each asset inherited from the previous period.

Now, the expected return is:

$$R_p = g_m r_m m + g_n r_n n$$

The variance is written as:

$$V_{pp} = m^2 g_m^2 V_{mm} + n^2 g_n^2 V_{nn} + 2 g_m g_n mn V_{mn}$$

The agent's program is therefore:

$$\begin{cases} \underset{g_m,\, g_n}{Min}\ V_{pp} = m^2 g_m^2 V_{mm} + n^2 g_n^2 V_{nn} + 2 g_m g_n mn V_{mn} \\ s.t. \quad R_p = g_m r_m m + g_n r_n n \end{cases} \tag{10.41}$$

The first case considered is $g_m > 0$ and $g_n > 0$. We obtain:

$$\begin{cases} g_m = \dfrac{r_p (r_m V_{nn} - r_n V_{mn})}{m (r_n^2 V_{mm} - 2 r_n r_m V_{mn} + r_m^2 V_{nn})} > 0 \\ g_n = \dfrac{r_p (r_n V_{mm} - r_m V_{mn})}{n (r_n^2 V_{mm} - 2 r_n r_m V_{mn} + r_m^2 V_{nn})} > 0 \end{cases} \tag{10.42}$$

The conditions in terms of correlation are the same as the ones found in Resolution (p. 208). However, the role of the amounts of each activity inherited is now enhanced. The higher the amount of one particular type of human capital inherited by the agent is, the less the agent is induced to invest in this type of human capital. This is due to the fact that the variance increases more than the expected return. As a result, he increases his investment in the other activity.

The second case is $g_m = 0$ and $g_n > 0$. The conditions are given by:

$$\begin{cases} g_n = \dfrac{R_p}{n r_n} > 0 \\ \rho_{mn} \geq \dfrac{V_n r_m}{V_m r_n} \end{cases} \tag{10.43}$$

Again, the conclusions in terms of correlation are the same and the amount of activity *n* decreases the part allocated to it.

The third case to be studied is $g_m > 0$ and $g_n = 0$. It occurs under the following conditions:

$$\begin{cases} g_m = \dfrac{R_p}{m r_m} > 0 \\ \rho_{mn} \geq \dfrac{V_m r_n}{V_n r_m} \end{cases} \tag{10.44}$$

The conclusions are symmetric to the ones of the previous case.

The Second Step: As in Section 10.3.3, after having determined the respective parts of each risky asset, the agent sets the parts allocated to risky human capital, on the one hand, and to risk-free human capital, on the other, in order to maximize his expected utility.

Taking into account the amounts inherited from the previous period, the agent's program is now:

$$\begin{cases} \underset{c_t,\, d_{t+1}}{Max} \; E\,[U(c_t) + \beta U(d_{t+1})] \\ s.t. \quad c_t \;=\; (1 - g_z - g_p)\, x_t \\ \qquad d_{t+1} \;=\; (1 + g_z r_z)\, z_t + p_t + R_p g_p = x_t + g_z R_z + g_p R_p \end{cases} \tag{10.45}$$

with

$$\begin{aligned} x_t &= p_t + z_t \\ p_t &= m_t + n_t \\ R_z &= r_z z_t \\ R_p &= g_m r_m\, m + g_n r_n\, n \end{aligned}$$

Following the same reasoning carried out in Section 10.3.3, three cases are characterized.

The first case: $g_z > 0$ and $g_p > 0$ occurs under the following conditions:

$$\begin{cases} g_z \;=\; \dfrac{(2ax_t + b)\,[(R_p + x_t)\,(R_p - R_z)x_t + V_{pp}(x_t - \beta R_z)]}{2a\,[x_t^2(R_p - R_z)^2 + V_{pp}(1 + \beta R_z^2)]} \;>\; 0 \\[2ex] g_p \;=\; \dfrac{(2ax_t + b)\,(R_z + x_t)\,(R_z - R_p)x_t}{2a\,[x_t^2(R_p - R_z)^2 + V_{pp}(x_t^2 + \beta R_z^2)]} \;>\; 0 \end{cases} \tag{10.46}$$

The agent chooses to invest both in vocational training and in general training if, for a higher expected vocational return, the variance of the random return is also high.

The resolution of *the second case*: $g_z = 0$ and $g_p > 0$ leads to the conditions:

$$\begin{cases} g_p \;=\; \dfrac{(2ax_t + b)\,(x_t - \beta r_p)}{2a\,(x_t^2 + \beta r_p^2 + \beta V_{pp})} \;>\; 0 \\[2ex] \dfrac{\beta(2ax_t + b)\,[x_t(r_p + x_t)\,(r_z - r_p) + V_{pp}(\beta r_z - x_t)]}{x_t^2 + \beta r_p^2 + \beta V_{pp}} \;<\; 0 \end{cases} \tag{10.47}$$

To induce the agent to allocate all his investment to risky assets, the expected return thereon must be very high relative to the one of the risk-free asset, while the variance is low.

The third case: $g_z > 0$ and $g_p = 0$ leads to symmetric conclusions, since the conditions are:

$$\begin{cases} g_z = \dfrac{(2ax_t + b)(x_t - \beta r_z)}{2a(x_t^2 + \beta r_z^2)} > 0 \\ \dfrac{\beta x_t(2ax_t + b)(r_p - r_z)(x_t + r_z)}{x_t^2 + \beta r_z^2} < 0 \end{cases} \tag{10.48}$$

If an asset simultaneously presents a higher return than the others and a lower variance (a fortiori if the return is certain), the agent obviously chooses to invest in it.

Effects on Growth: In the case of certainty, the lock-in effect leads to specialization in vocational training since its return is the highest in the short run even if this choice reduces growth in the long run.

Under uncertainty, the choice between the specific skills does not depend on the agent's preferences but on the level of each asset inherited and on the correlation coefficient. Since a high level of one inherited asset increases its variance more than its expected return, the incentive to invest in such a form of human capital weakens. Therefore, under uncertainty, the lock-in effect which can appear under certainty may disappear. Indeed, the lower the correlation coefficient is, the more the agent diversifies. The investment in the new technology may increase growth.

The choice between general education and specific types of vocational training is explained by the variance. If the agent inherits a high level of specific training then the variance is high. The higher it is, the more the agent is induced to invest in education, thereby increasing the education return (there is no negative feed-back as regards the education level since it is a safe asset, the return of which has no variance). If investments in education increase growth more than investments in specific training, then the lock-in effect, which prevails under certainty, vanishes under uncertainty, and growth is increased. It remains true if the agent has no initial education.

10.4 Conclusions

This paper offered an overlapping generation model of investment in several kinds of human capital considered to be heterogeneous. The role of multivalence under uncertainty compared to the one of specialization under certainty is emphasized.

One of the main results is that both the correlation coefficient and the variance have a bearing on growth through their impact on the agent's choice of diversification. Especially, they contribute to explain why people invest in education even if its short-run return is low.

All of the conclusions have been based on a very simple model where growth hinges only on human capital and a portfolio analysis is used. More general models are necessary to examine the implications of relaxing these restrictive assumptions.

However, there is a positive aspect in our choice. Because of its simple structure, it seems that this model could be a useful building block in more complex ones. First, adding a Markovian process to the returns on human capital would be an interesting extension. It would emphasize the conditions under which the agent specializes or becomes multivalent according to the shape of the Markovian matrix. Second, the model would also be a natural framework in which to consider both inter- and intra-generational equity problems.

Moreover, our results have direct and obvious implications in the context of economic and educational policies. Actually, since the agent's investment structure acts upon growth, it is of interest for governments to make policies to induce agents to choose the investment structure which increases economic growth.

References

Allais, M. (1947), *Economie et Intérêt.* Imprimerie Nationale.

Augier, L. and M.P. Merlateau (1991), *Training, Growth and Taxes.* Mimeo.

Arthur, W.B. (1988), "Self-Reinforcing Mechanisms in Economies" in *The Economy as an Evolving Complex System.*

Azariadis, C. and A. Drazen (1990), "Threshold Externalities in Economic Development", *Quarterly Journal of Economics,* Vol. 105, pp. 501–526.

Barham, W., R. Boadway, M. Marchand and P. Pestieau (1992), *Education and the Poverty Trap.* Mimeo.

Diamond, P. (1965), "National Debt in a Neoclassical Growth Model", *American Economic Review,* Vol. 55, pp. 1126–1150.

Eckstein, Z. and I. Zilcha (1991), *The Effects of Compulsory Schooling on Growth, Income Distribution and Welfare.* Mimeo.

Heiner, R.A. (1988), "Imperfect Decisions in Organizations", *Journal of Economic Behavior and Organization,* Vol. 9, pp. 25–44.

Henin, P.Y. (1981), *Macrodynamique, Fluctuations et Croissance.* Economica.

Krugman, P. (1991), "History versus Expectations", *Quarterly Journal of Economics.* Vol. 106, pp. 651–667.

Lucas, R. (1988), "On the Mechanics of Economic Development", *Journal of Monetary Economics,* Vol. 22, pp. 3–42.

Michel, P. (1992), *Bubbles Slowing Down Economic Growth.* Cahiers de Recherche d'Economie Mathématique et Applications.

Romer, P. (1986), "Increasing Returns and Long-Run Growth", *Journal of Political Economy,* Vol. 94, pp. 1002–1037.

Williamson, O.E. (1989), "Transaction Cost Economics", in Schmalensee R. and R.D. Willig (eds.), *Handbook of Industrial Organization, Volume 1.* Amsterdam: North-Holland.

GPSR Compliance

The European Union's (EU) General Product Safety Regulation (GPSR) is a set of rules that requires consumer products to be safe and our obligations to ensure this.

If you have any concerns about our products, you can contact us on ProductSafety@springernature.com

In case Publisher is established outside the EU, the EU authorized representative is:

Springer Nature Customer Service Center GmbH
Europaplatz 3
69115 Heidelberg, Germany

Batch number: 10725973

Printed by Printforce, the Netherlands